D1757971

Originality in EU Copyright

It was the best of times, it was the worst of times,
it was the age of wisdom, it was the age of foolishness,
it was the epoch of belief, it was the epoch of incredulity,
it was the season of Light, it was the season of Darkness,
it was the spring of hope, it was the winter of despair.

Charles Dickens

A Tale of Two Cities (1859)

Originality in EU Copyright

Full Harmonization through Case Law

Eleonora Rosati

*University of Cambridge, UK and European University
Institute, Italy*

Edward Elgar

Cheltenham, UK • Northampton, MA, USA

© Eleonora Rosati 2013

All rights reserved. No part of this publication may be reproduced, stored in a retrieval system or transmitted in any form or by any means, electronic, mechanical or photocopying, recording, or otherwise without the prior permission of the publisher.

Published by
Edward Elgar Publishing Limited
The Lypiatts
15 Lansdown Road
Cheltenham
Glos GL50 2JA
UK

Edward Elgar Publishing, Inc.
William Pratt House
9 Dewey Court
Northampton
Massachusetts 01060
USA

A catalogue record for this book
is available from the British Library

Library of Congress Control Number: 2013942242

This book is available electronically in the ElgarOnline.com Law Subject Collection, E-ISBN 978 1 78254 894 2

ISBN 978 1 78254 893 5

Typeset by Columns Design XML Ltd, Reading
Printed and bound in Great Britain by T.J. International Ltd, Padstow

This book has been published with a financial subsidy
from the European University Institute

EUROPEAN UNIVERSITY INSTITUTE

This publication is an extended and updated version of the author's PhD
thesis entitled 'Judge-Made EU Copyright Harmonisation: The Case of
Originality', which was successfully defended at the Department of Law of
the European University Institute in 2012.

Contents

Foreword

Over the past few years, political and academic attention has focused on the future of copyright at the EU level. Following two decades of piecemeal legislative interventions, which have resulted in a limited harmonization of the copyright laws of EU Member States, a debate has ensued as to the feasibility and desirability of achieving full copyright harmonization. This might be obtained either through an EU copyright code, encompassing a codification of the present body of copyright directives, or by way of a regulation (to be enacted pursuant to new Article 118(1) TFEU) aimed at creating a unitary copyright title.

Thus far, however, no such legislative initiatives have been undertaken. Despite this impasse, the CJEU has been acting in a proactive way, inching towards full harmonization. With its 2009 decision in Case 5/08 *Infopaq*, the Court provided an EU-wide understanding of an important principle of copyright: the originality requirement. The CJEU further elaborated upon this in subsequent case law (notably, Case C-393/09 *Bezpečnostní softwarová asociace*, Joined Cases C-403/08 and C-429/08 *Murphy*, Case C-145/10 *Painer*, Case C-604/10 *Football Dataco* and Case C-406/10 *SAS*).

The meaning of originality adopted by the CJEU as an EU-wide standard is akin to that traditionally envisaged in certain continental Member States' copyright laws, thus differing from the loose notion of originality under UK law. As such, an examination as to the implications of CJEU harmonizing jurisprudence in this Member State shall be undertaken, with regard to the scope of copyright protection and subject-matter categorization.

Overall, the contribution wishes to assess how, and to what extent, CJEU case law has resulted in *de facto* EU copyright harmonization. In addition, it will attempt to foresee the fate of EU copyright in light of copyright reform projects which are currently being discussed in political and academic circles both in the US and Europe.

Acknowledgements

Whenever I put my hands on a new 'literary work', I tend to read the acknowledgements section first. In the case of what were once PhD dissertations, this is often (not to say, invariably) structured as follows. Thanks go first to the author's supervisor for his/her 'invaluable support'. Then it is the turn of other advisors the new doctor has been so blessed to meet along his/her path. Finally, it is time to thank friends, family and, last but not least, the author's partner who has been invariably so supportive and patient as to read and comment upon every single page of this new *Ulysses*.

My acknowledgements section might have indeed followed this scheme. But, instead, I have decided to go a little astray in my application of this customary pattern. I am confident that this will allow me to claim at least a certain – yet modicum – degree of originality for the sake of copyright protection.

This *Originality in EU Copyright* may not be the new must-have accessory in the realm of copyright fashion this season. However, please do permit me to draft my acknowledgements as a backward journey (sort of a short *memoir*, if you will) through the time I have spent as a PhD candidate at the European University Institute, whilst researching and writing about the intoxicating topic of originality and EU copyright harmonization, from this the present contribution has ultimately emerged.

When I first thought of embarking on a PhD adventure, I was in Cambridge undertaking my LLM studies. For some, it may be easy to think that I took this resolution under the malicious effects of too much sherry and other decadent delights. As far as I remember, this was not the case. Instead, I fancied going for a PhD because – besides the college formal halls and May Balls – I was thoroughly enjoying being immersed in the study of copyright law. As such, the first person I feel indebted to is indeed Professor Lionel Bently, who supervised me during the preparation of my LLM dissertation. This concerned the charming principle known as the idea/expression dichotomy. Although at the time I was not as fluent in Shakespeare's language as I am now, and not nearly as skilled in the art of copyright as I currently pretend to be, Lionel patiently allowed me to grasp his passion and enthusiasm for this area of the law. Working with him was truly inspiring and a decisive step towards what came next.

After Cambridge, I arrived at the European University Institute. Here I met my supervisor-to-be: Professor Giovanni Sartor. At that time I could not have begun to imagine how prolific my time in Florence would have been. Thanks to Giovanni's friendly guidance and constant encouragement, I gained confidence and was given the possibility to develop my research interests in a context of absolute trust and intellectual freedom.

During my time in the enchanting world of copyright, I started to become familiar with the names and writings of great IP characters, whom I also eventually got to meet in person. When given my first chance to meet Professor Jeremy Phillips, I remember being just about as happy as I would have been, aged thirteen, had I just been told that I was about to meet a member of Take That (Jason, preferably). Jeremy's enthusiasm is infectious, and his wit and knowledge of IP have been – and still are – a constant source of inspiration. I am deeply indebted to Jeremy for all his constant support and help.

Thanks to my activity as a blogger for the IPKat and The 1709 Blog, I have had the chance to get in touch with enthusiastic IP folks, whose comments, insights and criticisms have allowed me to learn and, possibly, improve. Some of these readers even devoted time to reading my PhD thesis, and provided me with valuable suggestions. In particular, I would like to thank The Hon Mr Justice Richard Arnold, Lucky Belder, Stefan Kulk, Dominic McGonigal, Ben Hawes and his colleagues at the UK Intellectual Property Office, Peter Munkacsi, Tommy Ruane, and Trevor Cook for their help, which I appreciated greatly.

Needless to say that, if it is true that no man is an island, this truth applies to copyright lawyers, too. Indeed, amongst the non-IP people who have always been at my side with their love, patience, and curiosity, I cannot but mention and be particularly thankful to my parents.

Now, I guess it is high time for my thesis dedication.

As this is a work about the recent past and the making of copyright future at the EU level, some copyright-enthusiasts might think that I wished to dedicate my 'own intellectual creation' to those at Curia, who have been mostly involved in copyright cases lately. Dedicating my work to Advocate General Paolo Mengozzi would be therefore a great choice (and presumably fairly original, too), but it would fail to recognize and pay due tribute to what has been my mood and spirit whilst writing this work.

As a young woman, I am concerned with the future, but not only that of copyright. In relation to this, I am always impressed by stories of people who are able to beautifully represent the old and wise Latin motto *Homo faber suae quisque fortunae* ('every man is the maker of his own destiny').

This is what I have felt most deeply whilst researching and writing my PhD thesis. The future of the law (and particularly of copyright) is a matter of willingness, as is the fate of men. Therefore, I dedicate this little work of mine to my brother, Carlo Maria, whom I not only love tenderly, but whom I also admire for his courage, capacity and enthusiasm in constantly seizing and shaping the future he has been dreaming of.

Eleonora Rosati
Cambridge, April 2013

Abbreviations

AG	Advocate General
CDPA 1988	Copyright Designs and Patents Act 1988
CJEU	Court of Justice of the European Union
Conditional Access Directive	Directive 98/84/EC of the European Parliament and of the Council of 20 November 1998 on the legal protection of services based on, or consisting of, conditional access
Court of Justice	Court of Justice of the European Union
CPP	Copyright Principles Project
Database Directive	Directive 96/9 of the European Parliament and of the Council of 11 March 1996 on the legal protection of databases
DMCA	Digital Millennium Copyright Act
EC	European Community
ECJ	European Court of Justice
EEC	European Economic Community
EU	European Union
GPCCT	Communication from the Commission of the European Communities, *Green Paper on Copyright and the Challenge of Technology – Copyright Issues Requiring Immediate Action*
GPCKE	Communication from the Commission of the European Communities, *Green Paper on Copyright in the Knowledge Economy*, 16 July 2008, COM (2008) 466/3
GPCRRIS	Communication from the Commission of the European Communities Green Paper on *Copyright and Related Rights in the Information Society*, Brussels, 19 July 1995, COM (95) 382 final
GUI/GUIs	Graphic User Interface/Graphic User Interfaces

InfoSoc Directive	Directive 2001/29/EC of the European Parliament and of the Council of 22 May 2001 on the harmonization of certain aspects of copyright and related rights in the information society
IP	Intellectual Property
IPR/IPRs	Intellectual Property Right/Intellectual Property Rights
ISP/ISPs	Internet Service Provider/Internet Service Providers
OCILLA	Online Copyright Infringement Liability Limitation Act
OHIM	Office for Harmonization in the Internal Market
Software Directive	Directive 2009/24/EC of the European Parliament and of the Council of 23 April 2009 on the legal protection of computer programs (codified version)
Term Directive	Directive 2006/116/EC of the European Parliament and of the Council of 12 December 2006 on the term protection of copyright and certain related rights (codified version)
TEU	Treaty on the European Union
TFEU	Treaty on the Functioning of the European Union
TRIPS	Agreement on Trade-Related Aspects of Intellectual Property Rights (TRIPS)
UGC	user-generated content
WIPO	World Intellectual Property Organization
WTO	World Trade Organization

Table of cases (in chronological order)

Belgium

Canada

France

Germany

Italy

United States

Table of EU/EC/EEC legislation (in chronological order)

Table of EU/EC policy documents (in chronological order)

Introduction

1. COPYRIGHT HARMONIZATION: THE AGE OF INNOCENCE?

We are on the cusp of the convergence of two great trends: the pervading influence of the digital environment and the progression of European integration.

The process of European Union (EU) harmonization in the field of copyright has brought about several changes in the domestic legal systems of the Member States. The impetus behind EU legislative initiatives in this area has been the awareness that differences between the copyright laws of Member States had the potential to impede the full realization of the internal market objective. In the early days of European integration, intervention in the intellectual property (IP) laws of the Member States was infrequent and – when it happened – was justified in light of eliminating obstacles to free movement or competition. At the end of the 1980s, IP – and so copyright – became part of a broader strategy, aimed at favouring growth and competitiveness throughout Europe. During the 1990s, it became clear that copyright was to play a pivotal role in this respect. As such, the then European Community (EC) copyright agenda became gradually more ambitious. However, from the end of the century and throughout the 2000s, legislative interventions in the field of copyright have been piecemeal and more sporadic than they were previously. It was only at the end of the 2000s that the Commission's copyright agenda regained momentum. It is submitted that this was no accident as, in parallel, the Court of Justice of the European Union (CJEU, formerly the European Court of Justice, ECJ) gave a decisive boost to the area of copyright harmonization by touching upon a basic copyright principle: the originality requirement.

So far, legislative discourse on copyright at the EU level has mostly focused on the harmonization of the scope of exclusive rights, the delineation of protected subject-matter and the duration of protection. Although European harmonization has moved forward by strengthening the protection afforded to copyright owners, EU directives have allowed Member States to maintain what are differing regimes, at least in certain respects. The result has been that many major fields have been left untouched or quasi-harmonized. In the words of Advocate General Jääskinen: 'Copyright in the EU, as is the case elsewhere, remains largely a creature of national law ... Harmonisation of copyright law in the EU has been a mixed process of partial and full harmonisation.'[1]

Moreover, the harmonization process has been deemed to be 'blind to the structural impediment that territoriality presents to the free movement of goods and services, given that the copyrights and related rights that underlie these disparities are drawn along national borders'.[2] The inherent territoriality of current EU copyright is indeed likely to impede the operation of an internal market free from barriers to trade. In light of the development of the digital environment and the challenges it has brought with it, the establishment of a strong internal market for copyright-related goods and services calls for a definitive confrontation of the issue of territoriality. Although territoriality is a practical feature of the current copyright landscape, it is important to note that this term does not appear in any of the international IP treaties.[3]

It is submitted that a narrow and sporadic approach to EU copyright is no longer adequate. Further (more precisely: full) harmonization of copyright is currently at the centre of heated debates as to its desirability and feasibility. In the course of 2010, the Wittem Group published its European Copyright Code[4] and the Monti Report tackled the role of copyright in light of proposing a new strategy for the internal market.[5] In 2011, the Commission published its blueprint for intellectual property

---

[1] Opinion of Advocate General Niilo Jääskinen, Case C-5/11 *Criminal proceedings against Titus Donner*, 29 March 2012, [24]–[25].

[2] Mireille van Eechoud, P Bernt Hugenholtz, Stef van Gompel, Lucie Guibault and Natali Helberger, *Harmonizing European copyright law. The challenges of better law making* (Kluwer Law International 2009) 308.

[3] Paul Torremans, 'Copyright territoriality in a borderless online environment', in Johan Axhamn (ed), *Copyright in a borderless online environment* (Kluwer Law International 2012) 23, 25–6, highlights how the deepest cause of territorial approach to copyright lies on national treatment rules. For a discussion on territoriality in EU copyright law, *see* Philippe Jougleux, 'The plurality of legal systems in copyright law: an obstacle to European Codification?', in Tatiana-Eleni Synodinou (ed), *Codification of European copyright law* (Kluwer Law International 2012) 55, 61–3.

[4] Wittem Group, European Copyright Code, 26 April 2010, available at copyrightcode.eu.

[5] Mario Monti, *A new strategy for the single market at the service of Europe's Economy and Society. Report to the President of the European Commission José Manuel Barroso*, 9 May 2010.

rights to boost creativity and innovation,[6] and its follow-up to the Monti Report: the Single Market Act.[7]

An EU copyright, if construed as taking precedence over national titles, would remove the inherent territoriality with respect to applicable national copyright rules. Therefore, the idea of an EU-wide copyright law, which might be established by means of an EU regulation or through a codification of the relevant *acquis communauitarie*, has been receiving increasing attention in both political and academic circles. The benefits of having a strong harmonization law would be seen through the enhancement of legal security and transparency, as well as reduction in transaction costs.

2. THE TOPICALITY OF ORIGINALITY TO EU COPYRIGHT DISCOURSE

Traditionally, the originality requirement has been used in a different way between continental Member States and the UK. While the latter has adopted it as a loose notion referring to sufficient skill, labour and effort, continental European copyright laws have embraced stricter meanings of originality.

It is argued that originality, being at the basis of copyright protection, plays a fundamental policy role and, therefore, cannot be left outside the harmonization discourse. This contribution will attempt to show the policy implications which come about from the adoption of one understanding of originality over another. By referring to paradigmatic experiences in the US and the UK, this work will try to offer an insight into the way the legal understanding of this concept has changed over time. Further, above all, it will look at how originality has been shaped and re-shaped to achieve precise policy objectives.

---

[6] Communication from the Commission to the European Parliament, the Council, the European Economic and Social Committee of the Regions, *A Single Market for Intellectual Property Rights Boosting creativity and innovation to provide economic growth, high quality jobs and first class products and services in Europe*, Brussels, 24 May 2011, COM (2011) 287 final.

[7] Communication from the Commission to the European Parliament, the Council, the Economic and Social Committee and the Committee of the Regions, *Single Market Act – Twelve levers to boost growth and strengthen confidence – 'Working together to create new growth'*, Brussels, 13 April 2011, COM (2011) 206 final.

While the process of EU harmonization in the field of copyright has brought about several changes to the domestic legal systems of the Member States, originality has been harmonized to a very limited extent. Where this has happened (in relation to computer programs, databases and photographs), originality has been interpreted as 'the author's own intellectual creation'. This meaning of the originality requirement is akin to the standard adopted in continental Member States.

While the EU legislature has not deemed it necessary to adopt a harmonized understanding of originality for subject-matter other than computer programs, databases and photographs, the CJEU has acted in a proactive way towards the actual harmonization of copyright, by adopting an EU-wide notion of originality. The 2009 decision in *Infopaq International A/S v Danske Dagblades Forening* ('*Infopaq*'),[8] as followed in 2010 in *Bezpečnostní softwarová asociace – Svaz softwarové ochrany v Ministerstvo kultury* ('*Bezpečnostní softwarová asociace*'),[9] provided for the harmonization of the originality requirement. In these cases, the continental understanding of 'the author's own intellectual creation' was adopted as the standard for originality in EU copyright, for subject-matter other than computer programs, databases and photographs.

Later decisions have further clarified and developed the EU concept of originality. These are: *Football Association Premier League Ltd, NetMed Hellas SA, Multichoice Hellas SA v QC Leisure, David Richardson, AV Station plc, Malcolm Chamberlain, Michael Madden, SR Leisure Ltd, Philip George Charles Houghton, Derek Owen* and *Karen Murphy v Media Protection Services Ltd* ('*Murphy*');[10] *Eva-Maria Painer v Standard VerlagsGmbH, Axel Springer AG, Süddeutsche Zeitung GmbH, SPIEGEL-Verlag Rudolf AUGSTEIN GmbH & Co KG and Verlag M. DuMont Schauberg Expedition der Kölnischen Zeitung GmbH & Co KG* 8 ('*Painer*');[11] *Football Dataco Ltd and Others v Yahoo! UK Ltd and*

---

[8] Case C-5/08 *Infopaq International A/S v Danske Dagblades Forening* [2009] I-06569.

[9] Case C-393/09 *Bezpečnostní softwarová asociace – Svaz softwarové ochrany v Ministerstvo kultury* [2010] I-13971.

[10] Joined Cases C-403/08 and C-429/08 *Football Association Premier League Ltd, NetMed Hellas SA, Multichoice Hellas SA v QC Leisure, David Richardson, AV Station plc, Malcolm Chamberlain, Michael Madden, SR Leisure Ltd, Philip George Charles Houghton, Derek Owen* and *Karen Murphy v Media Protection Services Ltd.*

[11] Case C-145/10 *Eva-Maria Painer v Standard VerlagsGmbH, Axel Springer AG, Süddeutsche Zeitung GmbH, SPIEGEL-Verlag Rudolf AUGSTEIN GmbH & Co KG and Verlag M. DuMont Schauberg Expedition der Kölnischen Zeitung GmbH & Co KG.*

Others (*'Football Dataco'*);[12] and *SAS Institute Inc v World Programming Ltd* (*'SAS'*).[13]

The phrase the 'author's own intellectual creation' is to be found in the Software,[14] Database[15] and Term Directives.[16] As noted above, it was adopted as the standard for originality in *Infopaq*, and is to be understood as involving 'creative freedom' (*Murphy*), a 'personal touch' (*Painer*) and 'free and creative choices' (*Football Dataco*). To put it otherwise, originality is not simply a matter of sense, but also of sensibility. This is probably because, as was noted by Jean-Sylvestre Bergé back in 1996,

> Cette définition de l'œuvre protégée semble intégrer les deux éléments de la conception médiane de l'originalité-individualité: une création intellectuelle et une création personelle.[17]

The aforementioned judgments have also raised doubts as to whether a system of exhaustive subject-matter categorization (as it is under UK law, pursuant to what has been incisively called a 'pigeon-hole approach'[18]) is still in line with EU law. Following *Murphy*, *Painer* and *SAS*, the level of scrutiny in the EU for determining whether a work may qualify for copyright protection seems to require solely that the work is original, not that it also falls within a specific copyright-protected subject-matter. This may be somewhat at odds with the Berne Convention for the Protection of Literary and Artistic Works (Paris Act of 24 July 1971), as amended on 28 September 1979, which, although providing for a non-exhaustive

---

[12]   Case C-604/10 *Football Dataco Ltd and Others v Yahoo! UK Ltd and Others*.

[13]   Case C-406/10 *SAS Institute Inc v World Programming Ltd*.

[14]   Directive 2009/24/EC of the European Parliament and of the Council of 23 April 2009 on the legal protection of computer programs (Codified version) [2009] OJ L 111, 16–22.

[15]   Directive 96/9/EC of the European Parliament and of the Council of 11 March 1996 on the legal protection of databases [1996] OJ L 77, 20–28.

[16]   Directive 2006/116/EC of the European Parliament and of the Council of 12 December 2006 on the term of protection of copyright and certain related rights (Codified version) [2006] OJ L 372, 12–18.

[17]   Jean-Sylvestre Bergé, *La protection internationale et communautaire du droit d'auteur. Essai d'une analyse conflictuelle* (L.G.D.J. 1996), 141 (footnotes omitted) ('This definition of a protected work seems to combine the two elements of the intermediate notion of originality as individuality: an intellectual creation and a personal creation').

[18]   Jeremy Phillips and Alison Firth, *Introduction to intellectual property law* (4th edn, Butterworths 2001), 138.

list of copyright-protected works, seems to imply that any assessment of the actual originality of a work is only to be made once it has been determined that it is a production in the literary, scientific or artistic domain.

Finally, as was made clear in *Football Dataco*, not only has the CJEU harmonized the originality requirement and, with it, the standard for protection under EU copyright but – possibly in compliance with a strict application of the doctrine of pre-emption – also ruled out any possible alternative (quasi-copyright) protection for subject-matter such as databases. This may give rise to problematic gaps in a country – the primary example being the UK – which lacks a law of unfair competition and has traditionally relied on copyright and its low originality threshold (as well as passing off, although in a more limited way) to protect works.[19] In a continental Member State, these same works would probably not have qualified for such protection, due to their limited (even below the minimal) degree of originality. However, it is worth recalling that the doctrine of 'small change', which is to be found in some continental Member States' copyright laws, is actually intended to relax the originality threshold.

The impact of these judgments on UK copyright law is indeed likely to be relevant, as was (partially) made clear by the ruling of the High Court of England and Wales in *The Newspaper Licensing Agency Ltd and Others v Meltwater Holding BV and Others*,[20] as recently upheld by the Court of Appeal of England and Wales,[21] and also in the decision of Judge Birss QC (as he then was) in *Temple Island Collections Ltd v New English Teas Ltd and Nicholas John Houghton*.[22] In addition, as previously mentioned, the rulings in *Bezpečnostní softwarová asociace*, *Murphy*, *Painer*, *Football Dataco*, and *SAS* seem to imply that for copyright the subject-matter categorization is merely exemplificative as far as the EU legal architecture is concerned. As will be explained in relation to the recent decision of the UK Supreme Court in *Lucasfilm Ltd and Others v Ainsworth and Another*,[23] this may lead UK courts to adopt different perspectives in the future and, as a consequence, achieve different outcomes.

---

[19]   Daniel J Gervais, 'The compatibility of the skill and labour standard with the Berne Convention and the TRIPs Agreement' (2004) 26 EIPR 75, 78.
[20]   [2010] EWHC 3099 (Ch).
[21]   [2011] EWCA Civ 890.
[22]   [2012] EWPCC 1.
[23]   [2011] UKSC 39.

3. SCOPE AND AIM OF THIS CONTRIBUTION

Overall, the present work wishes to analyze and understand the reasoning underlying the aforementioned CJEU decisions, as well as their implications as far as UK copyright is concerned.

Particular attention to UK copyright experience is justified in light of the fact that the harmonization provided by CJEU jurisprudence now definitely means that EU copyright is in line with continental traditions. Hence, the UK is the Member State in which the effects of the *Infopaq* string of case law has the potential to be most relevant.

Although analysis of the actual legitimacy of CJEU harmonizing jurisprudence, as well as its merits, is of fundamental importance to EU political and legal discourse, this will not be part of the present work. Attention will be devoted mainly to the analysis of judicial decisions which have touched upon originality, so as to assess the current challenges facing EU copyright harmonization. The case of originality, which will be analyzed from a legal standpoint, serves the objective of showing that full harmonization is already in place at the EU level, outwith legislative and political initiatives. It is submitted that if EU legislative initiatives should in future decide to harmonize copyright fully, this process would result in CJEU case law being codified.

The structure of this work reflects the research themes it is meant to explore. These can be summarized as follows:

(1) EU copyright harmonization
   What have been the objectives and achievements of EU copyright harmonization so far?
   Have the scope and objectives of the harmonization process changed over time?
   How can harmonization be seen in light of its structural character, overall ambition and merits?

(2) Meaning and functions of the originality requirement
   What is originality and how is this to be seen in light of other basic concepts such as authorship and creativity, and in the context of copyright legal understanding?
   How has originality been understood in EU copyright reforms?
   Is the meaning of originality different in the EU Member States?
   Does originality play a policy role?

(3) EU policy on originality
   Why has originality been harmonized only to a limited extent?

(4) CJEU case law on originality
       What is the relevant CJEU case law in this respect and what are
       its implications, also in relation to internationally binding legal
       instruments?
       What does a harmonized concept of originality imply?
       What is the EU understanding of subject-matter categorization?
(5) UK copyright and the EU
       To what extent has the new EU originality standard affected the
       traditional UK understanding of originality?
       Is the bar to copyright protection higher after *Infopaq* and
       subsequent case law than previously?
       How is the bar to a finding of copyright infringement affected?
       Is the UK exhaustive subject-matter categorization at odds with
       EU law?
       Might having an open subject-matter categorization have led to
       different outcomes in cases such as *Lucasfilm*?
(6) The future of copyright at the EU level
       Is it possible to improve current copyright regimes?
       What are the terms of the debate in the US and Europe?
       Can the proposals of the Wittem Group and their Copyright Code
       be used to harmonize copyright further at the EU level?
       What are the legal tools that can be used to harmonize copyright
       further at the EU level?
       Is full harmonization a desirable objective?

4. METHODOLOGY

The approach this contribution adopts is mainly inductive. Significant
attention will be devoted to the study and analysis of recent decisions of
the CJEU, which shall be assessed in light of relevant EU policy
documents and discussions as to the future of EU copyright that are
ongoing at the Commission level and in leading academic circles. By
adopting a methodology which takes into account multiple legal and
judicial sources, as well as doctrinal approaches, this work wishes to
assess the impact that relevant CJEU judgments have had on Member
States' copyright laws, notably the UK, as well as drawing their
implications for the future of copyright at the EU level.
  Within this framework, attention will be paid firstly to relevant
legislative sources and policy documents, especially at the EU level. This
is necessary to outline the EU understanding and evolution of copyright

policy, along with the main objectives underlying EU intervention in this area of the law.

Secondly, in relation to the analysis of the originality requirement, relevant literature, mainly from EU and UK scholarships, will be reviewed. This is required to define the legal foundations of the concept of originality, as well as its understanding in the broader context of EU and UK copyright regimes.

Finally, the most relevant part of this work will be devoted to the reading and analysis of relevant judicial decisions, both at the level of the CJEU and of national (in particular, UK) courts.

This work shall attempt to combine the various rationales extracted from the sources mentioned above, in order to address the research themes it is meant to explore. As EU copyright harmonization is a work in progress, at the time of writing this contribution literature specifically tackling this issue was not particularly rich and, as far as the Author of this work was aware, no major contributions dedicated to the analysis of EU copyright harmonization in light of CJEU case law on originality had emerged yet.

1. The challenges of EU copyright: 'United in Diversity'[1] – Does it work?

SECTION I

1. THE EARLY DAYS OF EUROPEAN INTEGRATION: IP RIGHTS AND THE INTERNAL MARKET

In general, it can be said that European concerns with copyright and intellectual property grew steadily as information became more significant as an economic commodity.[2] So far, fourteen directives have been issued, directly or indirectly dealing with various aspects of copyright and related rights.[3] Accordingly, harmonization has resulted in a rich

---

[1] 'United in Diversity' is the motto of the European Union.
[2] Mireille van Eechoud, P Bernt Hugenholtz, Stef van Gompel, Lucie Guibault and Natali Helberger, *Harmonizing European copyright law. The challenges of better law making* (Kluwer Law International 2009), 1.
[3] These relate to protection of computer programs (Council Directive 91/250/EEC of 14 May 1991 on the legal protection of computer programs [1991] OJ L 122, 42–46; Directive 2009/24/EC of the European Parliament and of the Council of 23 April 2009 on the legal protection of computer programs (Codified version) [2009] OJ L 111, 16–22); enforcement (Directive 2004/48/EC of the European Parliament and of the Council of 29 April 2004 on the enforcement of intellectual property rights [2004] OJ L 195, 16–25); resale rights (Directive 2001/84/EC of the European Parliament and of the Council of 27 September 2001 on the resale right for the benefit of the author of an original work of art [2001] OJ L 272, 32–36); copyright in the information society (Directive 2001/29/EC of the European Parliament and of the Council of 22 May 2001 on the harmonization of certain aspects of copyright and related rights in the information society [2001] OJ L 167, 10–19); protection of databases (Directive 96/9/EC of the European Parliament and of the Council of 11 March 1996 on the legal protection of databases, [1996] OJ L 77, 20–28); term of protection (Council Directive 93/98/EEC of 29 October 1993 harmonizing the

body of case law, which has tackled copyright from several different perspectives.

Prior to the commencement of the harmonization process (the debate surrounding which flourished at the institutional and political level only at the end of the 1980s, although there had been earlier studies which tackled harmonization issues[4]), the intellectual property laws of the Member States had been affected by EC law to a limited extent. This was mainly through the treaty provisions on competition[5] and free movement of goods.[6] It is therefore apparent that, from its very onset, copyright harmonization at the EU level was viewed as functional to the broader internal market objective. The latter denotes an area without internal frontiers, in which the free movement of goods, persons, services and capital[7] is ensured in accordance with the provisions in the treaties.[8] Therefore, competence of the EU as regards the harmonization of the intellectual property laws of the Member States has been consistently

---

term of protection of copyright and certain related rights [1993] OJ L 290, 9–13; Directive 2006/116/EC of the European Parliament and of the Council of 12 December 2006 on the term of protection of copyright and certain related rights (Codified version), [2006] OJ L 372, 12–18; Directive 2011/77/EU of the European Parliament and of the Council of 27 September 2011 amending Directive 2006/116 on the term of protection of copyright and certain related rights [2011] OJ L 265, 1–5); satellite and cable (Council Directive 93/83/EEC of 27 September 1993 on the coordination of certain rules concerning copyright and rights related to copyright applicable to satellite broadcasting and cable retransmission [1993] OJ L 248, 15–21); rental rights (Council Directive 92/100/EEC of 19 November 1992 on rental right and lending right and on certain rights related to copyright in the field of intellectual property [1992] OJ L 346, 61–66; Directive 2006/115/EC of the European Parliament and of the Council of 12 December 2006 on rental right and lending right and on certain rights related to copyright in the field of intellectual property (Codified version) [2006] OJ L 376, 28–35); semiconductors (Council Directive 87/54/EEC of 16 December 1986 on the legal protection of topographies of semiconductor products [1987] OJ L 24, 36–40); and certain permitted uses of orphan works (Directive 2012/28/EU of the European Parliament and of the Council of 25 October 2012 on certain permitted uses of orphan works, [2012] OJ L 2995, 5–12).

[4]   A notable example is Adolf Dietz, *Copyright law in the European Community* (Sijthoff & Noordhoff 1978), which was prepared at the request of the then Commission of the European Communities.

[5]   Currently Title VII, Chapter I, of the consolidated version of the Treaty on the Functioning of the European Union (TFEU) [2010] OJ C 83, 47–199.

[6]   Currently Title II TFEU.

[7]   Title IV TFEU.

[8]   Article 26(2) TFEU.

justified in light of current Articles 26 and 114 TFEU. Article 26(1) TFEU sets out the EU competence to adopt measures aimed at establishing or ensuring the functioning of the internal market, in accordance with the relevant provisions of the treaties. Article 114(1) TFEU states that the European Parliament and the Council shall, acting in accordance with the ordinary legislative procedure and after consulting the Economic and Social Committee, adopt the measures for the approximation of the provisions laid down by law, regulation or administrative action in Member States which have as their object the establishment and functioning of the internal market. As has been noted, rooting EU competence in the area of copyright within objectives pertaining to the realization of the internal market has resulted in EU lawmaking competence being perceived as practically limitless.[9]

As is made clear by Article 36 TFEU, provisions relating to the free movement of goods shall not preclude prohibitions or restrictions on imports, exports or goods in transit that are justified to protect industrial property. This is because the treaties shall in no way prejudice the rules in Member States governing the system of property ownership.[10] However, in no case may such prohibitions or restrictions constitute a means of arbitrary discrimination or a disguised restriction on trade between Member States.[11]

This said, what exactly is meant by 'property' within the treaty system is far from clear. This can be explained because,

> In contrast, with the objective of establishing a common market, the rules aiming to guarantee competition and free movement of goods were listed amongst the fundamental principles of the European legal order. It is well known that the subsequent reconciliation of intellectual-property rights with the Treaty provisions on competition and free movement of goods did not proceed without conflicts and was only achieved by virtue of the judicial practice established by the Court of Justice … concerning the 'specific subject matter' and the 'essential function' of intellectual-property law.[12]

---

[9] Theodore Georgopoulos, 'The legal foundations of European copyright law', in Tatiana-Eleni Synodinou (ed), *Codification of European copyright law. Challenges and perspectives* (Kluwer Law International 2012) 31, 34.

[10] Article 345 TFEU.

[11] Article 36 TFEU.

[12] Christophe Geiger, 'Intellectual "property" after the Treaty of Lisbon: towards a different approach in the new European legal order?' (2010) 32 EIPR 255, 255–6, referring to Guy Tritton (ed), *Intellectual property in Europe* (3rd edn, Sweet & Maxwell 2008), 36 ff.

Indeed, the relationship between intellectual property and free movement provisions has been difficult to define,[13] not helped by the fact that the latter are concerned with state measures, rather than actions of private individuals. Therefore, it seems difficult to see how reliance on a patent, trademark, copyright or design right by an individual rightsholder who seeks to prevent the importation and sale of infringing goods can be tantamount to a measure within the scope of free movement provisions.[14]

In a series of cases[15] the CJEU attempted to clarify under what conditions and to what extent the rules on competition and free movement may interfere with Member States' IP laws. According to the Court, this happens when national legislation empowers IP rightsholders to exercise their rights in a manner that adversely affects the functioning of the internal market, thus resulting in an arbitrary discrimination or disguised restriction on trade between Member States. As was made clear by the CJEU in its seminal decision in *Metro*:[16]

> Among the prohibitions or restrictions on the free movement of goods which it concedes Article 36 [EEC Treaty, now Article 42 TFEU] refers to industrial and commercial property ... [I]t is ... clear from that article that, although the

---

[13] Guy Tritton, 'Articles 30 and 36 and intellectual property: is the jurisprudence of the ECJ of an ideal standard?' (1994) 16 EIPR 422, commenting on the then European Court of Justice's decision in Case C-9/93 *IHT Internationale Heitechnik GmbH and Uwe Danziger v Ideal Standard GmbH and Wabco Standard GmbH* [1994] I-2789. This was a reference for a preliminary ruling from the Oberlandesgericht (Higher Regional Court) Düsseldorf, seeking clarification as to the interpretation of Articles 30 and 36 EEC Treaty (now respectively, Articles 36 and 42 TFEU) in order to assess the compatibility with Community law of restrictions on the use of a name where a group of companies held, through subsidiaries, a trademark consisting of that name in several Member States but where it had been assigned to an undertaking outside the group, in one Member State only and covering only some of the products for which it had been registered.

[14] David T Keeling, *Intellectual property rights in EU law* (OUP 2003) Vol I, 23 ff.

[15] *See* Eechoud, Hugenholtz, Gompel, Guibault and Helberger, *Harmonizing, cit*, 3–4, and the case law cited therein.

[16] Case C-78/70 *Deutsche Grammophon Gesellschaft mbH v Metro-SB-Großmärkte GmbH & Co KG* [1971] 00487. This was a reference for a preliminary ruling from the Oberlandesgericht (Higher Regional Court) Hamburg, seeking clarification as to the interpretation of Articles 5, 85(1) and 86 EEC Treaty (now, respectively, Articles 5 of consolidated version of the Treaty on European Union (TEU) [2010] OJ C 83, 13–45, and Article 101(1) and 102 TFEU) concerning the distribution of sound recordings in various Member States.

Treaty does not affect the existence of rights recognized by the legislation of a Member State with regard to industrial and commercial property, the exercise of such rights may nevertheless fall within the prohibitions laid down by the Treaty. Although it permits prohibitions or restrictions on the free movement of products, which are justified for the purpose of protecting industrial and commercial property, Article 36 only admits derogations from that freedom to the extent to which they are justified for the purpose of safeguarding rights which constitute the specific subject-matter of such property.[17]

2. THE EMERGENCE OF COPYRIGHT AS A EUROPEAN ISSUE

Following this first phase during which attention focused on the relationship between Member States' intellectual property laws and the internal market objective, European policy- and law-makers adopted the view that Member States' intellectual property laws, if harmonized, would also have contributed to the realization of the internal market.

1988 was the year when the first seeds of IP harmonization were sown. Council Directive 89/104/EEC to approximate the laws of the Member States relating to trade marks was published on 21 December 1988.[18] This placed the legal foundations for the creation of an EC trademark system, and was shortly followed by the beginning of the copyright harmonization process. In June that year the Commission had already

---

[17]   *Ibid*, 11.

[18]   [1989] OJ L 40, 1–7 (now replaced by Directive 2008/95/EC of the European Parliament and of the Council of 22 October 2008 to approximate the laws of the Member States relating to trade marks (Codified version) [2008] OJ L 299, 25–33). The importance of harmonizing the Member States' trademark laws in view of establishing and ensuring the proper functioning of the internal market is highlighted at Recital 1 of the Directive. However, when Directive 89/104 was adopted, there was still the belief that the creation of an EC trademark system was not necessary: 'it does not appear to be necessary at present to undertake full-scale approximation of the trade mark laws of the Member States and it will be sufficient if approximation is limited to those national provisions of law which most directly affect the functioning of the internal market' (Recital 3). A Council Regulation appeared four years later (Council Regulation (EC) No 40/94 of 20 December 1993 on the Community trade mark [1994] OJ L 11, 1–36). This has now been replaced by Council Regulation (EC) No 207/2009 of 26 February 2009 on the Community trade mark (Codified version) [2009] OJ L 78, 1–42.

issued its Green Paper on Copyright and the Challenge of Technology (hereinafter, also the GPCCT).[19]

2.1 The 1988 Green Paper

As is made clear at §1.3. of the GPCCT, the concerns of the then European Economic Community (EEC) in the field of copyright were strong enough to call for EC legislative intervention in this field. The issues which called for consideration were four-fold.

Firstly, the proper functioning of the internal market was to be ensured. To this end, creators and providers of copyright goods and services should have been able to treat the Community as a single internal market. This required the elimination of obstacles and legal differences that substantially impaired the functioning of the market by obstructing or distorting cross-frontier trade in such goods and services, as well as distorting competition.

Secondly, intervention was deemed necessary in order to improve the overall competitiveness of Europe in relation to its trading partners, particularly in areas of potential growth, such as media and information.

Thirdly, intellectual property resulting from creative efforts and substantial investments within the Community should not be misappropriated by third parties outside the territorial frontiers of the Community.

Finally, the Commission acknowledged that, in developing Community measures on copyright, due regard must be paid not only to the interests of the rightsholders but also to those of third parties and the public at large.

The GPCCT also anticipated some of the problems facing the digital revolution which had to get underway shortly:

> New dissemination and reproduction techniques have developed with an ever-increasing speed and have added, at a corresponding rate of speed, to the complexity of this relationship. These new technologies have entailed the *de facto* abolition of national frontiers and increasingly made the territorial application of national copyright law obsolete, while, at the same time, permitting for better and for worse in every country ever more rapid, easy, cheap and high-fidelity reproduction. This has at one and the same time been a cause of satisfaction and concern.[20]

---

[19] Communication from the Commission of the European Communities, *Green Paper on copyright and the challenge of technology – copyright issues requiring immediate action*, Brussels, 7 June 1988, COM (88) 172 final.

[20] *Ibid*, para 1.4.1.

However, the GPCCT failed to acknowledge that differences in the laws of Member States had the potential to raise barriers to the functioning of the internal market. Instead, it noted that:

> Many issues of copyright law, do not need to be subject of action at Community level. Since all Member States adhere to the Berne Convention for the Protection of Literary and Artistic Works and to the Universal Copyright Convention, a certain fundamental convergence of their laws has already been achieved. Many of the differences that remain have no significant impact on the functioning of the internal market or the Community's economic competitiveness ... The Community approach should therefore be marked by a need to address Community problems. Any temptation to engage in law reform for its own sake should be resisted.[21]

This said, the Commission identified six areas that required immediate legislative intervention by the EC. These were: piracy (enforcement); audiovisual home copying; distribution right, exhaustion and rental right; computer programs; databases; and multilateral and bilateral external relations.[22]

3. HARMONIZATION THROUGH THE 1990s

Over the course of the 1990s, plans from the 1988 agenda were implemented and several directives on copyright and related rights were issued. These provided harmonization as regards computer programs (1991), rental right (1992), term of protection (1993), satellite and cable (1993), and databases (1996).

In addition, along with the harmonization of specific aspects of copyright, the agenda of the Commission gradually became more ambitious.

In 1993, the Commission published a White Paper,[23] in which the term 'information society' was used for the first time. This expression is intended to signify a society in which management, quality and speed of

---

[21]   *Ibid*, paras 1.4.9 and 1.4.10.

[22]   Further areas of possible intervention by the EC were identified in the *Follow-up to the Green Paper on copyright and the challenge of technology. Working programme of the Commission in the field of copyright and neighbouring rights*, Brussels, 17 January 1991, COM (90) 584 final.

[23]   European Commission, White Paper on *Growth, competitiveness, employment. The challenges and ways forward into the 21st century*, Brussels, 5 December 1993, COM (93) 700, Bulletin of the European Communities, Supplement 6/93.

information are key factors for competitiveness; as an input to the industries as a whole and as a service provided to ultimate consumers, information and communication technologies influence the economy at all stages.[24] The Commission acknowledged that the competitiveness of the European economy depended on both the development and application of such technologies, as well as the creation of a common information area within the then Community. Thus, it recommended that efforts should be undertaken to achieve those objectives linked to the building of an efficient European information infrastructure, as well as taking the measures necessary to create new services.[25]

Thus, in 1994 the Council convened a group of experts to report on the specific measures to be adopted by the Community and the Member States alike for the infrastructures in the sphere of information. The Bangemann Report[26] acknowledged the importance of intellectual property rights (IPRs) in developing a competitive European industry, both in the area of information technology and more generally across a wide variety of industrial and cultural sectors. Hence, it recommended common rules be agreed and enforced by the Member States.[27]

This led to the publication of a Communication on *Europe's way to the information society: an action plan,*[28] in which the Commission recommended that measures adopted in relation to intellectual property rights be reviewed and new initiatives undertaken.[29]

Subsequently, in 1995 the Commission published its Green Paper on *Copyright and related rights in the information society* (GPCRRIS).[30] Therein, it was said that, due to the very nature of the networks operating in the information society, a wide variation in the level of protection of works and other protected matter between Member States was likely to give rise to obstacles to the development of the information society,[31] as

---

[24]   *Ibid*, 92.

[25]   *Ibid*, 100.

[26]   European Commission, Growth, competitiveness and employment. White Paper follow-up, *Europe and the global information society. Recommendations of the high-level group on the information society to the Corfu European Council (Bangemann Group)*, Bulletin of the European Union, Supplement 2/94.

[27]   *Ibid*, 21.

[28]   Communication from the Commission to the Council and the European Parliament and to the Economic and Social Committee of Regions, *Europe's way to the information society: an action plan*, Brussels, 19 July 1994, COM (94) 347 final.

[29]   *Ibid*, 5.

[30]   Brussels, 19 July 1995, COM (95) 382 final.

[31]   *Ibid*, 4.

well as impairing the functioning of the internal market.[32] The position
was said to be aggravated by the fact that, in the age of the information
society, works would have been circulated increasingly in non-material
forms. This meant that compliance with rules pertaining to the freedom
to provide services ought to be ensured.[33] As a consequence,

> While respecting the principle of subsidiarity, … the Community has an
> obligation to take measures in respect of copyright and related rights in order
> to guarantee the free movement of goods and the freedom to provide services.
> This will involve harmonization of legislation, and mutual recognition too, in
> order to avoid creating distortions of competition which would confer an
> advantage on firms located in particular Member States.[34]

The following year the Commission issued its follow-up to the 1995
Green Paper,[35] in which four priority issues for legislative action were
identified in relation to the exploitation of copyright-protected works.
These concerned the reproduction right, the right of communication to
the public, the legal protection of anti-copying systems and distribution
right. While acknowledging that further harmonization was needed to
adjust and complement the existing legal framework on copyright and
related rights in light of the internal market objective, the Commission
highlighted that parallel progress at the international level was also
required. An isolated response from the EU would have not been
sufficient, on account of the global reach of the information society. In
1996 the World Intellectual Property Organization (WIPO) Copyright
Treaty and Performances and Phonograms Treaty were adopted. These
were signed by the Member States, as well as by the EC, which became
thus committed to implement the new international instruments and
ensured harmonized transpositions into Member States' laws.[36]

A directive on copyright and related rights in the information society
was first proposed in 1997 and finally adopted in 2001. As noted,

---

[32] *Cf ibid*, 10.

[33] *Ibid.*

[34] *Ibid.*

[35] Communication from the Commission, *Follow-up to the Green Paper on
copyright and related rights in the information society*, 20 November 1996,
COM (1996) 568 final.

[36] *Cf* the recent ruling of the CJEU in Case C-510/10 *DR and TV2 Danmark
A/S v NCB – Nordisk Copyright Bureau*, in particular [29] ff.

Directive 2001/29/EC[37] (the so-called 'InfoSoc Directive') is considerably broader than what was required by the digital agenda it was intended to implement. In particular, the Directive harmonized the basic economic rights (rights of reproduction, communication to the public, and distribution) in a broad and supposedly 'internet-proof' manner, and introduced special protection for digital rights management systems. In any case, the largest part of the Directive dealt with exceptions and limitations – a subject that was only incidental in the Green Papers which had been published prior to its adoption.[38] The InfoSoc Directive has been criticized under several angles, in particular with regard to the set of exceptions and limitations envisaged therein. Criticisms have focused – *inter alia* – on the apparent lack of flexibility in the system of exceptions and limitations then adopted by Member States,[39] as well as their narrow

---

[37]   *Cit.*

[38]   *See* Eechoud, Hugenholtz, Gompel, Guibault and Helberger, *Harmonizing, cit,* 9.

[39]   As highlighted by P Bernt Hugenholtz and Martin RF Senftleben, 'Fair use in Europe. In search of flexibilities' (2012), *Amsterdam Law School Research Paper No 2012-39 http://papers.ssrn.com/sol3/papers.cfm?abstract_id=1959554,* 14, despite certain features of the regulatory framework provided under the InfoSoc Directive (in particular, its closed enumeration of exceptions and limitations), it should not be overlooked that the list included therein covers a wide variety of use privileges, reflecting the diversity of national copyright traditions in EU Member States. In addition, a closer analysis of the individual elements of the enumeration shows that many exceptions listed in Article 5 of the Directive constitute prototypes for national lawmaking, rather than precisely circumscribed exceptions with no inherent flexibility. Martin RF Senftleben, 'Does the Directive provide enough flexibility and sustainability?', presentation at InfoSoc @ Ten. Ten years after the EU Directive on Copyright in the Information Society: looking back and looking forward, CRIDS – IviR conference, hosted by Marielle Gallo (Member of the European Parliament), European Parliament, Brussels, 13 January 2012, suggests Member States should re-implement the InfoSoc Directive, allowing for more flexibility in the system of exceptions and limitations. Senftleben also highlights how, in contrast with US copyright law, flexible elements (such as an open-ended fair use provision) are to be sought in vain in the EU copyright system, as the InfoSoc Directive encourages the further restriction of precisely defined statutory exceptions in light of the EC three-step test which has been modelled on similar international provisions. Hence, he advocates the introduction of an EU fair use doctrine, which would open up the current restrictive system, offer sufficient breathing space for social, cultural and economic needs, and enable the EU copyright infrastructure to keep pace with the rapid development of the internet (Martin RF Senftleben, 'Bridging the differences between copyright's legal traditions – the emerging EC fair use doctrine' (2010) 57 J Copyr Socy 521).

scope,[40] and ineptness as regards scientific research[41] and technological development.[42]

4. HARMONIZATION THROUGH THE 2000s

One of the goals of the Lisbon Strategy[43] was to make Europe the most competitive and dynamic knowledge-driven economy by 2010. However,

---

[40] Lucie Guibault, 'Has the directive achieved its goals of harmonization and greater legal certainty?', presentation at InfoSoc @ Ten. Ten years after the EU Directive on Copyright in the Information Society: looking back and looking forward, CRIDS – IviR conference, hosted by Marielle Gallo (Member of the European Parliament), European Parliament, Brussels, 13 January 2012, advocates more flexibility in the system of exceptions and limitations, as well as the need for guidance from the CJEU.

[41] Reto M Hilty, Sebastian Krujatz, Benjamin Bajon, Alfred Früh, Annette Kur, Josef Drexl, Christophe Geiger and Nadine Klass, 'European Commission – Green Paper. Copyright in the knowledge economy – Comments by the Max Planck Institute for Intellectual Property, Competition and Tax Law' (2008) *Max Planck Institute for Intellectual Property, Competition & Tax Law Research Paper Series No 08/05*, who highlight how limitations most relevant to scientific research provided for in the InfoSoc Directive are important tools to facilitate access to relevant information for end-users at the scientific research level and need to be preserved or, where possible, adequately extended. In particular, at the end-user level, limitations most relevant to scientific research should be mandatory, immune from contractual agreements and technological protection measures, and should be construed as providing a bottom line, which national legislation should not fall below. In return, original rightholders should receive adequate compensation. Legislative intervention is also recommended at the level of intermediaries. In particular, it is advised to follow up closely the developments in the scientific publication market, concerning the situation of (publicly funded) research institutions *vis à vis* publishing companies and database producers.

[42] Martin Kretschmer, 'Digital copyright: the end of an era' (2003) 25 EIPR 333, who highlights (335) that '[t]he European Information Society Directive forgoes straightaway the already limited opportunity to explore new user rights in the digital environment. It prescribes an exhaustive list of 20 possible exceptions that Member States of the European Union may introduce or maintain. No new exceptions can be introduced nationally, if the information society should develop unexpected services!'

[43] During the meeting of the European Council in Lisbon in March 2000, the Heads of State or Government launched a 'Lisbon Strategy' aimed at, amongst the other things, achieving full employment by 2010. The strategy was grounded on three pillars. Firstly, an economic pillar preparing the ground for the transition to a competitive, dynamic, knowledge-based economy; secondly, a

following the publication of the InfoSoc Directive and despite the increasing number of studies that showed the economic relevance of copyright industries to the European economy,[44] the harmonization agenda lost momentum.

In particular, intervention by the Commission was deemed necessary to build up a level playing field with regard to two aspects, these being enforcement (which was harmonized by an ad hoc directive issued in 2004[45]), and rights management (which was dealt with simply by way of a Communication from the Commission[46]).[47]

The 2004 Commission Staff Working Paper[48] was aimed at assessing whether any inconsistencies in the definitions or the rules on exceptions and limitations between the different copyright directives were such as to hamper the operation of the *acquis communautaire*, or would have a harmful impact on the fair balance of rights and other interests, including those of users and consumers. The paper supported only a minor adjustment to the definition of reproduction right and an extension in the application of the exception for certain temporary acts of reproduction under Article 5(1) of the InfoSoc Directive, to cover computer programs and databases. Since there were no apparent indications that the EU legislative framework in the field of substantive copyright law contained shortcomings that had a negative impact on the functioning of the internal market, no further harmonization measures were deemed necessary at that stage. In particular, the Working Paper contained an assessment of issues outside the current *acquis* (these being originality,

---

social pillar designed to modernize the European social model by investing in human resources and combating social exclusion; and finally, an environmental pillar, emphasizing the need to rely upon natural resources.

[44]   Robert G Picard, Timo E Toivonen and Mikko Grönlund, *The contribution of copyright and related rights to the European economy based on data from the year 2000*, final report prepared for European Commission – Directorate General – Internal Market, 20 October 2003.

[45]   Directive 2004/48/EC of the European Parliament and of the Council of 29 April 2004 on the enforcement of intellectual property rights, *cit.*

[46]   Communication from the Commission to the Council, the European Parliament and the European Economic and Social Committee, *The management of copyright and related rights in the internal market*, Brussels, 19 April 2004, COM (2004) 261 final.

[47]   Jörg Reinbothe, 'A review of the last ten years and a look at what lies ahead: copyright and related rights in the European Union', presentation at Fordham Intellectual Property Conference, New York, 4 April 2002.

[48]   Commission Staff Working Paper on the review of the EC legal framework in the field of copyright and related rights, 19 July 2004, SEC (2004) 995.

ownership, definition of the term 'public', points of attachment, moral rights, and the exhaustion of rights), and concluded that no harmonization was necessary in respect of these.[49]

Subsequently, former Commissioner for the Internal Market and Services Charlie McCreevy highlighted the need for Europe to improve drastically the economic performance of the internal market, by way of modernization.[50] To this end, he advocated the introduction of a modern, light-touch set of company law rules which could cut red tape while ensuring sound corporate governance, along with a reform of Europe's IP rules to promote innovation and reward innovators. In relation to the latter, McCreevy pointed out that:

> The protection of intellectual and industrial property – copyright, patents, trademarks or designs – is at the heart of a knowledge-based economy and central to improving Europe's competitiveness. This is a priority for reform: grounded on sound economics, not just legal concepts, and concentrating on solutions that foster innovation and investment in real life.[51]

With these words McCreevy indicated the approach to be taken in order to pursue a sensible intellectual property policy at the European level. In parallel to this, the need to promote free movement of knowledge and innovation was identified by the Commission as the 'Fifth Freedom' in the single market.[52]

However, the 2008 Commission's Green Paper on *Copyright in the knowledge economy* (GPCKE)[53] appeared to be 'remarkably less ambitious than its predecessors, at least when one views its objective and the means thought able to meet these.'[54] This was because the Green Paper directly tackled none of the aforementioned issues. Neither the scope of exclusive rights, nor the delineation of protected subject-matter, nor the

---

[49] *See* below *sub* Chapter 2, Section I, §3.

[50] Charlie McCreevy, 'Charlie McCreevy speaks to the European Parliament JURI Committee', Brussels, 21 November 2006, SPEECH/06/720.

[51] *Ibid.*

[52] Communication from the Commission to the European Parliament, the Council, the European Economic and Social Committee and the Committee of the Regions, *A Single Market for the 21st Century Europe*, 20 November 2007, COM (2007) 725 final, 9.

[53] Green Paper on *Copyright in the knowledge economy*, 16 July 2008, COM (2008) 466/3.

[54] Eechoud, Hugenholtz, Gompel, Guibault and Helberger *Harmonizing*, *cit*, 9.

duration of protection are dealt with therein.[55] The purpose of the GPCKE was instead to foster a debate on how knowledge for research, science and education would be best disseminated in the online environment. This was also in light of the fact that 'a forward looking analysis requires consideration of whether the balance provided by the [InfoSoc] Directive is still in line with the rapidly changing environment.'[56]

The first part of the GPCKE dealt with general issues regarding exceptions to exclusive rights introduced in the InfoSoc Directive. The second part tackled specific issues relating to those exceptions and limitations that are most relevant for the dissemination of knowledge, and whether these exceptions should evolve in the era of digital dissemination. In particular, the GPCKE focused on the exceptions to copyright for the benefit of libraries and archives; the exception allowing dissemination of works for teaching and research purposes; the exception for the benefit of people with a disability; and a possible exception for user-generated content (UGC). In addition, the GPCKE launched a public consultation, aimed at gathering the views of stakeholders as to whether technological and legal developments challenged the balance achieved by the law up until that point. In particular, due consideration was paid to the operation of broad exclusive rights as combined with specific and limited exceptions, most significantly asking whether these achieved a fair balance of rights and interests between the different categories of rightsholders and users.

The 2009 follow-up to the GPCKE[57] reported on the results of the public consultation in relation to the exceptions dealt with in the GPCKE. It concluded along the lines that 'copyright policy must be geared toward meeting the challenges of the internet-based knowledge economy',[58] while highlighting that '[a]t the same time a proper protection of Intellectual Property Rights is decisive to stimulate innovation in the knowledge-based economy. Different interests have to be carefully balanced.'[59] Just to add something more to such a 'Pontius Pilate-esque' approach, the Commission made it clear that '[i]n the immediate future, the preferred tool for many of the issues raised in the Green Paper [on

---

[55] *Ibid*, 10.

[56] GPCKE, 20.

[57] Communication from the Commission, *Copyright in the knowledge economy*, Brussels, 19 October 2009, COM (2009) 532 final.

[58] *Ibid*, 10.

[59] *Ibid*.

Copyright in the Knowledge Economy] is a structured dialogue between relevant stakeholders, facilitated by services of the European Commission.'[60]

The year 2009 was to remain a fairly irrelevant period for copyright policy, at least on the part of the Commission. However, as will be examined below, this was not the case for the EU judiciary.

Towards the end of 2009, DG INFSO and DG MARKET jointly published a Reflection Document,[61] aimed at starting (!) a reflection and broad debate about the possible responses of the EU to the challenges facing dematerialization of content. In particular, digital technologies were said to have brought about a number of changes to the way creative content is created, exploited and distributed. The Reflection Document thus addressed issues relating to UGC and rights management.

With regard to UGC, the Commission acknowledged that, whilst content is created by traditional players such as authors, producers and publishers, user-generated content plays a new and important role.[62] The co-existence of these two types of content was said to require a framework designed to guarantee both the freedom of expression and an appropriate remuneration for professional creators, who continue to play an essential role for cultural diversity.[63] However, the outcome of the public consultation launched by the GPCKE highlighted the sentiment that most of the stakeholders believed that it was too early to regulate UGC. This resulted from the uncertainty as to whether amateurs and professionals should benefit from special rules on UGC, or simply from existing exceptions to copyright such as criticism or review, incidental use and caricature, parody and pastiche.

If we now turn to consider rights management, traditional practices for licensing rights were said not to be always fit for digital distribution.

---

[60] *Ibid.*

[61] Reflection Document of DG INFSO and DG MARKT on *Creative Content in a European digital single market: challenges for the future*, 22 October 2009.

[62] *See* Nobuko Kawashima, 'The rise of "user creativity" – Web 2.0 and a new challenge for copyright law and cultural policy', presentation at the annual congress of the Society for Economic Research on Copyright Issues (SERCI), Berkeley, 9–10 July 2009, arguing that copyright law and policy have paid little attention to the contribution to cultural progress brought about by mini-creators, ie people who get inspiration from existing works and add to them to create new expressions. Thus, the need for copyright law to recognize the creativity present in those works is advocated, as well as the acknowledgement of their contribution to the enrichment of culture.

[63] Reflection Document, *cit*, 3–4.

Digital technologies have brought new actors and new roles into the value chain, with previously separate services now converging. This has implied a change in the way in which creative content is distributed, in particular due to the integration of mobile operators, internet service providers (ISPs), telecom companies, broadband technology companies, websites, online shops, online rights aggregators and social networking platforms. In addition, making professionally produced creative content available online was considered to be a risky business, because of market fragmentation, high development and production costs and the need to fund as yet unprofitable new services from the declining revenue streams of 'traditional' analogue and physical distribution.[64] However, as recently shown by some case studies,[65] the presence of a digital sales channel may be important for encouraging the legal acquisition and use of works. In fact, when a digital sales channel is not available, users will probably turn to piracy and begin to consume much more content through illegal channels than they had previously purchased legally. This is because piracy has high fixed costs but negligible variable ones, the fixed costs being those associated with the purchase/rental of copying devices and the variable ones those influenced by the level of output, ie the amount of pirated material.[66] Once the fixed costs are paid, it is unlikely that users, who have the choice between free pirated and lawful fee-paying content, will decide to switch back to obtaining content lawfully. These considerations demonstrate the importance of developing a level playing field for new business models and innovative solutions for the distribution of creative content[67] in order to counteract the growth and spread of pirated works.

---

[64] *Ibid*, 4.

[65] *See* Brett Danaher, Samita Dhanasobhon, Michael D Smith and Rahul Telang, 'Converting pirates without cannibalizing purchasers: the impact of digital distribution on physical sales and internet piracy', presentation at the annual congress of the Society for Economic Research on Copyright Issues (SERCI), Berkeley, 9–10 July 2009. The study concerns the removal of NBC content from Apple's iTunes store in December 2007, due to dissatisfaction with iTunes's price policy, and its restoration in September 2008. NBC's decision was causally associated with an 11.5% increase in the demand for pirated content, which led to a complete *revirement* of the decision taken in September 2008. The study also shows that the restoration of the content to the iTunes store led to a statistically insignificant decrease in piracy for the same content.

[66] *Ibid*, 10–11.

[67] *Cf* José Manuel Barroso, *Political guidelines for the next Commission*, 3 September 2009.

5. TOWARDS FULL COPYRIGHT HARMONIZATION?

For what was probably the first time in an official document, the Reflection Document (despite the flaws highlighted above) specifically tackled the issue of copyright full harmonization. This was in the context of discussions on to how improve the licensing framework at the European level.

According to the Commission, a 'European Copyright Law' might be established by means of an EU regulation, the legal basis for which might be new Article 118(1) TFEU, as introduced by the Lisbon Reform Treaty. This provision reads as follows:

> In the context of the establishment and functioning of the internal market, the European Parliament and the Council, acting in accordance with the ordinary legislative procedure, shall establish measures for the creation of European intellectual property rights to provide uniform protection of intellectual property rights throughout the Union and for the setting up of centralised Union-wide authorisation, coordination and supervision arrangements.

Although the introduction of an EU-wide copyright title was discussed along with other possibilities (such as alternative forms of remuneration), the Commission seemed to welcome such an option. It viewed this as beneficial, *inter alia*, to the functioning of the internal market, as well as to consumer access in relation to exceptions and limitations to copyright.[68] In the Reflection Document, it was stated that:

> A Community copyright title would have instant Community-wide effect, thereby creating *a single market* for copyrights and related rights. It would overcome the issue that each national copyright law, though harmonised as to its substantive scope, applies only in one particular national territory. A Community copyright would enhance *legal security and transparency*, for right owners and users alike, and greatly *reduce transaction and licensing costs*. Unification of EU copyright by regulation could also restore the

---

[68] Reflection Document, *cit*, 15 (footnotes omitted): 'Community rules on copyright have harmonised the scope and tenor of the exclusive rights without, however, providing clear boundaries for these rights by means of uniform exceptions. This is indeed a state of affairs that should not persist in a truly integrated internal market. The unclear contours of strong 'exclusive rights' are neither beneficial for the internal market in knowledge products nor for the development of internet services. Further harmonization of copyright laws in the EU, in particular relating to the different and optional limitations and exceptions, would create more certainty for consumers about what they can and cannot do with the content they legally acquire.'

balance between rights and exceptions – a balance that is currently skewed by the fact that the harmonization directives mandate basic economic rights, but merely permit certain exceptions and limitations. A regulation could provide that rights and exceptions are afforded the same degree of harmonization.

By creating a single European copyright title, European Copyright Law would create a tool for streamlining rights management across the Single Market, doing away with the necessity of administering a 'bundle' of 27 national copyrights. Such a title, especially if construed as taking precedence over national titles, would remove the inherent territoriality with respect to applicable national copyright rules; a softer approach would be to make such a Community copyright title an option for rightsholders which would not replace, but exist in parallel to national copyright titles.[69]

It is apparent that such an EU-wide copyright title would raise important issues for the organization of rights management. Hence, further reflection on the future of European rights management would have to precede the introduction of an EU-wide copyright title.[70] Finally, noting that new online services require a more dynamic and flexible framework in which they can legally offer diverse, attractive and affordable content to consumers, the Reflection Document recommended that careful analysis be undertaken as to the challenges facing the three main groups in the value chain – consumers, commercial users and rightsholders.[71]

5.1 The Legacy of the 2000s

From the GPCKE – as well as its follow-up and the Reflection Document – two main threads seem to emerge.

Firstly, that difficulties remain as regards the balancing of the different interests involved in copyright law and policy,[72] this being the so-called public/private divide which has been well highlighted by, amongst others, Peter Jaszi.[73]

Secondly, that increasing digitization and online distribution of cultural goods requires a reflection on the possible outcomes that might arise out of further and deeper harmonization of the copyright laws of EU Member

---

[69]   *Ibid*, 18–19 (emphasis added).

[70]   *Ibid*, 19.

[71]   *Ibid*, 9.

[72]   *Cf Follow-up* to the Green Paper on Copyright and the challenge of technology, 10, and Reflection Document, 9 ff.

[73]   Peter Jaszi, 'Toward a theory of copyright: the metamorphoses of "authorship"'(1991) 40 Duke LJ 455, 463 ff.

States.[74] As mentioned above, one of the goals of the Lisbon Strategy was to make Europe the most competitive and dynamic knowledge-driven economy by 2010. As expressly stated by the GPCKE, creation, circulation and dissemination of knowledge in the single market are directly linked to the broader goals of the Lisbon Strategy.[75] It is clear that a good protection model is the *condicio sine qua non* in order to achieve, or in the first instance, approach, these objectives.

6. THE DEBATE IN 2010–2013: THE INTERNAL MARKET, THE ROLE OF ACADEMIA AND EU LEGISLATION

Following the Reflection Document, debate around copyright full harmonization at the EU level has constantly increased.

In 2010 alone, two important documents were published.

The first was the European Copyright Code, released by the Wittem Group, composed of leading European copyright academics, in April of that year. The Code, as was clearly stated therein, 'might serve as a model or reference tool for future harmonization or unification of copyright at the European level'.[76] The contents of the Code will be discussed below, *sub* Chapter 6, Section I, §2.

The second document of some relevance was released just one month later. The report entitled *A new strategy for the single market at the service of Europe's economy and society* was produced by Mario Monti and addressed to the President of the European Commission, José Manuel Barroso.[77] This became known as the 'Monti Report'.

6.1   The Monti Report

The Report examines the challenges facing initiatives aimed at re-launching the internal market. Monti identifies three main obstacles to

---

[74]   *Cf* Reflection Document, 10–13.

[75]   GPCKE, 3.

[76]   Wittem Group, *European Copyright Code*, 26 April 2010, Introduction, 5, available at copyrightcode.eu.

[77]   Mario Monti, *A new strategy for the single market at the service of Europe's economy and society. Report to the President of the European Commission José Manuel Barroso*, 9 May 2010.

the functioning of the internal market.[78] The first challenge is said to come from the erosion of the political and social support for market integration in Europe. The second challenge comes from uneven policy attention given to the development of the various components of an effective and sustainable single market. The final challenge is due to what the Report defines as a 'sense of complacency', which has gained strength in the past decade. This sentiment has led to a belief that the single market has really already been completed, and can thus be put to rest as a political priority. Hence, the report advocates the adoption of a new strategy to safeguard the single market from the risk of economic nationalism, to extend it into new areas key for Europe's growth and to build an adequate degree of consensus around it. From these objectives, it is clearly not accidental that the actual Report is preceded by a quote from Paul-Henri Spaak:

> Tous ceux qui ont essayé de régler les problèmes économiques que posait le traité de Rome en oubliant le coté politique de la chose sont allés à un échec et aussi longtemps qu'on examinera [ces] problèmes uniquement sur le plan économique et sans penser à la politique, je le crains, nous irons à des échecs répétés.[79]

Indeed, it is important to highlight that EU integration and development in relation to copyright requires not just 'sound economics' (as was stated in 2006 by Charlie McCreevy), but also the political will to engage in such a debate.

The Monti Report specifically tackles the issue of copyright harmonization, saying that:

> The European markets for online digital content are still underdeveloped as the complexity and lack of transparency of the copyright regime creates an unfavourable business environment. It is urgent to simplify copyright clearance and management by facilitating pan-European content licensing, by developing EU-wide copyright rules, including a framework for digital rights management ... Additional measures should also be examined to take into

---

[78]   In a speech delivered at 'The State of the Union' conference in Florence on 9 and 10 May 2012, Mario Monti highlighted that the points raised in his 2010 Report were still those on which the EU should focus in order to favour the progression of the internal market.

[79]   'All those who, in trying to meet the economic challenges set out by the treaty of Rome, neglected the political dimension have failed. As long as [those] challenges will be addressed exclusively in an economic perspective, disregarding their political angle, we will run – I am afraid – into repeated failures.' (speech at the Chamber of Representatives, 14 June 1961).

account the specificities of all the different forms of on-line content, such as further harmonization of copyright, creation of an EU copyright title, considering that cross-border online transactions take place at the location of supply and extended collective licensing.[80]

The political dimension of EU copyright debate is apparent if one looks at the 2011 Commission's blueprint for intellectual property rights to boost creativity and innovation,[81] and, prior to this, the follow-up to the Monti Report: the Commission's Single Market Act.[82]

6.2   The Single Market Act

In April 2011, following the fifty proposals which it had put up for debate,[83] the Commission issued its action plan aimed at re-launching growth and strengthening confidence in the internal market. As the shortcomings of the latter had been highlighted in the Monti Report, the

---

[80]   Monti, *A new strategy, cit*, para 2.3, 45–6. Key recommendations as regards online digital content in the Report include: 1) proposals for an EU copyright law, including an EU framework for copyright clearance and management; and 2) proposals for a legal framework for EU-wide online broadcasting.

[81]   Communication from the Commission to the European Parliament, the Council, the European Economic and Social Committee of the Regions, *A single market for intellectual property rights boosting creativity and innovation to provide economic growth, high quality jobs and first class products and services in Europe*, 24 May 2011, COM (2011) 287 final.

[82]   Communication from the Commission to the European Parliament, the Council, the Economic and Social Committee and the Committee of the Regions, *Single Market Act – Twelve levers to boost growth and strengthen confidence – 'Working together to create new growth'*, Brussels, 13 April 2011, COM (2011) 206 final.

[83]   Communication from the Commission to the European Parliament, the Council, the Economic and Social Committee and the Committee of the Regions, *Towards a Single Market Act for a highly competitive social market economy – 50 proposals for improving our work, business and exchanges with one another*, Brussels, 27 October 2010, COM (2010) 608 final. The public consultation attracted more than 800 responses, reflecting the points of view of Member States, non-governmental organizations, social partners at national and European level, local and regional authorities, industrial and professional organizations, trade unions, businesses, consumer organizations, think tanks, academics and many individuals. As highlighted by the Commission, '[t]he consultation revealed high expectations from civil society, in terms both of the development of the Single Market's potential to foster growth and employment as well as the social dimension of the internal market and the protection of public services. Priorities identified by respondents in the economy confirm strong support for

adoption of a proactive and cross-cutting strategy was deemed necessary. In its Communication on the Single Market Act, the Commission set forth:

> This means putting an end to market fragmentation and *eliminating barriers and obstacles to the movement of services, innovation and creativity*. It means strengthening citizens' confidence in their internal market and ensuring that its benefits are passed on to consumers. A better integrated market which fully plays its role as a platform on which to build European competitiveness for its peoples, businesses and regions, including the remotest and least developed.[84]

The Single Market Act includes twelve levers to boost growth and strengthen confidence in the internal market. Among these, intellectual property rights are regarded as playing an important role. This is not only because between 45% and 75% of the value of large enterprises is linked to their intellectual property rights,[85] but also because industries which make intensive use of intellectual property rights have a fundamental role in the sustainable development of European states' economies.[86]

This said, the Commission's action plan suggested that legislation be enhanced to set up a unitary patent protection for the greatest possible number of Member States and a unified patent litigation system. The trademark system also requires updating, in order to improve the protection of trademarks and to make the European and national trademark systems more coherent, by simplifying procedures, reducing costs and enabling the system to benefit fully from new technologies to facilitate research.

In relation to copyright, the Single Market Act echoes Proposal No 2, which was part of the group of fifty proposals within the public consultation. This had followed from considerations as to how the absence of an EU-wide framework for the efficient management of copyright across the EU makes it difficult to disseminate knowledge and

---

the common goal of a highly competitive social market economy.' (Communication from the Commission to the European Parliament, the Council, the Economic and Social Committee and the Committee of the Regions, *Single Market Act, cit*, 4).

[84] Communication from the Commission to the European Parliament, the Council, the Economic and Social Committee and the Committee of the Regions, *Single Market Act, cit*, 3 (emphasis added).

[85] *Ibid*, 8.

[86] *Ibid*.

cultural goods online.[87] Therefore, current systems for the granting of copyright licences for legal online distribution should be simplified and made more transparent. In addition, collective management must be able to evolve towards European models, allowing for licences to cover several territories, whilst at the same time providing a high level of protection for rightsholders.

The hints contained in the Single Market Act were discussed and developed in the May 2011 blueprint for intellectual property rights.

6.3 The 2011 Commission's Blueprint

In May 2011, one month after the publication of the Single Market Act, the Commission issued its blueprint for intellectual property rights. This was aimed at setting an agenda to release the potential of European inventors and creators, as well as empowering them to turn ideas into high-quality jobs and promoting economic growth. In particular, according to the Commission, growth may be achieved only by putting in place a seamless, integrated and modern single market for intellectual property rights, which has not yet been realized. The fragmentation of the IP landscape in the EU is said to have problematic implications for Europe's growth, job creation and competitiveness. In particular, difficulties are deemed to exist in relation to both exploitation and enforcement of IP rights.[88] Licensing transactions are impaired by high costs and complexity. This results, *inter alia*, in ecommerce not having yet realized its full potential in the EU. In addition, existing intellectual property regimes have to cope with increasingly fast technological progress, which changes the way products and services are produced, disseminated and consumed. As a consequence, Europe is not always at the forefront of providing new digital services.

The enforcement of intellectual property rights within Europe and at its borders remains imperfect, not least because the EU enforcement regime is not in line with the new digital environment. In particular, enforcement needs to be strengthened, in order to effectively respond to the challenges facing dematerialization of works and their distribution.

---

[87]   Communication from the Commission to the European Parliament, the Council, the Economic and Social Committee and the Committee of the Regions, *Towards a Single Market Act*, cit, 8.

[88]   Communication from the Commission to the European Parliament, the Council, the European Economic and Social Committee of the Regions, *A Single Market*, cit, 6.

From the foregoing, it is apparent that the construction of a single market for intellectual property rights is to become a major objective of EU policy. This is considered necessary not only to favour growth, sustainable job creation and competitiveness of the EU economy, these being also key objectives of the EU 2020 agenda,[89] but also as an essential element to sustain the EU's recovery from the economic and financial crisis. Indeed, the development of sectors, such as ecommerce and digital industries, is deemed essential for EU economy, in that these offer the greatest potential for future growth.[90] Most of the new jobs in the EU which have been created over the past decade have been in the knowledge-based industries, where employment has increased by 24%. In contrast, employment in the rest of the EU economy has increased by

---

[89] Communication from the Commission, *Europe 2020 – A strategy for smart, sustainable and inclusive growth*, Brussels, 3 March 2010, COM (2010) 2020 final. The five targets for the EU in 2020 concern: employment: 75% of 20–64 year-olds to be employed; R&D/innovation: 3% of the EU's GDP (public and private combined) to be invested in R&D/innovation; climate change/energy: greenhouse gas emissions 20% (or even 30%, if the conditions are right) lower than 1990, 20% of energy from renewables, 20% increase in energy efficiency; education: reducing school drop-out rates below 10%, at least 40% of 30-34 year-olds completing third level education; poverty/social exclusion: at least 20 million fewer people in or at risk of poverty and social exclusion.

[90] As also recently highlighted by Neelie Kroes, 'What we are seeing at the moment is huge growth and diversity. First, growth in consumer expectations. They expect an offer that is open rather than limited, "on demand" rather than on a fixed schedule, interactive and targeted rather than passive and controlled. We cannot ignore that: because these days if consumers don't get what they want, they won't be afraid to switch off. Second, growth in the scope of creative content. It's not just about taking "old media" like music, TV and film and digitising them – although that is in itself lucrative. It's also about new media that didn't even exist before, content which is interactive, social, even user-created. Remember: the more widely we define culture and entertainment, the bigger are the market opportunities, the more unlimited our horizons ... And third, growth in the number of ways you can make money, and better reward creators, using content. Possibilities way beyond the old models ... As the range of consumer demands, the range of creative works and the range of business models become more diverse, then the ways to operate them have tended to converge.' (Neelie Kroes, 'Creativity for the creative sector: entertaining Europe in the electronic age', speech at European Parliament Intellectual Property Forum, European Parliament, Brussels, 24 January 2012, SPEECH/12/30).

just under 6%.[91] Copyright-based creative industries contributed 3.3% to the EU GDP in 2006.[92]

This said, the blueprint also contains proposals to improve the EU intellectual property framework. Starting with patents, the Commission discusses the advantages of having a unitary patent protection and litigation system. As regards trademarks, it is suggested that the EU trademark system is ameliorated by updating Regulation No 207/2009.[93] The blueprint also tackles issues pertaining to complementary protection of intangible assets, these being trade secrets, parasitic copies, and non-agricultural geographical indications. It also calls for a heightened fight against counterfeiting and piracy, to be instigated by improving the structure of the European Observatory on Counterfeiting and Piracy, which is meant to serve as a platform to join forces, exchange experiences and information and to share best practices on enforcement. On 19 April 2012, the European Parliament and the Council adopted Regulation No 386/2012.[94] This entrusts the Office of Harmonization in the Internal Market (OHIM) with tasks related to the enforcement of IPRs, including the assembling of public- and private-sector representatives as an EU Observatory on infringements of IPRs.

In addition, the Commission aims to pursue its objective of enhancing respect for intellectual property right standards at an international level

---

[91]   Ian Brinkley and Neil Lee, The Work Foundation – *The knowledge economy in Europe. A report prepared for the 2007 EU Spring Council*, 7. As reported at 4–5 of the blueprint, 1.4 million European SMEs operate in the creative industries. IP-based industries represent above average potential for growth and job creation. Creative industries account for 3% of employment (2008) and are among the most dynamic sectors in the EU. The number of employees in the creative industries in the EU-27 was 6.7 million in 2008. Overall employment in the creative industries increased by an average of 3.5% a year in the period 2000–2007 compared to 1% a year for the total EU economy. In 2009, it was estimated that intangible assets represented about 81% of the value of the S&P 500 market (Commission Staff Working Document, *European Competitiveness Report 2010*, Accompanying document to the Communication from the Commission to the European Parliament, the Council, the European Economic and Social Committee and the Committee of the Regions, *An integrated industrial policy for the globalisation era putting competitiveness and sustainability at the front stage*, Brussels, 28 October 2010, SEC (2010) 1276 final, Volume I,11).

[92]   Commission Staff Working Document, *European Competitiveness Report 2010*, *cit.*

[93]   Council Regulation (EC) No 207/2009 of 26 February 2009 on the Community trade mark, *cit.*

[94]   [2012] OJ L129, 1–6.

by engaging in cooperation with third countries in the context of the World Intellectual Property Organization (WIPO), the World Trade Organization (WTO) and the International Union for the Protection of New Varieties of Plants. It will also contribute to the promotion of technological innovation and to the transfer and dissemination of technology. Further, in the context of WIPO, it will continue to support large-scale ratification of the 1996 WIPO Internet Treaties and their proper implementation into domestic laws,[95] as well as to negotiate intellectual property right provisions in the EU's free trade agreements with third countries.[96] The Commission is also committed to enhancing intellectual property protection and enforcement at the EU borders. To this end, it proposes that a new regulation replacing Regulation No 1383/2003[97] be adopted with the objective of strengthening enforcement while streamlining procedures.[98]

At §3.3 the blueprint discusses the creation of a comprehensive framework for copyright in the digital single market, touching upon the following issues: copyright governance and management, user-generated content, private copying levies, access to Europe's cultural heritage and fostering media plurality, performers' rights, audiovisual works and artists' resale rights.

6.4 Full Harmonization is on its Way (via Licensing?)

The analysis carried out by the Commission is closely linked to what is considered as the state of the art in relation to dematerialization and dissemination of works through digital channels,[99] and raising awareness

---

[95] Communication from the Commission to the European Parliament, the Council, the European Economic and Social Committee of the Regions, *A Single Market, cit*, 20.

[96] *Ibid*, 21.

[97] Council Regulation (EC) No 1383/2003 of 22 July 2003 concerning customs action against goods suspected of infringing certain intellectual property rights and the measures to be taken against goods found to have infringed such rights [2003] OJ L 196, 7–14.

[98] Communication from the Commission to the European Parliament, the Council, the European Economic and Social Committee of the Regions, *A Single Market, cit*, 21.

[99] As recently highlighted by Neelie Kroes, 'More and more Europeans are going online. In 2004, a mere 40% of European households had access to the Internet at home. Just 6 years later, 70% of households are online … Because as more and more citizens get online, so they expect and demand more stuff to do online. This produces a virtuous circle of demand: in turn stimulating the supply

as to how territorial constraints of Member States' copyright laws are at odds with such a barrier-less environment:

> The internet is borderless but online markets in the EU are still fragmented by multiple barriers. Europe remains a patchwork of national online markets and there are cases when Europeans are unable to buy copyright protected works or services electronically across a digital single market. Technology, the fast evolving nature of digital business models and the growing autonomy of online consumers, all call for a constant assessment as to whether current copyright rules set the right incentives and enable right holders, users of rights and consumers to take advantage of the opportunities that modern technologies provide.[100]

This said, the agenda of the Commission includes a reform of copyright licensing, which has also recently been held to be of primary importance to future Commission actions.[101] The creation of a European framework for online copyright licensing is said to have the potential to stimulate greatly the legal offer of protected cultural goods and services across the EU and to benefit rights holders, collecting societies, service providers and consumers alike. The new framework for copyright licensing should establish common rules on governance, transparency and effective supervision, including collectively managed revenue streams. It is within this

---

of new content, new material, new services. These services are expanding rapidly, in terms of diversity, intensity and sophistication. Once it was about checking email or reading text online. Now Europeans increasingly want access to any content, at any time, on any device … More users, expecting more sophisticated services online, each consuming more bandwidth. That all means more traffic on our networks. And more traffic means we need a better infrastructure. An infrastructure that is the backbone, not the bottleneck, of the digital revolution. This is the kind of support that next generation access, NGA [next-generation access], can provide.' (Neelie Kroes, 'Investing in the future: meeting the internet's astonishing promise', speech at 'Talk in Brussels' – Deutsche Telekom Annual Reception, Brussels, 29 November 2011, SPEECH/11/857).

[100] Communication from the Commission to the European Parliament, the Council, the European Economic and Social Committee of the Regions, *A Single Market*, *cit*, 9.

[101] *See* the speeches of Maria Martin-Prat, current Head of Unit – Copyright, DG Internal Market & Services, at the Fordham IP Conference, New York, 12–13 April 2012 (as reported in Eleonora Rosati, 'EU copyright at Fordham: a report (Part I)' (The 1709 Blog, 17 April 2012) <http://tinyurl.com/ansc3lz> accessed 14 June 2013 and Neelie Kroes, 'What does it mean to be open online?', speech at World Wide Web Conference 2012, Lyon, 19 April 2012, SPEECH/12/275.

broader context that the 'Licences for Europe' initiative, which was launched at the beginning of 2013, is to be seen.[102] As was announced by the Commission at the end of 2012, this is a project which is aimed at tapping the potential and exploring 'the possible limits of innovative licensing and technological solutions in making EU copyright law and practice fit for the digital age.'[103]

The blueprint also addresses how to foster the development of new online services covering a greater share of the world repertoire. It suggests that an enforceable European rights management regime facilitating cross-border licensing should be put in place. Furthermore, effective cross-border management of copyright for online services should be taken into consideration. The Commission advises that means are provided to ensure that all operators comply with a high level of service standards for both rightsholders and users and that competition is not distorted.

In order to tackle a more far-reaching overhaul of copyright at the EU level, the Commission expressly suggests considering the adoption of a European Copyright Code. For the second time in an official document (the first being the 2009 Reflection Document) the Commission not only mentions the possibility of harmonizing copyright fully at the EU level, but also indicates how this objective might be achieved. In particular, the Commission explains that full harmonization may be sought through two distinct and alternative routes: either a codification of the current *acquis*, or the issuing of an ad hoc regulation aimed at creating an optional EU copyright title. The blueprint provides:

> [A European Copyright Code] could encompass a comprehensive codification of the present body of EU copyright directives in order to harmonise and consolidate the entitlements provided by copyright and related rights at EU level. This would also provide an opportunity to examine whether the current exceptions and limitations to copyright granted under the [InfoSoc] Directive need to be updated or harmonised at EU level. A Code could therefore help to clarify the relationship between the various exclusive rights enjoyed by rights holders and the scope of the exceptions and limitations to those rights.

---

[102] *See* the speeches of Androulla Vassiliou (member of the European Commission for Education, Culture, Multilingualism and Youth) on 'Culture and copyright in the digital environment', Brussels, 4 February 2013, SPEECH/13/94, and Neelie Kroes, 'Digital technology and copyright can fit together', Brussels, 4 February 2013, SPEECH/13/96.

[103] Communication from the Commission, *On content in the digital single market*, Brussels, 18 December 2012, COM (2012) 789 final, 3.

> The Commission will also examine the feasibility of creating an optional 'unitary' copyright title on the basis of Article 118 TFEU and its potential impact for the single market, rights holders and consumers.
>
> These issues require further study and analysis. The Commission will examine these issues, inter alia, in the context of the dialogue with stake-holders foreseen in the Digital Agenda for Europe and report in 2012, in particular on whether the [InfoSoc] Directive needs to be updated.[104]

As reported in the Annex to the blueprint, which contains a list of future Commission actions, the next couple of years promise to be crucial to the future of EU copyright. As recently as May 2011, the Commission issued its proposal for a Directive of the European Parliament and of the Council on certain permitted uses of orphan works,[105] and the relevant directive was eventually adopted in October 2012.[106] In the foreseeable future, following publication in 2012 of a proposal for a specific directive,[107] a legal instrument to create a European framework for online copyright licensing in order to create a stable framework for the governance of copyright at the European level should also be issued.

Other initiatives include an evaluation of whether further measures in the area of copyright should be implemented, a revision of the Enforcement Directive (this should have taken place in 2012), and a stakeholder consultation over user-generated content (also this should have been launched in 2012). In relation to the latter, the Commission notes that there is a growing realization that solutions are needed to make it easier and affordable for end-users to use third-party copyright-protected content in their own works. In other words, users who integrate copyright-protected materials into their own creations, which are then uploaded on the internet, should have access to a simple and efficient permissions system. This is found to be particularly pertinent in the case of amateur uses of copyright-protected materials for non-commercial purposes.

---

[104] *Ibid*, 11.

[105] Brussels, 24 May 2011, COM (2011) 289 final.

[106] Directive 2012/28/EU of the European Parliament and of the Council of 25 October 2012 on certain permitted uses of orphan works, *cit*. For a critical analysis of the directive, *see* Eleonora Rosati, 'The Orphan Works Directive, or throwing a stone and hiding the hand' (2013) 8 (4) JIPLP 303.

[107] Proposal for a Directive of the European Parliament and of the Council on collective management of copyright and related rights and multi-territorial licensing of rights in musical works for online uses in the internal market, Brussels, 11 July 2012, COM (2012) 372 final, 2012/0180 (COD), on which *see* João Pedro Quintais, 'Proposal for a Directive on collective rights management and (some) multi-territorial licensing' (2013) 35 EIPR 65.

According to the Commission, UGC of this type should not expose authors to infringement proceedings if they upload material without the rightsholders' consent. Discussion on this issue was scheduled to take place in the course of 2013, within the framework of a structured stakeholder diologue.[108] Indeed, a working group working on UGC and licensing for small-scale users of protected material has now been established within the Licences for Europe initiative. The Commission's objective is to 'foster transparency and ensure that end-users have greater clarity on legitimate and non-legitimate uses of protected material, and easier access to legitimate solutions'.[109]

Finally, as mentioned above and still in the course of 2012, the Commission should have reported on the application of the InfoSoc Directive and assessed whether this needed to be updated. However, as was recently announced by current Head of Unit for Copyright within DG Internal Market & Services, Maria Martin-Prat, the review of the InfoSoc Directive would not result in any legislative initiatives until 2013 at the very earliest.[110]

Closely linked to this, the Commission appeared also committed to assessing and discussing with concerned stakeholders the feasibility and desirability of producing a European Copyright Code. In relation to this, Martin-Prat made it clear that, whilst it is true that the priority of the Commission is to facilitate licensing across the EU and this implies facing the issue of territoriality, the possible establishment of an EU-wide licensing system is not going to affect the territoriality of EU Member States' copyright laws.[111] Therefore, debate as to the future of EU licensing is not necessarily linked to that on whether or not to adopt an EU-wide copyright.

7. WHY THE EU COPYRIGHT IS NOT JUST ABOUT COPYRIGHT

On 11 January 2012, the Commission published a Communication on *A coherent framework to build trust in the digital single market for*

---

[108] Communication from the Commission, *On content in the digital single market*, *cit*, 3–4.
[109] *See* http://ec.europa.uk/licences-for-europe-dialogue/node/5 (accessed 14 June 2013).
[110] *See* Rosati, 'EU copyright at Fordham', *cit*.
[111] *Ibid.*

e-commerce and online services.[112] The Communication highlights the advantages of building a genuine digital single market. This is said to favour several categories of stakeholders,[113] as well as to generate new types of growth, which the EU has not yet achieved[114] – not least because 'internet Europe' is still a patchwork of different laws,[115] rules, standards and practices with little or no interoperability. In particular, the Commission highlights that, '[t]he European Union cannot just resign itself to bearing the costs of a fragmented digital market after having set ambitious objectives for renewed, sustainable, smart and inclusive growth by 2020.'[116] Hence, the Commission is committed to working with all the

---

[112] Commission Communication to the European Parliament, the Council, the Economic and Social Committee and the Committee of the Regions, *A coherent framework for building trust in the digital single market for e-commerce and online services*, Brussels, 11 January 2012, COM (2011) 942.

[113] According to the Commission (*ibid*, 3–4), increased trust in the digital single market will be advantageous for consumers (who will benefit from lower prices, more choice and better quality of goods and services, due to cross-border trade and easier comparison of offer), small and medium-sized enterprises (which will have the possibility of accessing new markets beyond national and European borders), citizens (who will use the internet to carry out cross-border activities), workers (thanks to online services, high-quality jobs will be created, even in rural or isolated areas, and it will be possible to respond to job offers even outside the country), and the environment (growth generated through the development of ecommerce will be greener and more sustainable).

[114] The Communication reports (1–2) that in the G8 countries, South Korea and Sweden, the internet economy has brought about 21% of the growth in GDP in the last five years and generates 2.6 jobs for every job cut, at times accounting for 25% of net employment creation. Despite this, the share of the internet economy in European GDP remains small, as it was no more than 3% in 2010. Similarly, although the growth rate of ecommerce at national level is high, this new vector remains marginal at only 3.4% of European retail trade, which is much less advanced than in the United States or Asia-Pacific and tends not to go beyond national borders. Furthermore, according to the Copenhagen Economics – European Policy Centre (EPC), *The economic impact of a European digital single market*, final report, March 2010, 4, the cost of failure to complete the European digital single market is expected to be at least 4.1% of GDP between now and 2020, ie EUR 500 billion or EUR 1000 per EU citizen.

[115] *See* Communication from the Commission to the European Parliament, the Council, the European Economic and Social Committee of the Regions, *A Single Market*, *cit*, 9.

[116] Commission Communication to the European Parliament, the Council, the Economic and Social Committee and the Committee of the Regions, *A coherent framework*, *cit*, 2, referring to Communication from the Commission *Europe 2020*, *cit*.

stakeholders to enhance an EU digital single market. Such an objective is to be achieved by 2015, as also recently stated by the European Council, whilst highlighting that, to this end, priority should be given to measures aimed at further developing cross-border online trade, boosting demand for the roll-out of high-speed internet, modernizing Europe's copyright regime and facilitating licensing.[117] In relation to the latter, it is believed that any proposed measure should seek to reduce the administrative burdens and transaction costs associated with the licensing of content.[118]

Fragmentation of the legal framework pertaining to online services is said to be at odds with the growth objectives set out by the Commission. Copyright is within this legal framework and, although the Communication does not specifically tackle the issue of full copyright harmonization, from the identification of the main obstacles to the development of the digital single market it is apparent that, amongst other things, copyright needs to be discussed from this perspective.

According to the Commission itself, the following problems have to be solved: the supply of legal, cross-border online services, which is still said to be inadequate; the amount of information for online service operators or protection for internet users, which is not enough; payment and delivery systems, which are said to be poor; settlement of disputes, where this avenue is still difficult to pursue; and high-speed communication networks and hi-tech solutions, which remain insufficient.[119]

From the foregoing, it is apparent that the issue concerning the future of copyright at the EU level cannot be placed outwith the discourse concerning the enhancement of an EU digital single market. The development of legal and cross-border offers of online products and services cannot rely solely upon the kind of harmonization brought about by the Ecommerce Directive. This, indeed, did remove a series of obstacles to cross-border online activities. In particular, its internal market clause,[120]

---

[117] Conclusions of the European Council, CO EUR 4 CONCL 2, Brussels, 29 June 2012, EUCO 76/12, 10.

[118] European Parliament resolution of 11 September 2012 on the online distribution of audiovisual works in the European Union, 2011/2313(INI).

[119] Such obstacles are not an exhaustive list, points out the Commission, which stresses how (*ibid*, 4, footnotes partially omitted) '[t]he plan places emphasis on strengthening a single harmonised framework for e-commerce and other commercial online services. It opens a new chapter on this subject in the digital approach for Europe, continuing the logic, of the Single Market Act, and is part of a wider commitment from the European Union aimed at boosting the economy and the information society, ranging from promoting online administration and digital literacy to standardization and online security.'

[120] Article 3(2) of the Ecommerce Directive.

which forbids Member States from restricting the freedom to provide information society services from another Member State, is considered to be the cornerstone of the digital single market. Albeit a revision of the Ecommerce Directive is deemed unnecessary at this stage, an amelioration of its implementation, as well as clarification of certain aspects (such as the liability of ISPs), should be provided.

In order to achieve the objective of facilitating cross-border offers of online products and services, the Commission deems it necessary to assess the way in which a number of obstacles are still impeding the development of online services and access to them. In particular, businesses are said to be reluctant to commit to innovative activities, due to the costs and risks arising from the fragmentation of rules. This is a clear consequence of having co-existing national legal systems, each having special regard to consumer law. However, this is not the only field in which fragmentation is seen as detrimental to the achievement of the single digital market objective.[121]

As far as the market for digital content is concerned, legal offers of both music and audiovisual entertainment are evolving at different rates throughout the Member States. This does not always meet consumers' expectations, in part due to the limited availability of transnational or pan-European offers. This said, the Commission stresses the need for collective management of copyrights to become more European in structure, so as to allow for licences to cover a number of European regions. In addition, it is trusted that ambitious implementation of the recommendations included in the May 2011 blueprint of the Commission will foster the development of a richer and more suitable offer on a European scale.[122]

As has been mentioned, the Commission document of January 2012 does not expressly mention the issue of copyright full harmonization. However, this is implicit in the main actions that are indicated as being necessary. Among the other things, the Commission

---

[121] The complexity of the VAT system is also regarded as a factor which dissuades businesses from selling online in another Member State. Simplification of the administrative burden on businesses under the current VAT system, in particular the establishment of one-stop shops, would encourage and facilitate cross-border ecommerce (Commission Communication to the European Parliament, the Council, the Economic and Social Committee and the Committee of the Regions, *A coherent framework, cit,* 7).

[122] *Ibid,* 6.

will ensure that the European strategy for intellectual property rights [indicated in the May 2011 blueprint] is implemented rapidly and *ambitiously*, in particular by means of a legislative initiative on ... the review of the Directive on copyright in the information society ...[123]

The review of the InfoSoc Directive that the Commission intends to carry out sometime in the near future will involve a discourse on whether and to what extent full copyright harmonization is a desirable objective. As expressly stated in the May 2011 blueprint – and here recalled once again – one option aimed at ensuring a more far-reaching overhaul of copyright at the EU level would be to create an EU-wide copyright title, either by means of a codification of the present body of EU copyright directives, in order to harmonize and consolidate the entitlements provided by copyright and related rights at EU level, or by an ad hoc regulation issued pursuant to Article 118 TFEU. Discussion on this and other issues will be carried out in the context of the dialogue with relevant stakeholders. In the January 2012 document, the Commission made it clear that the EU intellectual property rights agenda is to be implemented rapidly and *ambitiously*. This rules out any possibility for full EU harmonization to be left outside the discourse on the possible amendments to the InfoSoc Directive.

SECTION II

Debate on copyright harmonization commenced about twenty-five years ago, with the 1988 GPCCT. Therefore, in relation to the history of EU integration as a whole, intellectual property (and copyright in particular) was not perceived, at first, as functional to achieving the internal market objective. It was only when awareness arose as to the key role of copyright in relation to its functioning that harmonization was pursued. Progress and assessment of EU copyright harmonization may be viewed from three different angles. The first angle concerns the structural character of harmonization; the second, its overall ambitiousness; and the third, its merits. These will be examined in turn.

---

[123]   *Ibid*, 7 (emphasis added).

1. THE STRUCTURAL CHARACTER OF COPYRIGHT HARMONIZATION

Since the 1988 GPCCT, harmonization of copyright at the EU level has been characterized by the interdependence of its objective(s) and overall scope.

As far as the objective of harmonization is concerned, measures taken in this respect have often (if not always) been justified in light of eliminating obstacles and legal differences between the laws of the EU Member States, which were such as to impair the functioning of the internal market.[124] In particular, this was because the presence of differing legal solutions distorted cross-frontier trade of goods and services, as well as competition. Thus, from the very beginning of copyright harmonization, removal of internal barriers has been at the centre of EU debate. This, however, has not been the only objective. Indeed, the enhancement of the overall competitiveness of the EU economy in relation to its trading partners has also been an important aspect. This can now rightly be considered as being at the centre of the EU harmonization model. In addition, effective enforcement of intellectual property rights, as well as the development of new business models aimed at favouring access to works by EU citizens, have become increasingly relevant to the harmonization discourse.

As regards the scope of harmonization, this has always occurred on an ad hoc basis and when differences in the laws of Member States were deemed to be detrimental to the internal market objective. Hence, the EU approach to copyright has occurred following a sector-by-sector approach, and has been both functional and fragmented. From this point of view, the political breadth of the harmonization process can be said to have been minimal, also (but not only) because intellectual property as such is an area in which the EU has no exclusive internal competence.

Compliance with the principle of subsidiarity requires that action at the EU level in an area of non-exclusive competence, such as intellectual property, shall occur only when the objectives of the proposed intervention may not be sufficiently achieved by Member States' action in the framework of their national constitutional system and are therefore to be

---

[124] In this sense also P Bernt Hugenholtz, Mireille van Eechoud, Stef van Gompel, Lucie Guibault, Natali Helberger, Mara Rossini, Lennert Steijger, Nicole Dufft and Philipp Bohn, *The recasting of copyright and related rights for the knowledge economy*, final report, November 2006, <http://tinyurl.com/ab9vlwy accessed> accessed 14 June 2013, 16.

better achieved by action at the EU level.[125] In addition, the principle of proportionality, which disciplines the method and intensity of EU intervention, requires that this does not go beyond what is necessary to achieve the objectives of the treaties.[126] Furthermore, the form of EU action shall be as simple as possible, consistent with satisfactory achievement of the objective of the measure and the need for effective enforcement. In addition, all things being equal, directives should be preferred to regulations and framework directives to detailed measures.[127]

In light of the foregoing, both the primary objective and scope of EU intervention in the field of copyright have been compliant with the principles of subsidiarity and proportionality. However, neither a fully functioning internal market nor a digital single market have been completely achieved as yet.

In relation to the internal market, it is true that – as highlighted by Monti in his 2010 report – obstacles to its functioning derive from a series of challenges. Among these, there is what the Report referred to as a 'sense of complacency', as if the single market had been really completed and could thus be put to rest as a political priority. Contrary to such a belief, the internal market still needs not only to be improved, but also modernized.[128]

As regards the digital single market, the Commission has clearly pointed out that digital technologies have brought about a number of changes and challenges to the way creative content is created, exploited

---

[125] *See* TEU, Section 5 of Protocol (No 30) on the application of the principles of subsidiarity and proportionality (1997), which clarifies that the following guidelines should be used in examining whether the principle of subsidiarity is respected: (1) the issue under consideration has transnational aspects which cannot be satisfactorily regulated by action by Member States; (2) actions by Member States alone or a lack of Community action would conflict with the requirements of the Treaty (such as the need to correct distortion of competition or avoid disguised restrictions on trade or strengthen economic and social cohesion), or would otherwise significantly damage Member States' interests; (3) action at Community level would produce clear benefits by reason of its scale or effects compared with action at the level of the Member States.

[126] *See* TEU, Section 1 of Protocol (No 30) on the application of the principles of subsidiarity and proportionality (1997).

[127] *See* TEU, Section 6 of Protocol (No 30) on the application of the principles of subsidiarity and proportionality (1997).

[128] *Cf* McCreevy, 'Charlie McCreevy speaks to the European Parliament JURI Committee', *cit.*

and distributed.[129] Differences in the laws of EU Member States have thus far impeded the achievement of a digital single market and the costs of a fragmented digital market are still to be borne.[130]

2. THE AMBITIOUSNESS OF THE COMMISSION'S COPYRIGHT AGENDA

Before copyright – and, more generally, intellectual property – harmonization got underway, the laws of the Member States had been affected by EU law through the EC treaties' provisions on competition and free movement of goods, although only to a limited extent. It was therefore apparent that in the early days of European integration an EU copyright policy as such did not exist. Any intervention in the field of copyright had to be justified in light of the broader objective pertaining to the realization of the internal market. However, awareness increased at the EU level as to the strategic importance of intellectual property to the overall competitiveness of the European economy. Such a role was expressly acknowledged by the Commission in its 1988 GPCCT. This marked a shift in the part the EU legislature was to play in the field of copyright in subsequent years. No longer was a negative approach to copyright adopted, ie legislative intervention aimed at eliminating obstacles to the functioning of the internal market, but also a positive approach came to play a role, seeking to favour growth and competitiveness throughout Europe, as well as to protect the creative efforts of European authors. This approach required stronger and more effective enforcement of copyright outside European borders.

The shift marked by the GPCCT inaugurated an ambitious agenda, which led to the adoption of five directives pertaining to various aspects of copyright over the course of the 1990s. Alongside these, awareness continued to increase as to the need for a level playing field for copyright to be created, in order to enhance the European IP model.

In parallel to the implementation agenda set out in 1988, the Commission started to address the challenges facing the information society, a term – as mentioned above – first used in 1993. In particular, the Commission indicated the need to favour both the development and

---

[129] Reflection Document of DG INFSO and DG MARKT on *Creative content, cit*, 3.

[130] Commission Communication to the European Parliament, the Council, the Economic and Social Committee and the Committee of the Regions, *A coherent framework, cit*, 2.

application of information and communication technologies, as well as the creation of a common information area. This was targeted at enhancing European competitiveness.

The documents published throughout the second half of the 1990s continued to emphasize the key role copyright plays both in light of the internal market objective and the overall competitiveness of the EU. In particular, attention was paid to economic rights (rights of reproduction, communication and making available to the public, and distribution), the harmonization of which quickly became a priority, not just in Europe, but also internationally.

From the end of the 1980s until the beginning of the 2000s, the EU copyright agenda continued to gain momentum and breadth. However, following the adoption of the InfoSoc Directive – and despite the ambitious objectives set out in the Lisbon Strategy – both the scope and results of the various measures adopted were modest. In particular, attention focused mostly on enforcement and rights management. Inconsistencies in definitions or rules on exceptions and limitations between the different directives were deemed to neither be in contrast to the building of an *acquis communautaire* nor to have a harmful impact on the fair balance of rights and interests. Moreover, the reviews which were carried out in the mid-2000s concluded that no further harmonization measures were necessary, as differences in the laws of Member States were not such as to impair the functioning of the internal market. Among the issues outside the current *acquis*, and for which harmonization was not deemed necessary, was originality. As will be explained below, such an attitude caused a marked delay in the harmonization process and, above all, resulted in a legislative gap which was only to be filled by EU judiciary at the end of the 2000s. Indeed, the relevance of the originality requirement to the determination of the scope of protection has been constantly overlooked, as its role was not understood fully until relatively recently. For instance, in his 1978 study on the copyright laws of the then nine EC Member States, Dietz did not consider the different thresholds to originality in the various national copyright laws, when addressing the ideal standard of protectability under EC copyright law. He argued that only the definition of 'work', which is to include the design, sketch or study (if these on their own have been expressed in a sufficiently concrete form and have not merely remained an unformed idea), ought to be retained to determine the protectability standard. Any characterization of the originality requirement was to be avoided and left to courts and case law to define. According to Dietz, even in those countries (Germany, Italy, UK, Ireland in his study) where the law provided additional hints as to the kind of 'work' protected by copyright, the actual meaning could be defined only by courts in each individual case.[131]

Lip-service was paid to the promotion of free movement of knowledge and innovation. However, there was still no sign of a return to an ambitious harmonization agenda by the second half of the 2000s. As such, the 2008 GPCKE was simply aimed at fostering a debate on how knowledge for research, science and education could be best disseminated in the online environment. Attention clearly focused on copyright exceptions and limitations. However, no actual legislative measures followed the Green Paper, as its 2009 follow-up merely acknowledged the need for copyright policy to address the challenges facing the internet-based knowledge economy and indicated that the preferred tool for many of the issues raised in the Green Paper was a structured dialogue between relevant stakeholders. Similarly, in its 2009 Reflection Document, the Commission indicated the issues arising from dematerialization of contents and their exchange that were such as to call for consideration. These only included user-generated content and rights management. However, the Reflection Document changed the approach followed by the Commission until then.

It can be said that from 2009 onwards, the Commission's copyright agenda quite suddenly regained momentum, thus marking a shift from the developments (or lack thereof) that occurred in the 2000s. In addition to the Reflection Document – which, overall, was not particularly ambitious – the following have contributed to reinvigorating discourse around copyright at the EU level. Firstly, the 2010 Monti Report. This, while examining the shortcomings of the internal market objective, contributed to highlighting its political dimension and, alongside this, the role of Member States in its re-launch. Moreover, the importance of copyright for this objective was highlighted by the Commission in its follow-up to the Monti Report, ie the Single Market Act, as well as in its 2011 Communication on *A single market for intellectual property rights*. The latter, in particular, confirmed the renewed interest of the Commission in pursuing an EU copyright policy. The blueprint contained a fairly detailed agenda aimed at realizing the broader objective of favouring European authors, as well as economic growth and competitiveness, by putting in place an integrated and modern single market for IPRs. In addition, following the acknowledgement in the Reflection Document of the debate surrounding copyright full harmonization, the 2011 blueprint went further and mentioned the possibility of issuing a European

---

[131]   Dietz, *Copyright law, cit*, 33–4.

Copyright Code, by means of a codification of the copyright directives adopted so far, or by a regulation pursuant to Article 118 TFEU.

3. THE ACHIEVEMENTS AND MERITS OF HARMONIZATION

As mentioned, the process of copyright harmonization has resulted in piecemeal legislation, which has firstly and primarily occurred where differences in the laws of Member States were deemed to impair the functioning of the internal market. Only at a later stage did legislative intervention occur for other reasons.

It has been noted[132] that, from the survey of EU directives constituting the current *acquis communautaire* and their implementation trends and pitfalls, there emerges a certain lack of consistency in the assumptions underlying current EU copyright law policy. In particular, though the harmonization process has been constantly rooted within the notion of 'adequate legal protection'[133] as a means to increase production and dissemination of works, this has resulted in harmonization moving upwards, even where economic evidence suggested that this would have led to unnecessary monopolies over non-rival resources such as cultural and information goods. There is no need to recall the heated debate

---

[132] Maria Lillà Montagnani and Maurizio Borghi, 'Promises and pitfalls of the European copyright law harmonization process', in David Ward (ed), *The European Union & the culture industries: regulation and the public interest* (Ashgate 2008) 213, 213 ff.

[133] *See, inter alia*, Recitals 10 ('Adequate legal protection of intellectual property rights is necessary in order to guarantee the availability of such a reward and provide the opportunity for satisfactory returns on this investment.') and 12 in the preamble to the InfoSoc Directive ('Adequate protection of copyright works and subject-matter of related rights is also of great importance from a cultural standpoint. Article 151 [of the Treaty of the European Community, now Article 167 TFEU] of the Treaty requires the Community to take cultural aspects into account in its action.'). Article 167(1–2) TFEU provides that '(1) The Union shall contribute to the flowering of the cultures of the Member States, while respecting their national and regional diversity and at the same time bringing the common cultural heritage to the fore. (2) Action by the Union shall be aimed at encouraging cooperation between Member States and, if necessary, supporting and supplementing their action in the following areas: improvement of the knowledge and dissemination of the culture and history of the European peoples, conservation and safeguarding of cultural heritage of European significance, non-commercial cultural exchanges, artistic and literary creation, including in the audiovisual sector.'

surrounding the extensions of the term of copyright protection, both at the time when the Term Directive[134] was issued and, more recently, with Directive 2011/77/EU, which was adopted on 12 September 2011.[135]

---

[134] According to Achilles C Emilianides, 'The author revived: harmonization without justification' (2004) 26 EIPR 538, the Term Directive was an important step forward in the copyright harmonization process in the EU, but it failed to pursue the significant policy issue of the justification of copyright duration in a convincing manner. The drafters of the Directive did not concern themselves with the philosophical foundations of copyright, or with the position of authors in literary interpretation: their sole objective was the immediate effectiveness of the Directive. The rationale underlying the term extension is indeed fairly vague. Recital 2 to the Directive states that as the 'differences between the national laws governing the terms of protection of copyright and related rights [were] liable to impede the free movement of goods and freedom to provide services, and to distort competition in the common market ... the laws of the Member States [were] harmoni[s]ed so as to make terms of protection identical throughout the Community'. This was not, however, the only rationale supporting the Directive: '[T]he minimum term of protection laid down by the Berne Convention, namely the life of the author and 50 years after his death, was intended to provide protection for the author and the first two generations of his descendants; ... the average lifespan in the Community has grown longer, to the point where this term is no longer sufficient to cover two generations' (Recital 5 to the Directive). As a result of such vague justifications, the provisions contained in the Directive were loosely drafted and confusing, and the harmonization process was unnecessarily perplexing, concludes Emilianides (541).

[135] Directive 2011/77/EU of the European Parliament and of the Council of 27 September 2011 amending Directive 2006/116/EC on the term of protection of copyright and certain related rights, *cit*. As highlighted by Recital 5: 'Performers generally start their careers young and the current term of protection of 50 years applicable to fixations of performances often does not protect their performances for their entire lifetime. Therefore, some performers face an income gap at the end of their lifetime. In addition, performers are often unable to rely on their rights to prevent or restrict an objectionable use of their performances that may occur during their lifetime.' As pointed out – *inter alia* – by Andrew Gowers in the review which former UK Prime Minister Tony Blair's Government had commissioned to establish whether UK intellectual property law was fit for purpose in an era of globalization, digitization and ever-growing economic specialization, '[i]ncreasing the length of sound term [from fifty to seventy years after the fixation in a record] increases the length of time during which royalties accrue. Once copyright in a sound recording ends, no royalties are due for that recording, and fewer licences are required to play those songs (copyright in the composition would continue, and therefore would continue to require a licence) ... Because the cost of the licences reflects the royalties payable on the copyrights, as those copyrights expire, so the cost of the licences will fall. Term extension would keep the cost of sound recording licences higher

This extended the term of protection for performers and sound recordings from fifty to seventy years. The main argument against excessive extension of the term of protection has been that, as a consequence, access to culture is denied, while no incentives to creation of new works are provided.[136] According to some commentators, term extension has contributed to the aggravation of issues concerning orphan works, in that it has made it more difficult to locate authors and so to seek and obtain licences for using third parties' works. The result is that '[i]f you can't track down who owns rights in the work, you can't use it no matter how beneficial your use may be and no matter how likely it is that the copyright owner has lost all interest in exploiting the work.'[137]

---

for longer. Extension would increase costs for all businesses that play music … The impact of extension would therefore be felt throughout the economy. In conclusion, the Review finds the arguments in favour of term extension unconvincing.' (Andrew Gowers, *Gowers review of intellectual property*, December 2006, <http://tinyurl.com/af3gyqc> accessed 14 June 2013, 56.) Arguments against extension of the term of protection for sound recordings in Europe are also presented and discussed in Susanna Monseau, '"Fit for purpose": why the European Union should not extend the term of related rights protection in Europe' (2009) 19 Fordham Intell Prop Media & Ent LJ 629.

[136] For a law and economics assessment of copyright duration, *see* William M Landes and Richard A Posner, *The economic structure of intellectual property* (Belknap Press of Harvard University Press 2003) 210 ff, who highlight, *inter alia*, that (238) empirical analysis suggests that most copyrights have very little economic value after twenty-eight years.

[137] William Patry, *How to fix copyright* (OUP 2011), 190, who reports the data according to which the British Library estimates that 40% of works in its collections are orphans and over 1 million hours of television programming from the BBC archives are not used due to the impossibility, or the disproportionate cost, of tracing rightholders, as well as the risk of subsequent legal actions (British Library, 'Orphan Works and Mass Digitisation', 29 September 2010). As was made clear by Neelie Kroes, 'Addressing the orphan works challenge', IFRRO (The International Federation of Reproduction Rights Organizations) launch of ARROW+ (Accessible Registries of Rights Information and Orphan Works towards Europeana), Brussels, 10 March 2011, SPEECH/11/163, the uncertainty due to the impossibility of identifying copyright owners benefits neither the rightholders, who cannot be traced, nor the creative industries or the wider public. In addition general copyright issues pertaining to preservation and access to cultural heritage arise in respect of public domain works, too. On problems facing restoration and, reconstruction and digitization of such works, *see* Andreas Rahmatian, 'Copyright protection for restoration, reconstruction and digitization of public domain works', in Estelle Derclaye (ed), *Copyright and cultural heritage: preservation and access to work in a digital world* (Edward Elgar Publishing 2010) 51.

As mentioned above, the InfoSoc Directive has not been immune from criticism. Some commentators have called it a 'badly drafted, compromise-ridden, ambiguous piece of legislation',[138] which has not only not contributed to improving legal certainty – a goal expressly stated at recitals 4, 6, 7 and 21 therein – but was the result of 'another round of lobbying and infighting at the national level'. This has led to additional work for the Court of Justice, which had 'to finish the job left largely undone by the European legislature.'[139] In relation to this last remark, the analysis Hugenholtz carried out more than ten years ago is impressively precise. This will be seen in relation to the issue of originality, which the EU legislature has deemed so far not necessary to address and harmonize.

Such a piecemeal approach has also given rise to concerns re the actual consistency of the EU legal framework, both at the level of the *acquis* and within national systems of intellectual property rights.[140] This is because:

> Although harmonization of copyright and related rights is the stated aim, the existing directives may in effect also contribute to the preservation and in theory even proliferation of differences between Member States' laws. One reason is that sometimes only a minimum level of protection is prescribed ... or that Member States may be allowed to introduce new rights ... Another reason is that rights and limitations may be optional ... But harmonization efforts so far have also attracted criticism for other reasons. The proportionality principle especially seeks to ensure that a legislative measure is fit for its purpose. Various elements of directives have been criticised for failing precisely that test.[141]

Even if the above lays down the flaws of the copyright harmonization process, it should be pointed out that its merits cannot be underestimated. The rationale underlying the entire process has been the removal of barriers that impeded the functioning of the internal market. Indeed, the copyright agenda of the Commission has always been functional to the broader objective of making a single market for copyright works. In addition, the process of harmonization has favoured the emergence of

---

[138] P Bernt Hugenholtz, 'Why the Copyright Directive is unimportant, and possibly invalid' (2000) 22 EIPR 499, 500.

[139] *Ibid.*

[140] *Cf* Michael Hart, 'The Copyright in the Information Society Directive: an overview' (2002) 24 EIPR 58, 58.

[141] Hugenholtz, Eechoud, Gompel, Guibault, Helberger, Rossini, Steijger, Dufft and Bohn, *The recasting of copyright, cit*, 17.

common principles, thus contributing to the creation of a peculiar EU copyright, and to strengthened legal certainty in EU commerce.[142] Harmonization, where it occurred, was needed since the differences in the laws of Member States were at odds with the internal market objective. It is now clear that it could have been better, with particular regard to the provisions relating to technology and technological impact. These lack the flexibility required in an ever-changing marketplace.

The real question which lies before us is not whether harmonization was necessary in the first place – it was – but whether, instead, it should go further with increased momentum, as recent case law developments and inputs from the Commission suggest. The answer to this issue is definitively 'yes'. This is for two reasons.

The first supports *further* harmonization because progress so far has involved only specific aspects of copyright. This has left untouched the very basics of copyright protection, for instance the meaning of 'work' or 'original'. These gaps have been filled by the Court of Justice. Some commentators (notably Lionel Bently) have argued that the harmonizing effects of CJEU jurisprudence touched upon concepts which could not possibly be harmonized with legislation alone.[143] In any case, an EU-wide copyright discourse cannot be construed without assigning an EU meaning to very basic concepts of copyright. As will be argued below *sub* Chapter 6, Section II, any legislative intervention aimed at harmonizing such concepts will be an *ex post* codification of principles developed by the CJEU.

The second reason supports *full* harmonization. As the market for copyright works is no longer bound to analogical barriers, but is characterized by instant transmission, availability and exploitation of digital works through digital channels, it is no longer conceivable that the EU lacks an EU-wide copyright title and remains instead a fragmented legal order. This is in contrast to a market (the EU one – to say the least) in which no fragmentation is actually supposed to exist.

---

[142]   *Cf* P Bernt Hugenholtz, 'Harmonization or unification of copyright in the EU?', presentation at InfoSoc @ Ten. Ten years after the EU Directive on Copyright in the Information Society: looking back and looking forward, CRIDS – IviR conference, hosted by Marielle Gallo (Member of the European Parliament), European Parliament, Brussels, 13 January 2012.

[143]   *See* the presentation of Lionel Bently at the Fordham IP Conference, New York, 12–13 April 2012, as reported in Eleonora Rosati, 'EU copyright at Fordham: a report (Part II)' (The 1709 Blog, 17 April 2012) <http://the1709blog.blogspot.it/2012/04/eu-copyright-at-fordham-report-part-ii.html.http://tinyurl.com/b2gkp54> accessed 14 June 2013.

2. Originality as a policy tool: Shaping the breadth of protection[1]

SECTION I

1. ON CREATIVITY, AUTHORSHIP AND ORIGINALITY

Poetic history ... is held to be indistinguishable from poetic influence, since strong poets make that history by misreading one another, so as to clear imaginative space for themselves.

My concern is only with strong poets, major figures with the persistence to wrestle with their strong precursors, even to the death. Weaker talents idealize; figures of capable imagination appropriate for themselves. But nothing is got for nothing, and self-appropriation involves the immense anxieties of indebtedness, for what strong maker desires the realization that he has failed to create himself? Oscar Wilde, who knew he had failed as a poet because he lacked strength to overcome his anxiety of influence, knew also the darker truths concerning influence. *The Ballad of Reading Gaol* becomes an embarrassment to read, directly one recognizes that every lustre it exhibits is reflected from *The Rime of the Ancient Mariner*; and Wilde's lyrics anthologize the whole of English High Romanticism. Knowing this, and armed with his customary intelligence, Wilde bitterly remarks in *The Portrait of Mr. W. H.* that: 'Influence is simply a transference of personality, a mode of giving away what is most precious to one's self, and its exercise produces a sense, and, it may be, a reality of loss. Every disciple takes away something from his master.' This is the anxiety of influencing, yet no reversal in this area is a true reversal. Two years later, Wilde refined this bitterness in one of Lord Henry Wotton's elegant observations in *The Picture of Dorian Gray*, where he tells Dorian that all influence is immoral: 'Because to influence a person is to give him one's own soul. He does not think his natural thoughts, or burn with his natural passions. His virtues are not real to him. His sins, if there are such

---

[1]   Some parts of this chapter represent an extended and updated version of the following contribution: Eleonora Rosati, 'Originality in US and UK Copyright Experiences as a Springboard for an EU-Wide Reform Debate' (2010) 5 IIC 524-543.

things as sins, are borrowed. He becomes an echo of someone else's music, an actor of a part that has not been written for him'.[2]

With his most significant *The anxiety of influence*, Harold Bloom developed the idea that, like criticism, which is either part of literature or nothing at all, great writing always strongly (or weakly) misreads previous writing.[3]

As pointed out incisively some years later by Roland Barthes, who reached the point of declaring the 'death of the author',[4] creativity and originality are concerned with the author's personal gaze or perspective on objects, no matter if these belong to the realm of mundane or to something more elevated.

> Representation is not defined by imitation: even if one gets rid of notions of the 'real', of the 'vraisemblable', of the 'copy', there will still be representation for so long as a subject (author, reader, spectator or voyeur) casts his gaze towards a horizon on which he cuts out the base of a triangle, his eye (or his mind) forming the apex.[5]

The very concept of the 'author', as an individual who is the sole creator of unique works whose originality warrants protection under laws of intellectual property is quite a recent one.[6] It is traditionally ascribed to the legacy of the romantic age and is in particular defined as the conception of the author as a genius who retains ownership of the intellectual endeavour on which he imparts his personality.[7]

The idea of an isolated genius, who creates solely by way of personal inspiration, has been challenged in the past few years, until the point that – as previously mentioned – postmodernist critique held it to be socially constructed and such as to disregard actual creative practices. It was

---

[2] Harold Bloom, *The anxiety of influence. A theory of poetry* (2nd edn, OUP 1973), 5–6.

[3] *Ibid*, xix.

[4] Roland Barthes, *Image Music Text* (first published 1977, Noonday Press edition 1988), 142–8.

[5] *Ibid*, 69 (emphasis in the original text).

[6] *See* Martha Woodmansee, 'On the author effect: recovering collectivity', in Martha Woodmansee and Peter Jaszi (eds), *The construction of authorship. Textual appropriation in law and literature* (Duke University Press 1994) 15, 15.

[7] Daniel Burkitt, 'Copyrighting culture – the history and cultural specificity of the Western model of copyright' (2001) 2 IPQ 146, 152.

Michel Foucault, in his seminal essay *What is an author?*,[8] who effectively suggested such a perspective on the rhetoric of authorship. The French philosopher held the view that, albeit the author is presented as a genius, as a perpetual surging of innovation, in reality this view of authorship is biased by an ideology that has no correspondence to actual creative practices. As pointed out by Mark Rose:

> Copyright is founded on the concept of the unique individual who creates something original and is entitled to reap a profit from those labours. Until recently, the dominant modes of aesthetic thinking have shared the romantic and individualistic assumptions inscribed in copyright. But these assumptions obscure important truths about the processes of cultural production.[9]

From this arises the need to engage with the realities of contemporary, polyvocal ways of intellectual production, which are increasingly collect-ive, corporate and collaborative, as suggested, *inter alia*, by Peter Jaszi.[10] The inaptness of romantic authorship at grasping the complexity of actual modes of creation is also emphasized by those scholars who analyze originality in the context of psychological theories of copyright. For instance, Jeanne Fromer observes that this is the case when creation is collaborative, as it is in the case of film production, computer software development, or jazz music performance. However, she also points out that individuals making up the collaboration still go through at least some of the four stages of creativity (these being preparation, incubation, illumination, and verification), and as a collective they go through all four.[11] More radical is the position of Gregory Mandel, who stresses the inaccuracy of the common cultural stereotype of artistic creativity. This is because

> Artistic creation often involves logical cognition and externally focused objectives. This is particularly true if we focus on joint endeavors ... As with inventors, artists' own descriptions of their creative processes demonstrate the

---

[8] Michel Foucault, 'What is an author?', in Donald F Bouchard (ed), *Language, counter-memory, practice: selected essays and interviews* (first pub-lished 1969, Cornell University Press 1977) 113.

[9] Mark Rose, *Authors and owners. The invention of copyright* (Harvard University Press 1993), 2.

[10] Peter Jaszi, 'On the author effect: contemporary copyright and collective creativity', in Martha Woodmansee and Peter Jaszi (eds), *The construction of authorship. Textual appropriation in law and literature* (Duke University Press 1994) 29, 38. *See* also Rose, *Authors and owners*, *cit*, 135.

[11] Jeanne C Fromer, 'A psychology of intellectual property' (2010) 104 NWL Rev 1441, 1484.

inaccuracies of the common stereotype. Edgar Allan Poe described authoring *The Raven*, one of the most famous poems of all time, as follows: 'It was my design to render it manifest that no one point in its composition is referable either to accident or intuition – that the work proceeded, step by step, to its completion with the precision and rigid consequence of a mathematical problem.' Poe goes on to describe how logic dictated his every decision in *The Raven*, from the optimal number of words to the individual words and imagery used. While it seems hard to believe that Poe was not exaggerating at least a little, it is also evident that logic and reason play a significant role in artistic creativity ... Artistic creativity, like technological creativity, depends significantly on more holistic, relational creativity as well [as] logical cognition.[12]

Although romantic conceptions of authorship (and hence, originality) fail to grasp the complexity of the mechanisms pertaining to creativity, this does not mean that the very idea of authorship must be rejected *tout court*. Instead, what is required is a new conceptualization of its meaning and a more sophisticated elaboration of the modes of joint authorship. Without authorship, copyright would have to be recast in materialist terms. Authorship and creativity would be tantamount to mere investments of labour power, with the consequence that the contributor would be entitled not to proprietorship but simply remuneration.[13] This would result in copyright being given a legal shape that departs from the very idea of property over the results of the creative process.[14]

In any case, even by maintaining the notion of authorship, a rethinking of what is meant by this would result in a new conceptualization of copyright. This is because '[a] claim that copyright laws sanctify romantic authorship does not require an argument that authors retain

---

[12]   Gregory N Mandel, 'Left-brain versus right-brain: competing conceptions of creativity in intellectual property law' (2010) 44 UC Davis L Rev 283, 339–40 (footnotes omitted).

[13]   *See* Lionel Bently, 'Copyright and the death of the author in literature and law' (1994) 57 MLR 973, 986, and Jessica Litman, 'The public domain' (1990) 39 Emory LJ 965.

[14]   Marieke van Schijndel and Joost Smiers, 'Imagining a world without copyright: the market and temporary protection, a better alternative for artists and the public domain', in Helle Porsdam (ed), *Copyright and other fairy tales. Hans Christian Andersen and the commodification of creativity* (Edward Elgar Publishing 2006) 147, 156 suggest copyright be replaced by temporarily protected usufruct. This, which derives from Roman law, is a more minor right than full property. The main characteristic of usufruct is that one does not have the ownership of an item, but rather the usage of the fruits of such an item for a given period.

perpetual right in their creations, or that copyright laws protect total ownership.'[15]

The quest for remuneration plays a necessary role in encouraging human cultural productions, but non-market rewards, such as recognition, professional advancement, credibility, generosity or even simple pleasure, also drive creativity and incentivize cultural production.[16] Hence, authorship is not just about exclusive rights. It also plays a fundamental role in terms of recognition and, as such, in determining the scope of the moral rights authors enjoy in their creations.[17] Therefore, even considering the pitfalls in the romantic theory of authorship, it would be difficult to imagine a legal landscape without authorship and, as a consequence, without copyright.

Any meaning given to authorship is to be read in conjunction with that of originality, although authorship as such is not based on originality, but rather entails the notions of 'individuality', 'responsibility' and 'unique work'.[18] This said, the more authorship is conceived in romantic terms, the higher the threshold to originality and, therefore, to copyright protection will be.

---

[15]   Lior Zemer, *The idea of authorship in copyright* (Ashgate 2007), 74. This author suggests that copyright should not be regarded as exclusive private property. Since copyright-protected works profit from significant public contribution, Zemer argues that both the public and authors should own them under a joint title.

[16]   Alina Ng, *Copyright law and the progress of science and the useful arts* (Edward Elgar 2011), 13. *See* also David A Simon, 'Culture, creativity, & copyright' (2011) 29 Cardozo Arts & Ent LJ 279, who argues (282) that, albeit authors create also out of monetary purposes, it is not necessary to separate out monetary motivations from nonmonetary ones. This is because the two have common traits which need to be jointly analyzed.

[17]   These are not yet subject to a coherent international approach. Therefore, inconsistent application and disparities in the level of protection cause problems when it comes to the enforcement of moral rights in different countries (*cf* Gillian Davies and Kevin Garnett, *Moral rights* (Sweet & Maxwell 2010), 1036 ff).

[18]   Anne Sechin, 'On plagiarism, originality, textual ownership, and textual responsibility. The case of *Jacques le fatalist*', in Reginald McGinnis (ed), *Originality and intellectual property in the French and English enlightenment* (Routledge 2009), 102, 103.

2. DIFFICULTIES IN DEFINING ORIGINALITY

Attempts to analyze originality in a theoretical fashion have been inevitably beset by difficulties. These are due to the vagueness of the very concept itself, as well as to uncertainties regarding its scope. As has been incisively pointed out:

> The trouble is that a theory of originality seems sometimes to amount to a theory of almost everything and sometimes to almost nothing. Worse, we often seem to oscillate between two platitudes: that the only constant is change and there is nothing new under the sun.[19]

In addition, the very meaning of originality inevitably differs between works of imagination and those of industrious collection. Yet, the legal test to be applied in order to determine whether a work is protected by copyright ought to be the same for both. Such (voluntary) incapability of copyright, justified by policy reasons,[20] to distinguish what is truly original from what is just industrious has inevitably led copyright-protected subject-matter to grow, sometimes even outwith all rational justifications. This may be considered as a 'vice' of copyright, as Benjamin Kaplan suggested, in that '[i]t is a question of sinning against flexibility by unwillingness to look closely at the works or to admit considerations of policy beyond the immediately obvious.'[21] However, as copyright protection is, broadly speaking, granted to 'works' (often these also have to meet the requirement of being 'fixed in a tangible form') which are 'original', it is apparent that the understanding of originality has the power to shape the breadth of any given copyright regime and, along with it, the scope of protection afforded to protected subject-matter.

In any case, as suggested by Richard Posner, any given notion of the originality requirement has implications as to the actual relevance of copyright to authors. This is because 'the less originality is valued, the less valuable to authors and readers is copyright protection, which encourages originality.'[22]

---

[19] John Vignaux Smyth, 'Originality in Enlightenment and beyond,' in Reginald McGinnis (ed), *Originality and intellectual property in the French and English enlightenment* (Routledge 2009), 175, 175–6.

[20] *See* below *sub* Section II, §1.5.

[21] Benjamin Kaplan, *An unhurried view of copyright* (Columbia University Press 1967), 77.

[22] Richard A Posner, *Law and literature* (revised and enlarged edn, Harvard University Press 1998), 391, who provides the following example: 'The absence of copyright law in Imperial China despite the fact that printing had begun there

While disregarding the philosophical foundations of this concept,[23] in legal terms originality is nowadays understood as falling within four families of standards. These, ranging from the most restrictive to the most generous, are continental Europe's and now the EU's 'author's own intellectual creation' standard, the US standard of a 'minimal degree of creativity' pursuant to the decision of the US Supreme Court in *Feist*,[24] Canada's *CCH*[25] standard of 'non-mechanical and non-trivial exercise of skill and judgment' and the UK's 'skill and labour' standard.[26]

---

centuries before it began in the West has been attributed in part to the emphasis that Chinese culture placed on continuity with the past and its suspicion of novelty, both of which encouraged copying.'

[23]   On which *see*, *inter alia*, Bruce Vermazen, 'The aesthetic value of originality' (1991) 16 MISP 266.

[24]   *Feist Publications, Inc, v Rural Telephone Service Co*, 499 US 340 (1991), on which *see* further below, *sub* Section II, §1.

[25]   *CCH Canadian Ltd v Law Soc'y of Upper Can*, [2004] 1 SCR 339, Section 15 (Can). The Law Society of Upper Canada maintained and operated the Great Library at Osgoode Hall in Toronto, a reference and research library with one of the largest collections of legal materials in Canada. The Great Library provided a request-based photocopy service for Law Society members, the judiciary and other authorized researchers. Under this 'custom photocopy service', legal materials were reproduced by Great Library staff and delivered to those requesting them. The Law Society also maintained self-service photo-copiers in the Great Library for use by its patrons. In 1993, three of the largest publishers of legal sources, CCH Canadian, Carswell Thomson and Canada Law Book sued the Law Society for copyright infringement of eleven specific works based on these activities. The Law Society denied liability and counterclaimed that copyright is not infringed when a single copy of a reported decision, case summary, statute, regulation or a limited selection of text from a treatise is made by the Great Library staff, or one of its patrons on a self-service copier, for the purpose of research. The Federal Court, Trial Division allowed the publishers' action in part, finding that the Law Society had infringed copyright in certain works and dismissed the Law Society's counterclaim. The Federal Court of Appeal allowed the publishers' appeal in part, holding that all of the works were original and therefore covered by copyright. It dismissed the Law Society's cross-appeal. The Supreme Court of Canada reversed, and held that the Law Society had not infringed copyright when a single copy of a reported decision, case summary, statute, regulation or limited selection of text from a treatise was made by the Great Library in accordance with its access policy. Moreover, the Law Society had not authorized copyright infringement by maintaining a photocopier in the Great Library and posting a notice warning that it will not be responsible for any copies made in infringement of copyright.

[26]   In this way, Elizabeth F Judge and Daniel Gervais, 'Of silos and constellations: comparing notions of originality in copyright law' (2009) 27 Cardozo Arts & Ent LJ 375, 377–8.

Given the scope of the present contribution, in the following paragraphs attention will be first dedicated to the legislative evolution (or lack
thereof) of originality within EU copyright reforms, including the
approach adopted in the relevant directives. Then, originality will be
considered under the lenses of the EU continental Member States and the
UK copyright traditions, respectively.

3. ORIGINALITY IN EU REFORM POLICY: THE INVISIBLE MAN

The 2004 Commission Staff Working Paper on the *Review of the EC
legal framework in the field of copyright and related rights*[27] was aimed
at evaluating the coherence of the *acquis communautaire* in the field of
copyright, in light of the set of directives which had harmonized some
aspects of copyright at the EU level until that point.[28]

The objective of the review was twofold: firstly, to improve the
operation of the *acquis communautaire* and its coherence; secondly, to
safeguard the proper functioning of the internal market.[29] The Working
Paper analyzed the provisions of the early *acquis* and compared them
with the standard set by the InfoSoc Directive.

The conclusions of the Working Paper were such as to advocate a
minor revision of the definition of the reproduction right and an extended
application of the exception for certain temporary acts of reproduction,
under Article 5(1) of the InfoSoc Directive, to computer programs and
databases.[30] The Working Paper included also a final section[31] dedicated
to the assessment of issues outside the current *acquis*, such as originality,
ownership, the definition of the term 'public', points of attachment,
moral rights and the exhaustion of rights.

---

[27] Commission Staff Working Paper on the review of the EC legal framework in the field of copyright and related rights, 19 July 2004, SEC (2004) 995.

[28] The Directives subject to revision in the Working Paper were the
following: Council Directive 91/250/EEC of 14 May 1991 on the legal protection
of computer programs; Council Directive 92/100/EEC of 19 November 1992 on
rental right and lending right and on certain rights related to copyright in the
field of intellectual property; Council Directive 93/98/EEC of 29 October 1993
harmonizing the term of protection of copyright and certain related rights;
Directive 96/9/EC of the European Parliament and of the Council of 11 March
1996 on the legal protection of databases.

[29] *Working Paper, cit*, 5.

[30] *Ibid*, 19.

[31] *Ibid*, para 3.

In particular, as far as originality and moral rights were concerned, the Working Paper, while acknowledging the different meanings and scope assigned to them by the various Member States' legislations, assessed such disparities in light of the functioning of the internal market. In particular, it recalled that EU legislation expressly dealt with the issue of originality whenever it was necessary to take account of the special features or the special technical nature of the categories of work in question.[32] So far, the originality requirement has in fact been referred to only in the following: Directive 2009/24/EC on the legal protection of computer programs (codified version, the 'Software Directive'); Directive 2006/116/EC on the term protection of copyright and certain related rights (codified version, the 'Term Directive') with regard to photographs; and Directive 96/9/EC on the legal protection of databases (the 'Database Directive').

Article 1(3) of the Software Directive provides that '[a] computer program shall be protected if it is original in the sense that it is the author's own intellectual creation. No other criteria shall be applied to determine its eligibility for protection.' Similarly, Article 6 of the Term Directive states that '[p]hotographs which are original in the sense that they are the author's own intellectual creation shall be protected in accordance with Article 1. No other criteria shall be applied to determine their eligibility for protection. Member States may provide for the protection of other photographs.' Article 3(1) of the Database Directive provides that '[i]n accordance with this Directive, databases which, by reason of the selection or arrangement of their contents, constitute the author's own intellectual creation shall be protected as such by copyright. No other criteria shall be applied to determine their eligibility for that protection.'

From the foregoing, it is apparent that, when harmonized, the originality requirement was intended as 'the author's own intellectual creation'. This means (as will be also explained further below) that the harmonization of the originality requirement for certain categories of works followed the continental model and thus the notion of originality implicitly embraced in the Berne Convention, as later incorporated into the Agreement on Trade-Related Aspects of Intellectual Property Rights (TRIPS).[33] Although copyright subject-matter has to be the result of the

---

[32]   *Ibid*, para 3.1.

[33]   Daniel J Gervais, 'The compatibility of the skill and labour standard with the Berne Convention and the TRIPs Agreement' (2004) 26 EIPR 75, 79. The same author however had previously noted that, when drafting the TRIPS Agreement, it was decided that originality should be applied in accordance with

individual's own intellectual efforts,[34] it is important to highlight that the degree of originality required for protection under Berne varies widely amongst the countries which are parties to the Convention.[35] In jurisdictions that conformed their own copyright systems to the French *droit d'auteur* tradition, originality is indeed meant as *la marque d'un apport intellectuel*.[36] This does not imply that a work, in order to be original, has to show a certain degree of novelty, but that the personality of the author has to be visible in the creative result.

The Working Paper highlighted that the understanding of originality is indeed not unique across the EU, as the legal systems of the various Member States interpret its meaning in different ways. As recalled by Silke von Lewinski, the differences between Anglo-Saxon and *droit d'auteur* systems have proved to be a major source of problems when discussing and then adopting internationally-binding agreements, or even when pursuing regional harmonization.[37] However, the conclusion of the Working Paper was that neither divergent originality requirements, nor the different scope of moral rights across Member States, might significantly impair the proper functioning of the internal market. Thus, an EU intervention in this sense was deemed to be unnecessary at that stage. In particular, there seemed to be no evidence that diverging requirements for the level of originality by Member States had the potential to create barriers to intra-Community trade. Only divergent economic rights might have impaired the proper functioning of the internal market.

It is submitted that to adopt this attitude is to neglect the fact that economic rights descend, in the first place, from the entitlement to copyright protection. One of the basic requirements is that a work must be original to be protected under copyright. Therefore, a discussion on copyright limited to the mere harmonization of economic rights (as has happened until very recently) is of reduced relevance, as any reform of

---

the law of the country where protection is claimed (Daniel Gervais, *The TRIPS Agreement. Drafting history and analysis* (2nd edn, Sweet & Maxwell 2003), 131).

[34]   *Cf* Article 2(5) of the Berne Convention: 'Collections of literary or artistic works such as encyclopaedias and anthologies which, by reason of the selection and arrangement of their contents, constitute intellectual creations shall be protected as such, without prejudice to the copyright in each of the works forming part of such collections.'

[35]   Kevin Garnett, Gillian Davies and Gwilym Harbottle, *Copinger and Skone James on copyright* (16th edn, Sweet & Maxwell 2012), Vol I, 138.

[36]   *See* below, *sub* Section I, §5.

[37]   *See* Silke von Lewinski, *International copyright law and policy* (OUP 2008), 33 ff.

the details should properly result from a comprehensive knowledge and careful analysis of the overall picture. It is regrettably parochial to proceed with a reform agenda under the assumption that disparities in the scope of copyright protection would harm the efficient functioning of the internal market only and expressly when such disparities relate to economic rights.

4. THE 'AUTHOR'S OWN INTELLECTUAL CREATION' STANDARD IN THE SOFTWARE, DATABASE AND TERM DIRECTIVES

Despite similar wordings, the author's own intellectual creation standard has been said not to have the same meaning within the Software, Database and Term Directives. This is because harmonization of the originality requirement in relation to, respectively, computer programs, databases, and photographs was supported by different rationales.[38]

As far as computer programs were concerned, the Software Directive was aimed at reconciling the stricter continental originality requirement with the more generous 'skill and labour' standard of UK copyright.[39] However, this conclusion is not uncontroversial, as some commentators hold the view that the phrase 'author's own intellectual creation' was adopted to indicate that the UK concept of originality was intended.[40]

Recital 8 in the preamble to the directive made it clear that 'in determining whether or not a computer program is an original work, no tests as to the qualitative or aesthetic merits of the program should be applied.' As recalled by Trevor Cook,[41] the inclusion of this recital was meant to address the consequences of the 1985 decision of the German Federal Supreme Court in *Inkassoprogram*,[42] in which it was held that under German law a computer program could be protected by copyright

---

[38]   *Cf* Mireille van Eechoud, P Bernt Hugenholtz, Stef van Gompel, Lucie Guibault and Natali Helberger, *Harmonizing European copyright law. The challenges of better law making* (Kluwer Law International 2009), 41.

[39]   *See* Catherine Seville, *EU intellectual property law and policy* (Edward Elgar Publishing 2009), 28.

[40]   Garnett, Davies and Harbottle, *Copinger and Skone James on copyright*, *cit*, Vol I, 1476, referring to Bridget Czarnota and Robert J Hart, *Legal protection of computer programs in Europe: a guide to the EC Directive* (LexisNexis 1991), 44.

[41]   Trevor Cook, *EU intellectual property law* (OUP 2010), 100.

[42]   BGH GRUR 1985, 1041/1047.

only if it displayed a degree of creativity which surpassed the general average of ability present in works of that kind. According to other commentators, the very adoption of the Software Directive was to be urged by the need to address the criticisms raised against the decision of the German Federal Supreme Court.[43]

In its report on the implementation and effects of the Software Directive, the Commission highlighted its striking feature, this being that for the first time the level of originality had been harmonized at the Community level for a specific copyright subject-matter. As a consequence of this, *droit d'auteur* countries (in particular Germany) were required to lower the protection threshold, whereas the UK and Ireland had to 'lift the bar'.[44] Apparently, the Commission did not find any particular problems with the practical application of the harmonized originality requirement in individual Member States. When implementing the Software Directive, the UK, which was one of the Member States most likely to be affected by the adoption of the author's own intellectual creation standard, did not deem it necessary to state explicitly what originality requirement ought to be intended in relation to computer programs, on consideration that originality under UK copyright was already consistent with the standard adopted in the directive. Although some commentators also shared this view,[45] it is unlikely that 'author's own intellectual creation' was to be intended as akin to the characterization of originality as 'sufficient skill labour and effort'.[46] This has now been confirmed by CJEU case law, in particular if one reads the Opinion of AG Mengozzi in *Football Dataco*.[47]

As far as the UK is concerned, it should be also noted that the standard envisaged in the directive requires that human intellectual effort is exercised in the production of a computer program, if that program is to

---

[43] Frederick M Abbott, Thomas Cottier and Francis Gurry, *International intellectual property in an integrated world economy* (2nd edn, Wolters Kluwer Law & Business 2011), 610–11.

[44] Report from the Commission to the Council, the European Parliament and the Economic and Social Committee on the implementation and effects of Directive 91/250/EEC on the legal protection of computer programs, Brussels, 10 April 2000, COM (2000) 199 final.

[45] *See* Dana Beldiman, *Functionality, information works, and copyright* (Lulu.com 2008), 68.

[46] In this sense, amongst the others, Stanley Lai, *The copyright protection of computer software in the United Kingdom* (Hart Publishing 2000), 17, and also 85, and Tanya Aplin and Jennifer Davis, *Intellectual property law. Text, cases, and materials* (1st edn, OUP 2009), 85.

[47] On which *see* below, *sub* Chapter 4, § 3.3.

be protected by copyright. This implies that computer programs produced without human input may not qualify for copyright protection under EU law, although computer-generated works are expressly protected under UK law.[48]

A somewhat clearer explanation as to why the originality requirement was harmonized at the EU level was provided with regard to databases.[49] In its report containing a first evaluation of the Database Directive,[50] DG Internal Market and Services explained that, prior to the adoption of the Directive, national laws differed with respect to the level of originality which was used to determine whether a database was protectable under copyright law (in some Member States there were also other forms of protection, like the so-called catalogue-rule in Scandinavian countries).[51] In particular, the threshold in common law jurisdictions was lower than that prevailing in *droit d'auteur* Member States. The best-known examples of compilations of data or information which were granted copyright protection under the common law standard (which is defined in the report as 'sweat of the brow') were the television programme listings which were the subject of the action in *Magill*.[52] The Commission found that

---

[48]   Cook, *EU intellectual property law*, *cit*, 100–01. Section 9(3) of the 1988 Copyright Designs and Patents Act (CDPA 1988) provides that in the case of literary – which include computer programs, pursuant to Section 3(1)(b) CDPA 1988 – dramatic, musical or artistic works which are computer-generated, the author shall be taken to be the person by whom the arrangements necessary for the creation of the work are undertaken.

[49]   For a thoughtful commentary on the history of the Database Directive, *see* Mark J Davison, *The legal protection of databases* (CUP 2003), 51 ff.

[50]   DG Internal Market and Services Working Paper, *First evaluation of Directive 96/9 on the legal protection of databases*, Brussels, 12 December 2005.

[51]   Denmark, Finland and Sweden granted protection to catalogues, tables or other similar productions in which a large number of information items were compiled.

[52]   Joined Cases C 241/91 P and C-242/91 P *Radio Telefis Eireann (RTE) and Independent Television Publications Ltd (ITP) v Commission of the European Communities*, [1995] I-00743. ITP, RTE and BBC used to provide their programme schedules free of charge, on request, to daily and periodical newspapers, accompanied by a licence for which no charge was made, setting out the conditions under which that information could be reproduced. Magill attempted to publish a comprehensive weekly television guide but was prevented from doing so by the appellants and the BBC, which obtained injunctions prohibiting publication of weekly television listings. Magill lodged a complaint with the Commission seeking a declaration that the appellants and the BBC were abusing their dominant position by refusing to grant licences for the publication of their respective weekly listings. The Commission found that the broadcasters

differences in legal protection between common law and *droit d'auteur* Member States had negative effects on the free movement of database products, the provision of information services and the freedom of establishment within the Community.[53] Hence, it was necessary to establish a uniform threshold of originality for original databases, and the author's own intellectual creation standard was chosen as the harmonized notion of originality. In fact, the Commission reasoned that copyright should vest just in databases which were original in the continental sense. In other words, the originality requirement 'imposes a significant qualitative factor ... , requiring some subjective contribution by the author.'[54] The introduction of the *sui generis* right in parallel to the introduction of the harmonized originality standard was aimed at compensating for the loss of the 'sweat of the brow' protection, and was as such a new form of intellectual property over non-original databases.[55]

Also in this case, the author's own intellectual creation standard was probably meant as a compromise between continental (in particular German) and UK originality requirements.[56] It was, however, in the UK that the harmonized meaning of originality for databases had the most dramatic impact, which resulted in the abandonment of authorities such as *Ladbroke (Football) Ltd v William Hill (Football) Ltd*,[57] as will be seen also below *sub* Section II, §2.2.[58]

With regard to photographs, although Article 6 of the Term Directive provides that copyright vests only in those which are their author's own intellectual creation, Recital 16 in the preamble to the directive clarifies

---

had abused their dominant position, and the decision was confirmed by the then Court of First Instance.

[53] *See* Terence Prime, *European intellectual property law* (Ashgate 2000), 259–61.

[54] Garnett, Davies and Harbottle, *Copinger and Skone James on copyright, cit*, Vol I, 158.

[55] DG Internal Market and Services Working Paper, *First evaluation, cit*, 8–9. On this, *see* also Seville, *EU intellectual property law, cit*, 41–2.

[56] *See* Annemarie C Beunen, *Protection for databases: the European Database Directive and its effects in the Netherlands, France and the United Kingdom* (Wolf Legal Publishers 2007), 76–7; Beldiman, *Functionality, cit*, 71, who interprets the harmonized meaning of originality as being tantamount to a standard of simple individuality.

[57] [1964] 1 WLR 273.

[58] For a discussion on the type of protection available to databases and tables and compilations other than databases following the implementation of the Database Directive into UK copyright, *see* Aplin and Davis, *Intellectual property law*, cit, 719 ff.

that a photographic work is to be considered original if it is the author's own intellectual creation reflecting his personality. It has been argued that this wording seems to imply a stricter test than that laid down for software and databases.[59] This conclusion would be required to comply with the stated intention of the framers of this provision, which was to clarify that the normal term of protection does not apply to simple (sub-original) photographs, which may nonetheless qualify for quasi-copyright or neighbouring right protection, in compliance with Member States' laws.[60] In any case, this standard of originality is rather different from that which could be discerned in UK law with regard to photographs.[61]

According to an influential commentary, the originality standard adopted by the Software, Database and Term Directives is to be found also in the 2001 InfoSoc Directive. Overall, also this directive is rooted within 'the principle that the protection of subject-matter as authors' works presupposes that they are intellectual creations, and that copyright as protected under the Directive applies only in relation to a subject-matter which is original in the sense that it is its author's own intellectual creation.'[62] This said, however, the same commentary concludes by saying that

> At present, the effect of these Directives has not been to alter the general law of the United Kingdom as regards originality as it is applied in practice (the originality required for a database is clearly an exception) and it seems likely that this will remain the position. The Directives do not lay down any very clear test of originality and although the test for originality under UK law is low in comparison to that of some Member States, it is generally based on the principle that a work should be the author's own intellectual creation.[63]

---

[59]   Eechoud, Hugenholtz, Gompel, Guibault and Helberger, *Harmonizing*, *cit*, 41, referring to Gunnar WG Karnell, 'European originality: a copyright chimera', in Jan JC Kabel and Willy Alexander (eds), *Intellectual property and information law: essays in honour of Herman Cohen Jehoram* (Kluwer Law International 1998), 201, 203.

[60]   For instance, Article 92 of the Italian Copyright Act (Legge 22 April 1941, No 633) provides that exclusive rights on simple photographs last for twenty years from the realization of the photograph.

[61]   Christina Michalos, *The law of photography and digital images* (Sweet & Maxwell 2004), 133.

[62]   Garnett, Davies and Harbottle, *Copinger and Skone James on copyright*, *cit*, Vol I, 140 (footnotes omitted).

[63]   *Ibid* (footnotes omitted).

The present contribution holds a view to the contrary, ie that the understanding of originality in the UK has been different from the EU notion of this basic principle. This has also been confirmed by recent decisions of the CJEU, which have clarified that an author's own intellectual creation is not just the result of sufficient skill, labour and effort.

5. UNDERSTANDING ORIGINALITY: THE CONTINENTAL APPROACH

Whilst common law copyright systems have been traditionally ascribed to incentive-based views of copyright (although in its early days copyright was intended just to protect the rightsholder against unauthorized use or reproduction of his material),[64] civil law traditions have adopted different approaches to copyright, which descend from rights-based views of it. The latter may be traced back to the philosophies of Kant,[65] Fichte[66] and Hegel.[67]

As explained by Andreas Rahmatian:

> While the Common law copyright systems focus on the work and its potential economic value, the author's rights systems concentrate on the author and protect his work because it bears traces of the author's personality. It is not the work that protects (indirectly) the author/maker and his economic interests, but the author's protection as a person which extends to works emanating from that person.[68]

---

[64] *See, ex multis*, F Willelm Grosheide, 'Paradigms in copyright law', in Brad Sherman and Alain Strowel (eds), *Of authors and origins. Essays on copyright law* (Clarendon Press 1994), 203, 207–09.

[65] Immanuel Kant, 'Von der Unrechtmässigkeit des Büchernachdruckes' (1785), Italian Translation: 'Dell'illegittimità dell'editoria pirata', in Riccardo Pozzo (ed), *L'autore e i suoi diritti. Scritti polemici sulla proprietà intellettuale* (Biblioteca di Via Senato Edizioni 2005), 39.

[66] Johan Gottlieb Fichte, 'Beweis der Unrechtmäßigkeit der Büchernach-druckes: Ein Räsonment und eine Parabel' (1791), Italian Translation: 'Dimostrazione dell'illegittimità dell'editoria pirata: un ragionamento e una parabola', in Pozzo (ed), *L'autore e i suoi diritti. Scritti polemici sulla proprietà intellettuale* (Biblioteca di Via Senato Edizioni 2005), 73.

[67] Georg Wilhelm Freidric Hegel, *Grundlinien der Philosophie des Rechts* (1820), English Translation, in Allen W Wood (ed), *Elements of philosophy of right* (CUP 1991), 67.

[68] Andreas Rahmatian, *Copyright and creativity. The making of property rights in creative works* (Edward Elgar Publishing 2011), 47, citing F Willelm

However, the differences between copyright and *droit d'auteur* regimes have been scaled down on account of both historical evidence[69] and critical assessments of relevant legislative developments.[70] Indeed, it has been highlighted how, while *in principle* the copyright and *droit d'auteur* traditions rest on sharply differing premises, *in fact* these two systems are far more alike than they are unlike. This is on account of both legislative and practical developments. As to legislative developments, it can be said that the Berne Convention has bridged the two systems, with the result that its extensive minimum standards have dictated substantively similar rules. In addition, similarities in economic, political and social structures across the two systems have also led to a certain convergence.[71]

This said, however, there remain aspects which are reminiscent of diverging theoretical approaches. One of them concerns the characterization of the originality requirement.[72]

The contemporary continental understanding refers to the personal, individual input of the author. In other words, the work has to be an

---

Grosheide, 'Moral rights', in Estelle Derclaye (ed), *Research handbook on the future of EU copyright* (Edward Elgar Publishing 2009), 242, 243.

[69]   For instance, Jane C Ginsburg, 'A tale of two copyrights: literary property in revolutionary France and America', in Brad Sherman and Alain Strowel (eds), *Of authors and origins* (Clarendon Press 1994), 131, highlights that, despite the traditional understanding of the US Copyright Clause (on which *see* below *sub* Section II, §1.1.) as being opposed to the *esprit* enshrined in the French revolutionary copyright laws of 1791, the differences between revolutionary US and French copyright systems were neither as extensive nor as venerable as typically described.

[70]   According to Lyman Ray Patterson, *Copyright in historical perspective* (Vanderbilt University Press 1968), 143, the Statute of Anne (this was the first copyright statute of modern history and has been traditionally considered rooted within an incentive-based view of copyright) was not intended to benefit primarily authors. It was instead a trade regulation statute enacted, among the other things, to put an end to the booksellers' monopoly.

[71]   Paul Goldstein and Bernt Hugenholtz, *International copyright. Principles, law and practice* (2nd edn, OUP 2010), 14–15, citing, amongst others, William R Cornish, 'Sound recordings and copyright' (1993) 24 IIC 306, 307: 'Over primary issues of making the rights granted legally effective and so economically meaningful, the two approaches flow together in a single stream. Where there are divergences, they are often more the product of low political lobbying than of high and disinterested thought.'

[72]   *Cf* Gillian Davies, *Copyright and the public interest* (2nd edn, Sweet & Maxwell 2002), 329–30, who holds the different view that, while differences between the various standards of originality have had (especially in the past) an important impact on the concept of authorship and protectable subject-matter, these are currently to be scaled down.

œuvre de l'esprit ('work of the mind')[73] – not just the result of skill and labour – to enjoy copyright protection. This definition is to be found in the French intellectual property code.[74] As a consequence of this approach, and contrary to what is the law in the US,[75] French courts have found that copyright subsisted even in very short phrases or titles, such as *'Les hauts de Hurlevent'*,[76] *'Clochemerle'*,[77] *'Vol de nuit'*,[78] and *Les liaisons dangereous*,[79] whilst protection has been denied, *inter alia*, to *Guele d'amour*,[80] *Éducation anglaise*,[81] *Le Meuf Show*,[82] and *Vogue*.[83] As noted by Lucas and Lucas, in instances pertaining to copyright protection of titles, in assessing their originality or lack thereof, courts have often employed a language similar to that of trademark law.[84] This observation serves to highlight, on the one hand, the difficulties relating to a proper and independent understanding of the notion of originality in copyright law and, on the other hand, the circumstance for which its appreciation has often relied either on the concept of novelty in patent law (as it was, among the other things, in *Feist*[85]) or distinctive character in trademark law.

---

[73] André Lucas and Henri-Jacques Lucas, *Traité de la propriété litéraire et artistique* (3rd edn, Litec 2006), 53.

[74] 'L'auteur d'une oeuvre de l'esprit jouit sur cette oeuvre, du seul fait de sa création, d'un droit de propriété incorporelle exclusif et opposable à tous.' ('The author of a work of the mind has upon such work, for the very act of creation, an intellectual property right which is exclusive and can be opposed to anyone', Article L111-1(1) of the Code de la propriété intellectuelle – consolidated version as to 1 January 2012).

[75] CFR 37 §202.1(a) excludes, among the other things, that copyright may vest in words and short phrases such as names, titles, and slogans.

[76] Tribunal de commerce Seine, 26 June 1951.

[77] Cour d'appel Lyon, 5 July 1979.

[78] Tribunal de Grande Instance de Nanterre, 28 April 1998.

[79] Cour d'appel Paris, 4e ch, 30 April 1963.

[80] C Cass, 2 February 1937,

[81] Cour d'appel Paris, 4e ch, 23 January 1995.

[82] Cour d'appel Paris, 4e ch, 16 September 2005.

[83] C Cass com, 17 January 2006. For further references, *see* Lucas and Lucas, *Traité, cit,* 91–92.

[84] '[L]a protection des titres relève autant, sinon plus, des signes distinctifs que de la propriété littéraire, ce qui explique la terminologie spontanément utilisée, par exemple les références à l'antériorité, à la nouveauté, au caractère descriptif, générique, distinctif, attractif, et aussi l'imbrication avec le droit des marques.' (Lucas and Lucas, *Traité, cit,* 94, footnotes omitted).

[85] *See* below, *sub* Section II.

In France references to novelty have been made to highlight the differences between this and the criterion of originality. In other countries, however, a 'comparative' approach has been sometimes employed by courts. As explained by Sterling, this is said not to be dissimilar to 'the novelty test in patent law, and looks at the question whether the work in suit may be regarded as unique.'[86]

In other instances, references have been made to trademark law to mark the continuity between the notion of originality in copyright and that of distinctive character in trademark law. This has been the case also under EU copyright law, especially if one looks at the Opinion of Advocate General Trstenjak in *Infopaq*,[87] which contains an express reference to originality as being tantamount to distinctiveness. When discussing the notion of 'reproduction in part', the Advocate General made it clear that its interpretation must not be excessively technical and such as to include any form of reproduction of a work. Reproduction in part of a work subsists when what has been copied includes 'a content, a distinctive character and – as part of a given work – a certain intellectual value, for which reason it is necessary to give it copyright protection.'[88]

Coming to legislative definitions of originality, French law does not contain a general reference to the originality requirement, nor do other civil law countries.[89] For instance, the Italian copyright act provides for copyright to vest in *opere dell'ingegno di carattere creativo* ('intellectual creations having creative character'),[90] while German law grants protection to *persönliche geistige Schöpfungen* ('personal intellectual creation'),[91] which is very similar to the relevant provision under Portuguese

---

[86]   JAL Sterling, *World copyright law*, (2nd edn, Sweet & Maxwell 2003), 338. For the position under UK law, *see* below *sub* Section II, §2.1.

[87]   Case C-5/08 *Infopaq International A/S v Danske Dagblades Forening* [2009] I-06569, Opinion of Advocate General Verica Trstenjak, delivered on 12 February 2009.

[88]   *Ibid* [58].

[89]   *See* Ramon Casas Vallés, 'The requirement of originality', in Estelle Derclaye (ed), *Research handbook on the future of EU copyright* (Edward Elgar Publishing 2009), 102, 106 for more legislative definitions of originality in various countries.

[90]   Article 1(1) of Legge 22 April 1941 No 633 – *Protezione del diritto d'autore e di altri diritti connessi al suo esercizio* ('Protection of copyright and other rights connected to its exercise') and Article 2575 of Codice Civile ('Civil Code').

[91]   Article 2(2) of Urheberrechsgestetz, UrhG 1965 as last amended on 8 May 1998.

copyright law: *criações intelectuais do domínio literário, científico e artístico* ('intellectual creations in the literary, scientific or artistic areas').[92]

Laconic formulas used in continental Member States' copyright laws, or the lack of a specific definition of originality *tout court*, have led some commentators to conclude that courts in Member States cannot give substance to the EU criterion in interpreting originality.[93] Others[94] have suggested that the continental understanding of originality is akin to the standard envisaged by the US Supreme Court in *Feist Publications v Rural Telephone Service Co*,[95] which will be explained below *sub* Section II, §1.

Despite these criticisms, one can agree with Lucas and Lucas, who highlight how:

> Faute de pouvoir scruter les intentions d'un législateur qui semble avoir évité soigneusement le débat, on peut tenter de cerner la notion d'œuvre de l'esprit en opposant schématiquement deux démarches. Dans une approche objective, on dira que le cheminement importe peu et que seul compte le résultat. Dans une approche subjective, on mettra l'accent sur le lien entre l'œuvre et le créateur ...
>
> Le deux démarches doivent ... être combinées. Une œuvre de l'esprit, c'est une création intellectuelle ..., se concrétisant dans une forme perceptible aux sens ... [96]

---

[92]   Article 2(1) of the Código do direito de autor e dos direitos conexos – decreto lei No 63/85, de 14 de março ('Code of copyright and neighbouring rights – law decree No 63 on 14 March 1985').

[93]   Karnell, 'European originality', *cit*, 76.

[94]   Sterling, *World copyright law*, *cit*, 309, as reported in Tanya Aplin, *Copyright law in the digital society. The challenges of multimedia* (Hart Publishing 2005), 56.

[95]   *Cit.*

[96]   Lucas and Lucas, *Traité*, *cit*, 53–4 (footnotes omitted; emphasis added): 'Although it is difficult to identify the intentions of a legislator, who appears to have carefully avoided such a debate, we can try to define the concept of a work of the mind by contrasting two approaches. On the one hand, the objective approach, according to which the [creative] path is of little importance and only the result is relevant. On the other hand, the subjective approach, according to which the link between the work and the author must be emphasized. Such approaches must be combined. A work of the mind is an intellectual creation ... which may be perceived by the senses.' A similar distinction between *l'originalité 'subjective'* and *l'originalité 'objective'* can be found also in Jean-Sylvestre Bergé, *La protection internationale et communautaire du droit d'auteur. Essai d'une analyse conflictuelle* (L.G.D.J. 1996), 24 ff.

This said, understanding the continental meaning of originality as being tantamount to 'the author's own intellectual creation' (which is to be found expressly under German law in respect of computer programs)[97] may be considered as a correct assumption, although different formulations of originality have been adopted by courts and scholars throughout civil law jurisdictions. Sometimes, originality has been defined as *la marque d'un apport intellectual* ('the mark of an intellectual contribution').[98] Other times it has been found to subsist when the work reflected *la personalità dell'autore* ('the personality of the author');[99] elsewhere, where it was the result of an *atto creativo* ('creative act') which had been given an external existence.[100] Despite reductive interpretations of the notion of originality under Italian law,[101] also recently the Milan Court of

---

[97]   Article 69a(3) of Urheberrechsgestetz, UrhG 1965 as last amended on 8 May 1998 provides that 'Computerprogramme warden geschützt, ween sie individuelle Werke in dem Sinne darstellen, daß sie das Ergebnis der eigenen geistigen Schöpfung ihres Urhebers sind. Zur Bestimmung ihrer Schutzfähigkeit sind keine anderen Kriterien, insbesondere nicht qualitative oder ästhetische, anzuwenden.' ('Computer programs shall be protected if they constitute original works in the sense that they are the result of their author's own intellectual creation. No other criteria, particularly of a qualitative or aesthetic nature, shall be applied to determine their eligibility for protection.' – English Translation by WIPO).
[98]   *Cf* the decision of the French Court of Cassation in *Babolat Maillot Witt v Pachot,* C Cass, Assemblée plénière, 7 March 1986,   No 82, regarding computer programs, in which it was held that 'l'originalité … est définie comme "la marque d'un apport intellectuel", c'est-à-dire un effort personnalisé dépassant la logique automatique et contraignante' ('originality … is defined as 'the mark of an intellectual contribution', ie a personal effort which supersedes automatic logic and association').
[99]   *Cf* Nicola Stolfi, *Il diritto d'autore* (Società Editrice Libraria 1932), 518 ff.
[100]   *RTI Reti Televisive Italiane and Another v Rai and Another,* Rome Court of First Instance, 21 October 2011. For further references, *see* Paolo Galli, 'Commento all'articolo 1 della Legge 22 aprile 1941 n. 633', in Luigi C Ubertazzi (ed), *Commentario breve alle leggi su proprietà intellettuale e concorrenza* (4th edn, CEDAM 2007), 1487, 1493.
[101]   According to Vittorio M De Sanctis, *Il diritto d'autore* (Giuffré 2012), 32 (footnotes omitted), 'è possibile equiparare la creatività alla paternità esclusiva dell'opera dell'ingegno, ma tenendo conto del fatto che vi sono personalità diverse per intensità e del fatto che alcune opere dell'ingegno non hanno bisogno di essere compiute da una forte personalità.' ('it is possible to consider the creativity and the paternity of a work as being the same, yet one has to take account of the fact that there are personalities which differ on the grounds of

First Instance, while discussing copyright protection as applied to industrial designs, held that the presence of a creative character ('*carattere creativo*') is a basic requirement of copyright protection for any subject-matter.[102]

6. UNDERSTANDING ORIGINALITY: THE UK APPROACH

A different concept of originality can be discerned in UK copyright law, which has traditionally taken to intend it as synonymous with 'originating' from the author. In other words, the originality requirement has been understood as implying just the presence of a direct causative link between the author's mental conception and the work which emanated from his hand.[103]

After the introduction of the prerequisite of originality in statutory copyright law in 1911, the authority cited to define its meaning has been consistently *University of London Press, Ltd v University Tutorial Press, Ltd*,[104] in which Peterson J held that:

> The word 'original' does not in this connection mean that the work must be the expression of original or inventive thought. Copyright Acts are not concerned with the originality of ideas, but with the expression of thought ... The originality which is required relates to the expression of the thought. But the Act does not require that the expression must be in an original or novel form, but that the work must not be copied from another work – that it should originate from the author.[105]

---

intensity and that there are some works of the mind which do not have to be the result of a strong personality.')

[102] *Flos SpA v Semeraro Casa & Famiglia SpA*, Milan Court of First Instance, 12 September 2012, 18.

[103] Jeremy Phillips and Alison Firth, *Introduction to intellectual property law* (4th edn, Butterworths 2001), 142, who exemplify as follows: 'where twenty artists all make a sketch of the Changing of the Guard, what gives them each an entitlement to copyright, even if their works are identical, is the fact that each has executed his work by reference to his own judgement and not by copying another'.

[104] [1916] 2 Ch 601.

[105] *Ibid*, 608. For critical considerations (yet with an exclusively domestic approach), *see* Burton Ong, 'Originality from copying: fitting recreative works into the copyright universe' (2010) 2 IPQ 165, 170–1.

Such a concept of originality has been little challenged since 1911,[106] and still today it is said to explain the requirement of originality under UK law.[107] As pointed out by Cornish, Llewelyn and Aplin, there are two explanations why such a requirement to copyright protection has been read in a limited sense. First of all, a loose understanding of originality reduces the element of subjective judgment in deciding what qualifies for protection to a minimum, thus avoiding having to engage with questions which are inherently subjective and 'not amenable to the forensic process'.[108] Secondly, it allows protection for any investment of labour and capital which in some way produces a literary result.[109] In addition, it can be said with Jane Ginsburg that the persistence of a sweat-of-the-brow standard[110] 'has less to do with originality than it does with the absence of an unfair competition remedy against "misappropriation". That is, the solicitude for seat may seem more to protect investment than creativity'.[111]

The 1988 Copyright Designs and Patents Act ('CDPA 1988') contains a laconic reference to the originality requirement. Section 1(1) defines 'copyright' as a property right which subsists in the following descriptions of work – (a) *original* literary, dramatic, musical or artistic works, (b) sound recordings, films or broadcasts, and (c) the typographical arrangement of published editions. As explained by Flint, Thorne and Williams,

> Presumably the reason for the omission of the word 'original' in relation to works other than literary, musical or artistic works, is due to the fact that works listed in Section 1(1)(b) and (c) incorporate other original works by

---

[106]   As will be shown below *sub* Section II, §2, however, the history of originality in the UK is not as simple as this.

[107]   *See* Garnett, Davies and Harbottle, *Copinger and Skone James on copyright, cit,* Vol I, 141.

[108]   In this sense, Richard Arnold, 'Are performers authors?' (1999) 21 EIPR 464, 467.

[109]   William Cornish, David Llewelyn and Tanya Aplin, *Intellectual property: patents, copyright, trade marks and allied rights* (7th edn, Sweet & Maxwell 2010), 448.

[110]   On which *see* below *sub* Section II, §1.

[111]   Jane C Ginsburg, 'The concept of authorship in comparative copyright law' (2003) *Columbia Law School Public Law & Legal Theory Research Paper Group – Paper No 03-51,* 19.

their very nature – a sound recording will incorporate a literary, musical and/or artistic work, etc.[112]

Still today, one of the most respected commentaries on copyright in the UK, points out that:

> A literary, dramatic or musical work is not protected by the law of copyright unless it is original. In the case of a literary work (other than a database), a dramatic work or a musical work this means that its author did not merely copy it slavishly from elsewhere, but produced it independently by the expenditure of a sufficiently substantial amount of his own skill, knowledge, mental labour, taste or judgement. However, the amount of skill, labour etc which is required to establish a copyright is not large, and essentially it suffices if it is not insubstantial. It is not necessary that the work should be the expression of inventive thought, because a substantial amount of purely routine mental labour may equally well satisfy the statutory requirement; conversely, however, skill, knowledge etc may make up for a paucity of mental labour.[113]

Because of the loose significance of originality under UK copyright law, a few actions (eg a work written when drunk[114]) have failed in UK courts on the ground that a work was not sufficiently original to be protected by copyright. Although originality is relevant to the topic of infringement (where there has been incomplete or inexact imitation),[115] scrutiny as to whether there has been infringement is usually carried out under the lens of 'substantiality', rather than 'originality'. This is because, to establish infringement, the CDPA 1988 requires that a substantial part of the plaintiff's work has been copied by the defendant.[116] However, as

---

[112] Michael F Flint, Clive D Thorne and Alan P Williams, *Intellectual property – The new law. A guide to the Copyright, Designs and Patents Act 1988* (Butterworths 1989), 6.

[113] Hugh Laddie, Peter Prescott and Mary Vitoria and Others, *The modern law of copyright and designs* (4th edn, LexisNexis 2011), Vol I, 80 (footnotes omitted).

[114] *Fournet v Pearson Ltd* (1897) 14 TLR 82, as reported in Garnett, Davies and Harbottle, *Copinger and Skone James on copyright*, cit, Vol I, 142, who, however, note that in principle there is no reason why a work created under the influence of alcohol or drugs should not be regarded as original if it has some meaning or significance.

[115] Laddie, Prescott and Vitoria and Others, *The modern law* (4th edn), cit, Vol I, 82.

[116] *Cf* Section 16(3) CDPA 1988, which provides that the acts restricted by copyright include – *inter alia* – the work as whole or any substantial part of it.

famously pointed out by Lord Reid in *William Hill*,[117] 'the question whether the defendant has copied a substantial part depends much more on the quality than the quantity of what he has taken.'[118] Such approach to copyright infringement can now be considered as established law. Also recently, Kitchin J (as he then was) confirmed that:

> In assessing the crucial question as to whether a substantial part has been taken, the court must have regard to all the facts of the case including the nature and extent of the copying; the quality and importance of what has been taken; the degree of originality of what has been taken or whether it is commonplace; and whether a substantial part of the skill and labour contributed by the author in creating the original has been appropriated.[119]

In relation to the requirement of 'substantial part of the skill and labour', the precise amount is difficult to define.[120] In any case, it is evident that this is a question of degree, to be determined on the facts of each case:

> What is the precise amount of the knowledge, labour, judgment or literary skill or taste which the author of any book or other compilation must bestow upon its composition in order to acquire copyright in it … cannot be defined in precise terms. In every case it must depend largely on the special facts of that case, and must in each case be very much a question of degree.[121]

Indeed, save where the circumstances make it obvious that the work must have been original (or the defendant acknowledges this), originality must be proven in a copyright action. However, the CDPA 1988 includes a statutory presumption in Section 104(5)(a) that, if the author is dead or his identity cannot be ascertained by reasonable inquiry, it shall be presumed that, in the absence of evidence to the contrary, his work is original. However, such presumption does not go further than saying that the work as a whole is original. No degree of originality is presumed nor is any particular part in isolation presumed to be original.[122]

---

[117] *Ladbroke (Football) Ltd v William Hill (Football) Ltd, cit.*
[118] *Ibid* [276] (Lord Reid).
[119] *Paul Gregory Allen (acting as trustee of Adrian Jacobs (deceased)) v Bloomsbury Publishing Plc and Joanne Kathleen Murray (professionally known as JK Rowling)* [2010] EWHC 2560 (Ch) [85].
[120] Laddie, Prescott and Vitoria and Others, *The modern law of copyright* (4th edn), *cit*, 85.
[121] *Macmillan & Co Ltd v Cooper* (1923) 93 LJPC 113 [121] (Atkinson J).
[122] Laddie, Prescott and Vitoria and Others, *The modern law of copyright* (4th edn), *cit*, 97.

The meaning of originality in UK copyright has been deemed to be something akin to the 'sweat of the brow' approach, famously rejected in the US by the decision of the Supreme Court in *Feist*.[123] As recalled above, originality under UK law is synonymous with a work originating from the author. As will be seen below *sub* Section II, §2, such a conceptualization is problematic. As explained by Lior Zemer:

> If I write a poem and did not copy it from another source, then the work does not only represent a thing that has been originated in me, but also, due to differences between people, it contains a modicum of originality in the sense of creating a different substance.[124]

In any case, a loose understanding of originality in UK copyright aims at granting protection to the creative labour (even if minimal) of authors. As such, it can be said that overall, labour – rather than creativity – is at the basis of copyright protection in UK copyright.

Despite the traditional understanding of UK originality, this concept has undergone an evolution, which serves the purpose of highlighting the policy role of this concept. In other words, it may be wrong to assume that UK originality is just sweat of the brow. In any case, although there may be a certain rapprochement between UK and *droit d'auteur* countries in terms of practical outcome, the conceptual approaches to originality remain different.[125]

Before turning to the analysis of the evolution of originality in UK copyright, the parallel experience of US copyright will be described, as recent studies have shown that its evolution has not been as linear as has traditionally been understood. In the following pages the policy role of originality will be examined. A study will be undertaken as to the evolution of its concept in the US, whose rich case law serves the purpose of showing its impact in shaping copyright regimes, and in the UK, even prior to the decision of the Court of Justice of the European Union in *Infopaq International A/S v Danske Dagblades Forening*.[126] In

---

[123] *Feist Publications, Inc, v Rural Telephone Service Co, cit. See* Daniel Gervais, '*Feist* goes global: a comparative analysis of the notion of originality in copyright law' (2002) J Copyr Socy 949, 958 and Alasdair Bleakley, Edward Baden-Powell and Jeffrey Eneberi, *Intellectual property and media law companion* (4th edn, Bloomsbury Professional 2010), 4.

[124] Zemer, *The idea of authorship, cit*, 55 (emphasis in the original text).

[125] In this sense, Eechoud, Hugenholtz, Gompel, Guibault and Helberger, *Harmonizing, cit*, 42.

[126] *Cit.*

particular, the UK experience is meant to show that the concept of originality has changed over the years and, even before the *de facto* harmonization carried out by the CJEU and despite received wisdom, the UK bar to originality had been occasionally raised so as to get closer to the continental standard.

SECTION II

1. FOLLOWING THE ORIGINALITY BRICK ROAD IN THE US

1.1   The 'Originality' of *Feist*

The US Supreme Court's unanimous decision in *Feist* was deemed to represent a shift in US copyright, as it was ruled that copyright protection was not granted to works of information which fail to manifest a modicum of creative input in selection or arrangement. The Court ruled that copyright does not secure the sweat of the brow or the investment of resources in a work of information. In other words, mere industry and effort are not sufficient to establish originality.

Rural Telephone Service Company was a certified public utility providing telephone services to several communities in Kansas. Pursuant to state regulation, Rural had published a telephone directory, consisting of white pages and yellow pages. It had obtained data for the directory from subscribers, who had had to provide their names and addresses to obtain a telephone service.

Feist Publications was a publishing company that specialized in area-wide telephone directories covering a much larger geographic range than directories such as Rural's. When Rural refused to licence its white pages listings to Feist for a directory covering eleven different telephone service areas, Feist extracted the listings it needed from Rural's directory without Rural's consent.

Both the District Court for the District of Kansas and the Court of Appeals for the 10th Circuit ruled in favour of Rural, holding that telephone directories were subject to copyright protection.

The Supreme Court reversed the judgment of the Court of Appeals and held that no copyright subsisted in the telephone directories. The Court grounded its decision on the text of both Section 102(a)[127] of the 1976 Copyright Act, and Article I, Section 8, Clause 8 of the US Constitution (the so-called, *inter alia*, 'Copyright Clause').[128]

In particular, Justice O'Connor (who delivered the Opinion of the Court) found that, as the Copyright Clause mandates originality as a prerequisite for copyright protection,[129] this is to be meant as independent creation plus a modicum of creativity. Indeed:

> The originality requirement is not particularly stringent. A compiler may settle upon a selection or arrangement that others have used; novelty is not required. Originality requires only that the author make the selection or arrangement independently (i.e., without copying that selection or arrangement from another work), and that it display some minimal level of creativity. Presumably, the vast majority of compilations will pass this test, but not all will. There remains a narrow category of works in which the creative spark is utterly lacking or so trivial as to be virtually nonexistent … Such works are incapable of sustaining a valid copyright.[130]

Facts do not owe their origin to an act of authorship. Therefore, they are not original and cannot enjoy copyright protection. Nonetheless, a compilation of facts may possess the requisite originality because the author typically chooses which facts to include, in what order to place them, and how to arrange the data so that readers may use them effectively. However, copyright protection extends only to those components of the work that are original to the author, not to the facts themselves.

The 1976 Copyright Act provides for copyright to subsist in compilations, these being intended as works 'formed by the collection and

---

[127] 'Copyright protection subsists, in accordance with this title, in original works of authorship fixed in any tangible medium of expression, now known or later developed, from which they can be perceived, reproduced, or otherwise communicated, either directly or with the aid of a machine or device …'

[128] 'The Congress shall have Power … To promote the Progress of Science and useful Arts, by securing for limited Times to Authors and Inventors the exclusive Right to their respective Writings and Discoveries.'

[129] As highlighted by Jane C Ginsburg, 'No "sweat"? Copyright and other protection of works of information after *Feist v. Rural Telephone*' (1992) Colum L Rev 338, 339–40, the frequent references to Constitution were not dictated by mere rhetorical flourishes. Firstly, they implemented a policy favouring general and free access to disclosed data. Secondly, they paved the way for uncertainties concerning both the availability of state law intervention and the power of Congress to issue other forms of federal anti-copying protection.

[130] *Feist Publications, Inc, v Rural Telephone Service Co, cit*, [1294].

assembling of preexisting materials or of data that are selected, coordin-
ated, or arranged in such a way that the resulting work as a whole
constitutes an original work of authorship.'[131] Therefore, as Justice
O'Connor found, some ways of selecting, coordinating, and arranging
data which are not sufficiently original cannot trigger copyright protection.

The 'sweat of the brow' or 'industrious collection' test (adopted by
lower courts) had extended a compilation's copyright protection beyond
selection and arrangement to the facts themselves. Therefore, the
Supreme Court held that the lower courts had misconstrued the copyright
statute and eschewed the fundamental axiom of copyright law that no one
may claim copyright in facts or ideas.

1.2 Did *Feist* Raise the Bar of Protection?

The US Supreme Court held that originality is not something akin to
novelty. Congress had previously clarified this when it had expressly
stated that the 'standard [for originality] does not include requirements of
novelty, ingenuity or esthetic merit, and there is no intention to enlarge
the standard of copyright protection to require them'.[132] Furthermore,
prior to the adoption of the current Copyright Act, the Register of
Copyrights had taken the opportunity to point out that, in order to be
protected, a work 'must represent an appreciable amount of creative
authorship'.[133] At the end of the day, however, it was deemed preferable
not to expand the meaning of originality, as there would have been the
danger of interpreting it as implying further requirements of aesthetic
value or novelty.

The importance of *Feist* has been reassessed under various angles.
Among other things, Miriam Bitton has recently argued that the Supreme
Court did not offer any actual guidance to lower courts on the question of
creativity of compilations.[134] This is because the Supreme Court articu-
lated the originality standard by choosing the weakest possible case, that

---

[131] Section 101 of the 1976 Copyright Act.
[132] HR Rep No 1476, 94th Cong, 2nd Sess 51 (1976); S Rep No 473, 94th
Cong, 1st Sess 50 (1975).
[133] Report of the Register of Copyrights on the General Revision of the US
Copyright Law, House Committee on the Judiciary, 87th Cong, 1st Sess 9
(Committee Print, 1961).
[134] Miriam Bitton, 'Protection for informational works after Feist Publications Inc. v. Rural Telephone Service' (2011) 21 Fordham Intell Prop Media &
Ent LJ 611, 625 ff.

of a white-page directory, organized in alphabetical order and, indeed, lacking minimal creativity. *Feist* did not really involve 'sweat of the brow' or human effort as was historically understood, nor did it exemplify the classical free riding scenario. Therefore, its relevance is scaled down due to its fact-specific background. Indeed, this finding may be confirmed if one considers that, also on account of lack of congressional clarification regarding originality following *Feist*, ad hoc originality standards have been subsequently embraced by US courts in relation to various copyright-protected subject-matter.[135]

In addition, the judgment in *Feist* is said not to have raised the standard for copyright protection, since it did not invalidate protection of databases and compilations *tout court*. This interpretation has received judicial confirmation in *Key Publications, Inc v Chinatown Today Publishing Enters*,[136] in which the Court of Appeal for the 2nd Circuit acknowledged that after *Feist* the scope of copyright protection was 'thin', but not 'anorexic'.[137] Thus, in assessing infringement cases, '[t]he key issue is not whether there is overlap or copying but whether the organizing principles guiding the selection of businesses for the two publications is in fact substantially similar'.[138] By clarifying the meaning of originality as not involving any requisite novelty or aesthetic merit, the Supreme Court did not threaten to deny copyright protection to any work intended as a creative effort by its author.[139] In fact, as far as databases and compilations are concerned, copyright protection is prevented only where the creativity in selection, coordination and arrangement of facts is so minimal so as to be non-existent. Thus, it has been said that copyright protection is dictated by the features of the work at stake[140] and, therefore, so long as the creative effort is more than minimal, copyright protection should be accorded.

---

[135] *See* Justin Pats, 'Originality standard as applied to photographs and other derivative works: a need for change' (2006) 17(2) NYSBA Entertainment, Arts and Sports Law Journal 37, and the case law cited therein.

[136] 945 F 2d 509, 511 (2d Cir 1991).

[137] *Ibid* [514].

[138] *Ibid* [514]–[516].

[139] *Cf* Simon Stern, 'Copyright, originality, and the public domain', in Reginald McGinnis (ed), *Originality and intellectual property in the French and English enlightenment* (Routledge 2009), 69, 89 and Howard B Abrams, 'Originality and creativity in copyright law' (1992) Law and Contemp Probs 3, 16.

[140] Hector MacQueen, Charlotte Waelde and Graeme Laurie, *Contemporary intellectual property. Law and policy* (1st edn, OUP 2008), 235–6.

1.3 The Unveiled Story of Originality

It has been argued that the decision in *Feist* should be interpreted in light of earlier cases in which the issue of originality had been addressed, and the fact that for most of the nineteenth century the notion that copyright embraced an originality requirement was fairly unknown to Anglo-American courts. As far as information works (such as maps, charts, road-books, directories and calendars) are concerned, courts found infringement on the basis of the copying of their actual content and on account of the efforts expended in their creation.[141]

In this respect, *Feist* may be said not to have represented a strong innovation in the US concept of originality. However, judgments such as those in *Emerson v Davies*[142] and *Bleistein v Donaldson Lithographic Co*[143] were not the only precedents as far as originality is concerned. As clarified by Diane Leenheer Zimmerman:

> The addition in *Feist* of the creativity requirement seems to make sense only if seen as an acknowledgment by the Court that *Bleistein* and its progeny simply express an inadequate understanding of the constitutional requirements for copyright and of the modern Court's understanding of its purposes.[144]

Seen in this light, the decision in *Feist* was not aimed at creating a new standard for copyright protection. Instead, it simply restated the approach that had been followed by the US Supreme Court in decisions such as the *Trademark Cases*[145] and *Sarony*.[146]

The notion of originality in US copyright has thus been subject to different evolutions, and has been given different meanings throughout copyright history. Indeed, it can be said that the evolution of US

---

[141] Robert Brauneis, 'The transformation of originality in the progressive-era debate over copyright in news' (2009) *The George Washington Law School Public Law and Legal Theory Working Paper No 463 – Legal Studies Research Paper No 463*, 1, who highlights that transformation in conceptions of originality followed debate over legal protection for news in the last decades of the nineteenth century.

[142] 8 F Cas 615 (CCD Mass 1845).

[143] 188 US 239 (1903), on which *see* further below.

[144] Diane Leenheer Zimmerman, 'It's an original!(?): in pursuit of copyright's elusive essence' (2005) 28 Colum J L & Arts 187, 205–06.

[145] *Trademark cases* 100 US 82 (1879).

[146] *Burrow-Giles Lithographic Co v Sarony*, 111 US 53 (1884). *See* Gervais, '*Feist* goes global', *cit*, 954.

copyright is twofold. At the end of the nineteenth century, two different approaches co-existed.[147]

1.4 Originality as Creativity

On the one hand, there were cases that supported the originality doctrine, by requiring something akin to novelty or merit. For instance, in *Clayton v Stone*,[148] in which a price catalogue was refused copyright protection, the need for substantive merit was held necessary in order to claim protection successfully. This was because the Copyright Clause in the Constitution was not intended to protect mere industry, unconnected with learning and science. Analogously, in *Jolly v Jacques*,[149] which involved copyright protection of a composition adapted from a pre-existing tune, Justice Nelson held that '[t]he musical composition contemplated by the statute must, doubtless be substantially new and original work; and not a copy of a piece already produced, with additions and variations, which a writer of music with experience and skill might readily make'.[150] Therefore, the judge found that no copyright subsisted in the musical composition that was adapted from an earlier work.

In 1879, the Supreme Court addressed the issue of originality and held that Congress did not have the power to regulate trademarks on the grounds of the Constitution's Copyright Clause.[151] The Court held that copyright protection could be granted only to works which were 'original, and ... founded in the creative powers of the mind'.[152]

1.5 Originality as the Market Value of a Work

As distinct from this first string of decisions, there is a line of case law that shares a negative attitude towards the romantic concept of authorship. While rejecting any criterion of aesthetic merit, this attitude rooted copyright protection within the market value of the work. Accordingly,

---

[147] For an accurate analysis of these issues, *see* Oren Bracha, 'The ideology of authorship revisited: authors, markets, and liberal values in early American copyright' (2008) 118 Yale LJ 186.

[148] 5 F Cas 999, 1000, CCSDNY [1829].

[149] 13 F Cas 910, CCSDNY [1850].

[150] *Ibid*, [914]–[915].

[151] *The Trademark cases, cit*. In 1881, the Congress had to rely upon the Commerce Clause (Article I, Section 8, Clause 3) to pass the Trade Mark Act.

[152] *Ibid* [94].

this should be the sole parameter worth considering and includes the time and cost expenditures in producing it.

In *Emerson v Davies*,[153] a case concerning the infringement of copyright in an arithmetic book, Justice Story held that for a work to be original it is sufficient that it has not been copied and had been created by relying on one's own skill, labour and financial resources. Indeed, the judge intended the creative process as cumulative, the result of continuous borrowing from existing works:

> In truth, in literature, in science and in art, there are, and can be, few, if any, things, which, in an abstract sense, are strictly new and original throughout. Every book in literature, science and art, borrows, and must necessarily borrow, and use much which was well known and used before. No man creates a new language for himself, at least if he be a wise man, in writing a book. ... The thoughts of every man are, more or less, a combination of what other men have thought and expressed, although they may be modified, exalted or improved by his own genius or reflection. If no book could be the subject of copy-right which was not new and original in the elements of which it is composed, there could be no ground for any copy-right in modern times, and we should be obliged to ascend very high, even in antiquity, to find a work entitled to such eminence.[154]

The same minimalist originality standard was adopted by Justice Holmes in *Bleistein v Donaldson*,[155] a case concerning whether copyright vested in a poster advertisement for a circus. Here it was held that if a work is not copied, then it is original and deserving of protection. Despite the presence of a dissenting opinion arguing that being unable to discover anything useful or meritorious prevents granting any protection,[156] the Supreme Court's decision in *Bleistein* showed a reductive approach to copyright, in that it was held that copyright subsisted in such a work. This was found to be because:

> It would be a dangerous undertaking for persons trained only to the law to constitute themselves final judges of the worth of pictorial illustrations, outside of the narrowest and most obvious limits. At the one extreme, some works of genius would be sure to miss appreciation. Their very novelty would make them repulsive until the public had learned the new language in which their author spoke. It may be more than doubted, for instance, whether the etchings of Goya or the paintings of Manet would have been sure of

---

[153]   *Cit.*
[154]   *Ibid* [619].
[155]   *Cit.*
[156]   *Ibid* (Justice Harlan).

protection when seen for the first time. At the other end, copyright would be denied to pictures which appealed to a public less educated than the judge. Yet if they command the interest of any public, they have a commercial value, – it would be bold to say that they have not an aesthetic and educational value, – and the taste of any public is not to be treated with contempt.[157]

It has been pointed out[158] that the *Bleistein* decision brought about two sets of consequences. Firstly, it eliminated from copyright discourse any reference to the promotion of science, as was dictated in the Constitution's Copyright Clause. Secondly, *Bleistein* represented the end of any attempt to make originality a meaningful threshold requirement to copyright protection.[159]

The issue at stake in *Sarony*[160] was whether copyright could vest in photographs.[161] Justice Miller, writing on behalf of the Supreme Court, held that the Copyright Clause was broad enough to cover an act authorizing copyright in photographs, in so far as they are the result of 'original intellectual conceptions of the author'.[162] The Court located authorship not in the act of capturing the image or in the post-photographic manipulation of the photograph, but in its preparatory stages. What is important about this decision is that the Court wanted to reach the policy objective of granting copyright protection to photographs and, by locating the creative moment in pre-shooting activities, it held that photographs could be protected by copyright.[163]

When rewriting the Copyright Act in 1909, Congress extended protection to all writings by an author.[164] Hence, there was less room left for

---

[157] *Ibid* [250]–[251].

[158] Leenheer Zimmerman, 'It's an original!(?)', *cit*, 204–05.

[159] *Cf Alfred Bell & Co Ltd v Catalda Fine Arts, Inc*, 191 F2d 99, 2d Cir [1951].

[160] *Burrow-Giles Lithographic Co v Sarony*, *cit*.

[161] For an analysis and assessment of the evolution of copyright protection for photographs in the US, *see* Justin Hughes, 'The photographer's copyright – photograph as art, photograph as database' (2011) Benjamin N Cardozo School of Law – Yeshiva University – Jacob Burns Institute for Advanced Legal Studies, *Faculty Research Paper No 34*, 7 November 2011.

[162] *Ibid*, 58.

[163] In order to achieve this result, the Court had to undergo a rationalization of copyright, which was not effortless. On that, *see* Christine Haight Farley, 'The lingering effects of copyright's response to the invention of photography' (2004) 65 U Pitt L Rev 385, 425–32.

[164] According to Section 4 of the Act of 4 March 1909, to Amend and Consolidate the Acts Respecting Copyright, 'the works for which copyright may be secured … shall include all the writings of an author'.

assessing whether a work over which copyright protection was sought actually favoured the progress of science and useful arts.

In light of the foregoing, as well as on a broader scale, from *Feist* and its preceding history three mains threads emerge.

Firstly, the meaning of originality has changed over time, as well as having had concurrent meanings at any given time.

Secondly, any meaning given to originality reflects the one assigned to other basic principles, such as authorship. The more this concept is akin to the romantic concept of genius and creativity, the more originality becomes an effective threshold to protection.

Thirdly, as the decisions in *Sarony*, *Bleistein* and *Feist* in particular show, the actual scope of originality can be used as a tool to either grant or deny copyright protection. In other words, by relying on originality, courts have achieved and continue to achieve policy objectives, thus showing the instrumental role of originality in defining the categories of works which can be protected by copyright.

2. ORIGINALITY IN UK COPYRIGHT: A TALE OF TWO CITIES

Any IP textbook[165] clarifies that the originality standard in the UK has traditionally been akin to that set forth in the leading case, *University of London Press*.[166] According to this case, a work is original if it has not been copied from another work and shows a certain (modicum) amount of skill, labour and judgment.

This said, as highlighted by Lord Atkinson, originality depends largely on the facts of the case and must in each instance be very much a question of degree.[167] Such an approach has also been followed more recently in *Express Newspaper Plc v News (UK) Ltd*,[168] in which V-C Sir Nicolas Browne-Wilkinson decided to follow the old case of *Walter v*

---

[165] *Cf* Lionel Bently and Brad Sherman, *Intellectual property law* (3rd edn, OUP 2008), 93–107; MacQueen, Waelde and Laurie, *Contemporary intellectual property*, *cit*, 50–7; Catherine Colston and Kirsty Middleton, *Modern intellectual property law* (2nd edn, Cavendish 2005), 261–3; Paul Torremans, *Holyoak and Torremans: intellectual property law* (4th edn, Butterworths 2005), 175.

[166] *University of London Press, Ltd v University Tutorial Press, Ltd*, *cit*.

[167] *Macmillan v Cooper*, *cit*.

[168] [1990] FSR 359 (Ch D).

Lane.[169] There it was held that the originality requirement is met whenever a sufficient degree of (above minimal) skill, labour or judgment are found.

As already mentioned,[170] the limited level of original achievement required in order to enjoy copyright protection may be explained in two ways. Firstly it reduces to a minimum the element of subjective judgment in deciding what qualifies for protection. Secondly, it allows protection for any investment of labour and capital that in some ways produces a literary result. The latter has to be read in conjunction with the fact that the UK lacks a law of unfair competition. As such, intellectual property rights are used to accomplish this further task, where no other forms of relief are available.[171]

As a preliminary remark, it should be recalled that the concept of originality is approached differently depending on the type of work at stake: the treatment depends on whether the work is new or derivative, a table, compilation or a computer-generated work.[172] In particular, as far as the latter two are concerned, the standard of originality is that descending from the process of EU harmonization. In order to be deemed

---

[169]   [1900] AC 539. The case concerned a newspaper report of an oral speech and whether copyright could vest in it. The court responded affirmatively, as considerable labour, skill and judgment are requested in order to produce a verbatim transcript of a speech.

[170]   *Supra sub* Section I, §6.

[171]   *Cf Exxon Corp v Exxon Insurance Consultants International Ltd* [1981] 1 WLR 624; [1981] 2 All ER 495 and 3 All ER 241. An oil company had invented the word 'Exxon' as its corporate name and trademark. An insurance company had borrowed the name for itself without the oil company's consent. The oil firm therefore claimed injunctions against the insurance company restraining it from passing off their goods or services as its own, and from infringing the oil company's copyright in the name. The first instance judge granted the first injunction but refused the second one, stating that no copyright subsisted in a name. The oil company appealed, contending that the word 'Exxon' was protected by copyright. The Court of Appeal dismissed the appeal and held that copyright could not exist in words merely because they could not be described as an original work having literary character. The Court pointed out that the phrase 'original literary work' is a composite expression to be constructed as such and not as three individual words. Therefore, a work is something that affords either information, instruction or pleasure in the form of literary enjoyment and that the word 'Exxon', being simply an artificial combination of four letters of the alphabet and serving only for identification purposes when used in juxtaposition with other words, was not within the definition of an 'original literary work'. Therefore, it did not qualify for copyright protection.

[172]   *See* Bently and Sherman, *Intellectual property, cit*, 97–111.

original, these works have to be the result of the 'author's own intellectual creation'. In light of the influence of EU law on UK copyright law,
one may wonder whether the presence of two different originality
standards in UK copyright undermines the overall coherence of the
system, and, if so, which of the two approaches should prevail. However,
before moving to this question, it is worth addressing a different issue:
whether the understanding of originality in UK copyright has always
been akin to that envisaged in the *University of London Press* case, in
which it was held that copyright subsisted in the papers of the matricu-
lation examination of the University of London.

2.1   Originality over Time: Hard Times

A preliminary point to be stressed is that, despite received wisdom, there
is not a single UK concept of originality. As highlighted by Lord Oliver
of Aylmerton in *Interlego v Tyco Industries*:[173]

> Originality in the context of literary copyright has been said in several well
> known cases to depend upon the degree of skill, labour and judgment
> involved in preparing a compilation ... To apply that, however, as a universal
> test of originality in all copyright cases is not only unwarranted by the context
> in which the observations were made but palpably erroneous. Take the
> simplest case of artistic copyright, a painting or a photograph. It takes great
> skill, judgment and labour to produce a good copy by painting or to produce
> an enlarged photograph from a positive print, but no one would reasonably
> contend that the copy painting or enlargement was an 'original' artistic work
> in which the copier is entitled to claim copyright. Skill, labour or judgment
> merely in the process of copying cannot confer originality.[174]

Lord Oliver went even further and, although he did not accept the
defendant's argument that to qualify for copyright protection there must
be original creative input by the author, he acknowledged that the
University of London Press standard was incomplete, because '[s]kill,
labour or judgment merely in the process of copying cannot confer

---

[173]   [1989] AC 217. The case involved an action for copyright infringement
over modifying designs for Lego toy bricks. Artistic copyright over the engineering drawings was denied, as the second set of designs differed from the first
one only in relation to technical information such as dimensions and tolerances.
The Court held that the bricks qualified for registered design protection, and not
for copyright protection (under Section 10 of the Copyright Act 1956 copyright
and design protections were not cumulative), since the new designs were not new
works for the purpose of artistic copyright.
[174]   *Ibid* (Lord Oliver).

originality'.[175] Therefore, the Privy Council (Hong Kong) held that copyright protection in engineering drawings could not be sought merely out of reproduction of earlier drawings with alterations to the instructions for the manufacturing process written thereon. That was because these were not alterations to the artistic nature of the drawing: instead, they were of a mere technical nature.

Just as the history of originality in the US is not the result of a single and constant evolution, nor is that in the UK.[176] It has been pointed out that at the beginning of intellectual property history, one of the overriding concerns was with creativity:

> One of the factors that the various areas of intellectual property had in common was not only a concern with creative labour but also a similar image of what it meant to create: they adopted, if you like, a shared model of creativity. In particular, it is clear that while God may have provided the starting blocks for the creative process, it was the contribution made by the author, engraver, designer or inventor who individualised the subject matter they worked with which the law protected. Put differently, what intellectual property law protected was the creative or human element embodied in the resulting product.[177]

The late Sir Hugh Laddie[178] argued that the current view of originality, which he traced back to *Walter v Lane*,[179] has not always been the law. In fact, in *Dick v Yates*,[180] the Court of Appeal had to decide whether *Splendid Misery* – the title of a book – enjoyed copyright protection. Jessel MR stressed the analogies between originality in copyright and novelty in patent law, arguing that a title could not be considered original as such. Lush LJ concurred by taking it 'to be established law that to be the subject of copyright the matter must be original, it must be a composition of the author, something which has grown up in his mind, the product of something which if it were applied to patent rights would be called invention. Nothing short of that would entitle a man to

---

[175]   *Ibid* [971].

[176]   *See* Simon Stokes, *Art and copyright* (1st edn, Hart Publishing 2001), 21–2.

[177]   Brad Sherman and Lionel Bently, *The making of modern intellectual property law. The British experience, 1760–1911* (CUP 1999), 46.

[178]   Hugh Laddie, 'Copyright: over-strength, over-regulated, over-rated?' (1996) 5 EIPR 253, 259–60.

[179]   *Cit.*

[180]   (1881) 18 Ch D 76. This case was however in distinction in *Walter v Lane, cit.*

copyright.' It was therefore held that no copyright subsisted in the title of the book.[181]

Recent decisions have also shown a different approach to the issue of originality. In the *Designers Guild* case,[182] the House of Lords was asked to decide whether copyright in the artwork for a fabric design had been infringed by a later design. It was held that the test to be followed to assess infringement cases is to see whether the alleged infringer has incorporated a substantial part of the independent skill, labour and judgment contributed by the original author in creating the work. Substantiality is a matter of impression, principally concerned with a work's derivation. Therefore, it was decided that, where it was alleged that an entire design had been copied, a finding that the similarities between the works were of a sufficient extent and nature to support a finding of copying, this was also likely to be determinative of the issue of substantiality and, so, of copyright infringement.

Furthermore, in *The Newspaper Licensing Agency Ltd v Marks & Spencer*,[183] Lord Hoffmann not only insisted on the need for original skill and labour but, while discussing *Designers Guild*, he explained that

> [The] copying of certain of the ideas expressed in that design which, in their conjoined expression, had involved original artistic skill and labour, constituted the copying of a substantial part of the artistic work ... The notion of reproduction ... is sufficiently flexible to include the copying of ideas abstracted from a literary, musical or artistic work, provided that their expression in the original work has involved sufficient of the relevant original skill and labour to attract copyright protection.[184]

The House of Lords thus held that, whilst copying of a literary, dramatic or musical work meant – pursuant to Section 17(2) of the CDPA 1988[185] – reproducing the work in any material form, in the case of the

---

[181]   On this, *see* also *sub* Section I, § 5.

[182]   *Designers Guild, Ltd v Russell Williams (Textiles), Ltd*, [2000] 1 WLR 2416. The case concerned the alleged infringement of a fabric design. Judge Lawrence Collins QC found that, notwithstanding that there were numerous differences between the design of the claimant and the one of the defendant, the defendant had derived the later design from the one of the claimant. The House of Lords confirmed this finding.

[183]   [2001] UKHL 38.

[184]   *Ibid* [19]–[20].

[185]   'Copying in relation to a literary, dramatic, musical or artistic work means reproducing the work in any material form. This includes storing the work in any medium by electronic means.'

typographical arrangement, nothing short of a facsimile copy would suffice for a finding of copyright infringement.

In light of the foregoing it has been argued that such an approach would be a new one with regard to originality. If further elaborated,

> it may get to a clear-creativity test, because 'original skill and labour' cannot have the same meaning as 'skill and labour' ... In other words, if 'original' means something, which it must, it is more than mere skill and labour, and that additional element is likely the intellectual creativity which seems to be required by EU directives.[186]

2.2   UK and EU Originality: Great Expectations?

If we now examine the changes brought about by the implementation of EC directives, as mentioned above, the requirement of 'the author's own intellectual creation' is expressly provided with regard to databases, computer programs and photographs.

As clarified by Bently and Sherman,[187] as far as databases are concerned, EU originality criterion differed from the traditional UK standard, as envisaged in *Ladbroke (Football) Ltd v William Hill (Football) Ltd*[188] where football pool coupons were granted copyright protection. The new originality requirement, in contrast to the traditional UK one, does not permit a court to take into account the creation of the information included in a database. In other words, it does not allow copyright protection for pre-expressive stages in the creation of a database.

With regard to computer programs, as already mentioned, it was not deemed necessary to amend the CDPA 1988, in order to comply with the Software Directive.[189] This was because it was thought that the UK position was already compliant with the one required by the Directive.[190]

Finally, as far as the protection of photographs is concerned, the discourse calls for a preliminary consideration as to the relevant provision in the Term Directive, Article 6. With regards to photographs, the position of UK copyright law has always been ambiguous, since judicial decisions in this area have given little guidance in determining what originality means in this context. Prior to the adoption of the Term

---

[186]   Gervais, '*Feist* goes global', *cit*, 959–60.
[187]   Bently and Sherman, *Intellectual property*, *cit*, 108.
[188]   *Cit*.
[189]   *Cf* Articles 1(a) and 3 of the Copyright, Designs and Patents Act.
[190]   In this sense, Bently and Sherman, *Intellectual property*, *cit*, 109.

Directive, the leading authority was deemed to be the *Graves' Case*,[191] in which the photograph of the engraving of a painting was held to be deserving of protection. However, as highlighted by Bently and Sherman,[192] it is doubtful whether this case could actually be of any help today, as the technological apparatus for taking photographs is so different from in 1869. Also, *Interlego*[193] raised doubts as to the usefulness of the *Graves' Case* as an authority. Similarly, in the US case *The Bridgeman Art Library Ltd v Corel Corp*,[194] Justice Kaplan considered that because of the antiquity of the *Graves' Case* it should be overlooked, along with the development of the law of originality in the UK. However, despite the *dicta* in *Interlego* and *The Bridgeman Library*, subsequent case law has not completely abandoned the loose approach to originality as envisaged in the *Graves' Case*. So, for instance, copyright has been found to subsist in simple photographs of three-dimensional objects.[195] Even after the implementation of the Term Directive, the situation, as far as photographs are concerned, remained unclear. While the Directive leaves Member States free to grant protection to unoriginal photographs if so they wish, thus allowing the UK to maintain its lower standard (as compared to other EU Member States),[196] for some commentators the standard envisaged by the Term Directive does not differ from what was already the understanding of originality under UK law. According to Ysolde Gendreau,

---

[191]   (1869) LR 4 QB 715.

[192]   Bently and Sherman, *Intellectual property*, *cit*, 109–110.

[193]   *Tyco Industries v Interlego, cit.*

[194]   25 F Supp 2d 421, 36 F Supp 2d 191 [1998]. The plaintiff, the Bridgeman Art Library, founded by Lady Bridgeman, had a rich collection of photographs taken of works of art for which copyright protection had expired, but to which The Bridgeman Library claimed copyright protection in the photographs. The software house Corel had started marketing a series of CD-ROMs which reproduced European master paintings. The Bridgeman library alleged copyright infringement in more than one hundred of its photographs. The conclusion was that no copyright could vest in Bridgeman's photographs, as a photograph which duplicates another work is the equivalent of a photocopy, thus lacking the requisites for protection. On the *Graves' case* and *The Bridgeman Library*, *see* Simon Stokes, 'Graves' Case and copyright in photographs', in Daniel McClean and Karsten Schubert (eds), *Dear images. Art, copyright and culture* (Ridinghouse 2002), 109.

[195]   *Antiquesportfolio.com v Rodney Fitch & Co Ltd*, [2001] FSR 345; [2001] ECDR 51.

[196]   In this sense, Bently and Sherman, *Intellectual property*, *cit*, 111. On this issue, *see* below *sub* Chapter 5, § 1.

The originality criterion for photographs which is stated in the EC Directive on the Term of Protection of Copyright, 'the author's own intellectual creation', may indeed appear to be an appropriate rewording of the UK test for originality, if one interprets 'own intellectual creation' as a reference to a physical person's independent work of the mind. The result of this person's activity can only betray some skill and labour, however minimal they are.[197]

2.3 Traditionally Intended Originality: The Old Curiosity Shop

In light of the foregoing, it is possible to argue that the traditional UK understanding of originality, as envisaged in *University of London Press*, does not represent a complete picture. On the one hand, courts have not always been keen, over the course of copyright history, to embrace such a standard. On the other hand, recent decisions have shown an increasingly restless attitude towards maintaining *University of London Press* as an authority.

If the meaning of originality in the UK has changed over time, this has been the result of a combined dissatisfaction with the traditional test of the 'sufficient skill, labour and judgment', and the legislative innovations brought about by the process of EU harmonization. As clarified by MacQueen, Waelde and Laurie,[198] the simultaneous presence of two originality standards in UK copyright forces a reflection as to which would be best suited to the digital environment. So far, the continental approach has been favoured, particularly because EU directives that harmonized the meaning of originality with regard to specific subject-matter have modelled this requirement in accordance with continental copyright laws.

However, what matters most is that it can be shown that even a tradition like that of the UK, which has been deemed homogeneous over time, has not in fact been so. These findings lead us to welcome the developments of CJEU case law. The *de facto* harmonization of the originality requirement provided by the decision in *Infopaq*[199] will be explained below *sub* Chapter 3. In any case, it may be anticipated that the new EU-wide originality requirement may be such as to permit UK courts to adopt solutions that

---

[197] Ysolde Gendreau, 'United Kingdom', in Ysolde Gendreau, Axel Nordemann and Rainer Oesch (eds), *Copyright and photographs. An international survey* (Kluwer Law International 1999), 283, 286 (footnotes omitted).

[198] H MacQueen, C Waelde and G Laurie, *Contemporary intellectual property*, cit, 235.

[199] Case C-5/08 *Infopaq International A/S v Danske Dagblades Forening*, cit.

overcome the problems highlighted above and associated with the
traditional originality standard in this Member State.

Such reflections are to be seen in the context of a more general debate
concerning the scope of copyright, as well as of its possible reform. In
the words of Laddie:

> Maybe time has come to look forward, rather than backwards. Perhaps we
> should consider whether the current law on originality makes sense or serves
> a useful purpose. To reduce it to its simplest, you can have too much of a
> good thing and I suggest we have got too much copyright.[200]

CONCLUSION

So far, EU Member States have embraced different originality standards
and this has been deemed acceptable in so far as it did not create barriers
to intra-Community trade. In a few cases, EU directives have harmonized
the concept of originality, in accordance with that resulting from *droit
d'auteur* traditions. Behind this limited harmonization, there was the
belief that such an operation was necessary only with regard to
technology-related categories of works. As far as traditional copyright
subject-matter is concerned, Member States have been left free to
maintain their own originality standards.

From the evolution of copyright in the US and in the UK, it has been
shown that the concept and the scope of originality have changed over
time. It has been stretched to grant copyright protection to photographs
(*Sarony*) and advertisements (*Bleistein*) and re-interpreted in a restrictive
way when it became clear that the outcomes descending from the
adoption of a broad meaning were undesired (*Feist*).

As can also be seen the history of UK copyright, which has traditionally been thought of as understanding originality in a fairly loose way,
this too has experienced moments when different alternatives were on the
table (*Dick v Yates*). More recently, a certain feeling of dissatisfaction
with the traditional standard set up by the *University of London Press*
case has arisen (*Interlego*, *The Newspaper Licensing Agency*, *Designers
Guild*). From these decisions, it is apparent that the originality requirement, on account of its flexible nature, has also played a fundamental
policy role and contributed to defining the scope of copyright protection.

---

[200]   Laddie, 'Copyright: over-strength', *cit*, 260.

3. Originality in a work, or a work of originality: The effects of the *Infopaq* decision[1]

1. RECALLING THE DEBATE ON COPYRIGHT IN 2010

Copyright has never been as intensely discussed at the EU level as it is now. In particular, attention is currently directed at both evaluating the coherence of the *acquis communautaire* and at assessing whether copyright harmonization should go further, to the point of issuing of an EU-wide copyright law. It is sufficient to recall that in 2010 alone, two important documents were published.[2]

Firstly, in April, the Wittem Group, composed of leading European copyright academics, released a European Copyright Code, which, as was clearly stated therein, 'might serve as a model or reference tool for future harmonization or unification of copyright at the European level'.[3]

Secondly, in May, Mario Monti addressed the President of the European Commission José Manuel Barroso with a Report containing *A new strategy for the single market at the service of Europe's economy and society* (also known as the Monti Report), in which due attention was paid to the issue of further harmonization of copyright.

2. A DIFFERENT APPROACH

From the foregoing, it is apparent that in the past few years, as compared to positions previously endorsed, the approach to copyright at the EU

---

[1]   Some parts of this chapter represent an extended and updated version of the following contribution: Eleonora Rosati, 'Originality in a Work, or a Work of Originality: The Effects of the *Infopaq* Decision' (2011) 58(4) J Copyr Socy 795–817, and 33(12) EIPR 746–755.

[2]   For a more detailed analysis, *see supra sub* Chapter 1, Section I, § 6.1-2 and below *sub* Chapter 6, Section I, § 2.

[3]   Wittem Group, *European Copyright Code*, Introduction, 5.

level has taken a different shape. Indeed, a relatively insignificant length of time has passed since the publication of the Commission Staff Working Paper on the review of the EC legal framework in the field of copyright and related rights,[4] which was released in 2004. Yet, one can doubt that today a review of the *acquis communautaire* in the field of copyright would reach the same conclusions as contained therein. This is with particular regard to the assessment of issues outside the current *acquis*, such as originality.

As already mentioned, so far the originality requirement has in fact been referred to only in Article 1(3) of the Software Directive in relation to computer programs, Article 6 of the Term Directive with regard to photographs and Article 3(1) of the Database Directive as regards databases. As recalled by the Working Paper,[5] the originality requirement was harmonized to take account of the special features or the special technical nature of the category of work in question and was held to be found whenever a work was its 'author's own intellectual creation'.

Such meaning of the originality requirement is akin to the French (and continental) concept of copyright (*droit d'auteur*), in which protection is granted to works which bear 'l'empreinte du talent créateur personnel'.[6]

With regard to whether the originality requirement should be harmonized further, the Working Paper concluded that:

> In theory, divergent requirements for the level of originality by Member States have the potential of posing barriers to intra-Community trade. In practice, however, there seems to be no convincing evidence to support this ... [T]here are no indications that the lack of harmonization of the concept of originality would have caused any problems for the functioning of the Internal Market with respect to other categories of works, such as compositions, films or books. Therefore, legislative action does not appear necessary at this stage.[7]

In light of the foregoing, two threads seem to emerge. Firstly, that at the moment both academic and political attention is firmly focused on the

---

[4]   Commission Staff Working Paper on the review of the EC legal framework in the field of copyright and related rights, 19 July 2004, SEC (2004) 995. On this *see supra sub* Chapter 2, Section I, § 3.

[5]   *Ibid*, § 3.1, 14.

[6]   *See supra sub* Chapter 2, Section I, para 5.

[7]   Commission Staff Working Paper on the review of the EC legal framework in the field of copyright and related rights, *cit*, para 3.1, 14.

issue of further harmonization of copyright at the EU level.[8] Secondly, that the approach to harmonization has changed, in the sense that the possible implications and advantages of this are now openly discussed.[9] As was recently stated by Ms Neelie Kroes, current Vice-President of the European Commission responsible for the Digital Agenda:

> [T]oday our fragmented copyright system is ill-adapted to the real essence of art, which has no frontiers … [W]e must look beyond national and corporatist self-interest to establish a new approach to copyright. We want 'une Europe des cultures' and for this we need a debate at European level.[10]

If the full copyright harmonization project were to be commenced, first of all it would be necessary to achieve political consensus as regards the terms and options available for this objective. However, as will be shown below, it seems that this process is already in place and, moreover, has taken place by means of neither policy reports nor legislative innovations. Indeed, copyright harmonization has been boosted by the jurisprudence of the CJEU which, through the decisions in *Infopaq International A/S v Danske Dagblades Forening*[11] and *Bezpečnostní softwarová asociace –*

---

[8] *See ex multis*, Mireille van Eechoud, P Bernt Hugenholtz, Stef van Gompel, Lucie Guibault and Natali Helberger, *Harmonizing European copyright law. The challenges of better law making* (Kluwer Law International 2009).

[9] Indeed, the Monti Report had been commissioned by President Barroso with the intention of obtaining helpful and valuable inputs for an initiative meant to re-launch the single market as a key strategic objective, due to the fact that, *inter alia*, 'the full potential of the Single Market has not yet been delivered. In many areas the Single Market is far from being completely in place. In addition, there are missing links which prevent a still fragmented market from acting as a powerful engine for growth and delivering the full benefits to consumers.' (Monti Report, *Mission letter from the President of the European Commission*, 3).

[10] Neelie Kroes, 'A digital world of opportunities', speech at the Forum d'Avignon – *Les rencontres internationals del de la culture, de l'économie et des medias*, Avignon, 5 November 2010, SPEECH/10/619. In the same sense, also Neelie Kroes, 'Copyright and innovation in the creative industries' speech at *The 2012 intellectual property and innovation summit*, The Lisbon Council Brussels, 10 September 2012, SPEECH/12/592 (for a critical appraisal of this speech, *see* Jeremy Phillips, 'At the apex of the Summit: "real world" invoked in copyright debate' (The IPKat, 11 September 2012) <http://tinyurl.com/ao9u8s6> accessed 14 June 2013).

[11] Case C-5/08 *Infopaq International A/S v Danske Dagblades Forening* [2009] I-06569.

Svaz softwarové ochrany v Ministerstvo kultury,[12] has *de facto* harmonized the originality requirement at the EU level.

3. PRECEDENT IN THE CJEU

Before turning to the analysis of the decisions of the CJEU which have
tackled originality, a brief examination as to the value of precedent in the
CJEU system shall be undertaken.

Unlike common law jurisdictions, there is no formal system of
precedent under EU law. This is because there was the fear that a system
of binding precedent would have been inappropriate in what was meant
to be a court of first and last resort, many of whose decisions could have
been overcome only by amending the treaties, thus implying the agreement of and ratification by all the Member States.[13]

However, just like courts in civil law countries, the CJEU tries to
maintain consistency in its judgments.[14] Indeed, the Court seldom departs
from its prior case law, and even more rarely does so explicitly.[15] The
latter feature has resulted in uncertainties as to under what circumstances
the Court may decide to amend its previous interpretation.[16]

---

[12] Case C-393/09 *Bezpečnostní softwarová asociace – Svaz softwarové
ochrany v Ministerstvo kultury* [2010] I-13971.

[13] Anthony Arnull, *The European Union and its Court of Justice* (OUP
1999), 529.

[14] Nigel G Foster, *EU law directions* (OUP 2008), 62.

[15] David Anderson, *References to the European Court* (1st edn, Sweet &
Maxwell 1995), 301.

[16] Jan Komárek, 'Judicial lawmaking and precedent in supreme courts'
(2011), *LSE Law, Society and Economy Working Papers 4/2011*, 34, who also
highlights that there have been different approaches even among advocates
general: whilst Advocate General Miguel Poiares Maduro in his opinion in
Joined Cases C-94/04 and C-202/04 *Federico Cipolla v Rosaria Fazari, née
Portolese*, and *Stefano Macrino and Claudia Capodarte v Roberto Meloni* [2006]
ECR I-11421 expressly explained (paras 26–30) the value of precedent for the
Court and the need to have additional reasons for reversing well-established case
law, Advocate General Philippe Léger, in his first opinion in Case C-280/00
*Altmark Trans GmbH and Regierungspräsidium Magdeburg v Nahverkehrs-
gesellschaft Altmark GmbH* [2003] ECR I-07747, merely invited (paras 73–98)
the Court to review its previous interpretation.

As was first clarified in the *Da Costa* decision[17] and then codified in Article 104(3) of the Rules of Procedure of the Court,[18] the obligation imposed by current Article 234(3) TFEU[19] upon national courts or tribunals of last instance may be deprived of its purpose by reason of the authority of an interpretation already given by the Court under this provision in those cases in which the question raised is materially identical with a question which has already been the subject of a preliminary ruling in a similar case. According to one of the most authoritative textbooks on EU law, the decision in *Da Costa* initiated what is in effect a system of precedent under EU law.[20]

Furthermore, there are numerous instances in which the CJEU has employed the terminology of precedent and reviewed earlier decisions to confirm or distinguish from past cases. The result is that, albeit unofficially, the case law developed by the CJEU has increasingly come to resemble a 'true case law system relying on precedents to take forward new cases.'[21]

In any case, as a corollary of the absence of a system of binding precedent, any distinction between the *ratio decidendi* of a case and its *obiter dicta*, which represents a basic feature of the doctrine of *stare decisis* as developed by English courts,[22] is to be scaled down. Indeed,

---

[17] Joined Cases C-28/62, C-29/62 and C-30/62, *Da Costa en Schaake NV, Jacob Meijer NV, Hoechst-Holland NV v Netherlands Inland Revenue Administration*, [1963] 00061.

[18] Rules of Procedure of the Court of Justice of the European Communities of 19 June 1991 [1991] OJ L 176, 7–32.

[19] 'Where any [question concerning: (a) the interpretation of this Treaty; (b) the validity and interpretation of acts of the institutions of the Community and of the ECB; (c) the interpretation of the statutes of bodies established by an act of the Council, where those statutes so provide.] is raised in a case pending before a court or tribunal of a Member State against whose decisions there is no judicial remedy under national law, that court or tribunal shall bring the matter before the Court of Justice.'

[20] Paul Craig and Grainne de Búrca, *EU law. Text, cases and materials* (5th edn, OUP 2011), 450.

[21] Foster, *EU law*, *cit*, 63.

[22] As explained by Eric Tjong Tjin Tai and Karlijn Teuben, 'European precedent law' (2008), *Tilburg Institute of Comparative and Transnational Law Working Paper No 2008/4*, 3, the development of the doctrine of *stare decisis* culminated in the 1898 decision in *London Tramways v London County Council* [1898] AC 375, in which (379) the House of Lords declared itself absolutely bound to follow its own decisions in future cases. This rule was mitigated just in 1966, when the House of Lords indicated in a Practice Direction that it would be prepared in appropriate cases to overrule its earlier decisions.

contrary to decisions in common law jurisdictions, in principle everything that is said in a judgment of the CJEU expresses the Court's opinion and has therefore the potential to have some persuasive force.[23]

This being in brief the overall value of precedent under EU law, attention will now be turned to the decisions of the CJEU which have *de facto* harmonized the concept of originality at the EU level. As will be explained below, the harmonizing effects of CJEU case law have gone far beyond mere compliance with earlier decisions and their interpretation of relevant EU law provisions. The Court has indeed kept elaborating upon its case law, in a manner which can be rightly (and worryingly) considered as being tantamount to actual lawmaking.

4. THE *INFOPAQ* DECISION: A *COUP DE MAIN*?

This reference for a preliminary ruling was made by the Højesteret (the Danish Supreme Court) in the context of proceedings between Infopaq International A/S ('Infopaq') and Danske Dagblades Forening ('DDF'), concerning the dismissal of Infopaq's application for a declaration that it was not required to obtain the consent of the copyright owners for acts of reproduction of newspaper articles that were obtained using an automated process, consisting of the scanning, conversion into digital format and electronic processing of the resulting files.

4.1 Facts and Questions Referred to the CJEU

Infopaq operated a media monitoring and analysis business that mainly involves writing up summaries of selected articles from Danish daily newspapers and magazines. The selection followed certain subject criteria agreed with customers and was carried out by means of a data capture process. This had five stages. Firstly, the relevant publications were registered manually by Infopaq employees in an electronic registration database. Secondly, the publications were scanned and an image file was created for each page of the publication. The image file was then transferred to an optical character recognition ('OPC') server. Thirdly, the OPC server converted the image file into a text file and eventually the original image file was deleted. Fourthly, the text file was processed to find predefined search words. Each time a match for the search word was found, the relating publication, section and page number on which the

---

[23] Arnull, *The European Union, cit*, 529.

match was found were indicated, along with a percentage showing how far into the text this was to be found. Furthermore, in order to facilitate the locating of the search word when reading the article, the five words that preceded and followed the search word were captured (this resulted in an extract of eleven words). Upon completion of the process, the text file was deleted. Finally, a document was printed out for each page of the publication in which the search word appeared, which contained the extract of eleven words.

In 2005, the DDF (the professional association of Danish daily newspapers whose function is to offer assistance with regard to copyright issues), informed Infopaq that it required authorization from the copyright owners in order to carry out its activities. Infopaq therefore brought an action against DDF before the Østre Landsret (the High Court of Eastern Denmark) to obtain a declaration that it had the right to apply the data capture process without the consent of DDF or its members. The Court dismissed the action as unfounded and Infopaq appealed the decision before the Højesteret.

The Højesteret held that it was not disputed that consent from copyright owners was not required in press monitoring activities and the writing up of summaries which involved the manual reading of each publication, the selection of relevant articles on the basis of predetermined search words and the production of a manually prepared cover sheet for the summary writers, providing an identified search word in an article and its position in the newspaper. Also, the national court found that there was no dispute as to the fact that the data capture process involved two acts of reproduction: the creation of the image file, when the printed articles were scanned; and the consequent conversion into a text file. However, the Højesteret noticed that there was disagreement between the parties as to whether this amounted to reproduction within the meaning of Article 2 of the InfoSoc Directive.[24] The parties also

---

[24] Article 2 of the InfoSoc Directive states that: 'Member States shall provide for the exclusive right to authorise or prohibit direct or indirect, temporary or permanent reproduction by any means and in any form, in whole or in part: (a) for authors, of their works; (b) for performers, of fixations of their performances; (c) for phonogram producers, of their phonograms; (d) for the producers of the first fixations of films, in respect of the original and copies of their films; (e) for broadcasting organisations, of fixations of their broadcasts whether those broadcasts are transmitted by wire or over the air, including by cable or satellite.'

disagreed as to whether, if there was reproduction, the acts in question, when taken as a whole, were covered by the exemption envisaged by Article 5(1) of the InfoSoc Directive.[25]

Therefore, the Højesteret decided to stay the proceedings and refer a significant number of questions (thirteen in total) to the CJEU.

For the purposes of the present contribution, it is sufficient to limit the analysis to the first question only, which concerned whether the concept of 'reproduction in part' as meant by the InfoSoc Directive, was to be interpreted as encompassing the storing and subsequent printing out on paper of a text extract consisting of eleven words. In this respect, the CJEU held that an act occurring during a data capture process, which consisted of storing an extract of a protected work comprising eleven words and printing out that extract, was such as to come within the concept of reproduction in part within the meaning of Article 2 of the InfoSoc Directive, if the elements thus reproduced were the expression of the intellectual creation of their author. By doing that, and as will be further explained below, the CJEU concretized a real revolution in EU copyright. In all likelihood, neither policy papers nor legislative instruments have ever been capable of providing such abrupt and radical changes as those brought about by the CJEU in the *Infopaq* decision.

4.2   The InfoSoc Directive and a Harmonized Concept of Originality

As a preliminary matter, the CJEU wanted to make it clear that the InfoSoc Directive does not define the concept of either 'reproduction' or 'reproduction in part'. Therefore, following *Rafael Hoteles*,[26] the CJEU

---

[25]   According to Article 5(1) of the InfoSoc Directive: 'Temporary acts of reproduction referred to in Article 2, which are transient or incidental [and] an integral and essential part of a technological process and whose sole purpose is to enable: (a) a transmission in a network between third parties by an intermediary, or (b) a lawful use of a work or other subject-matter to be made, and which have no independent economic significance, shall be exempted from the reproduction right provided for in Article 2.'

[26]   Case C-306/05, *Sociedad General de Autores y Editores de España (SGAE) v Rafael Hoteles SA*, [2006] I-11519, concerned the interpretation of Article 3 of the InfoSoc Directive, ie the right of communication to the public of works and right of making available to the public other subject-matter. This reference for a preliminary ruling was made in the context of proceedings between SGAE and Rafael Hoteles, in relation to the alleged infringement, by the latter, of intellectual property rights managed by SGAE. SGAE had in fact taken the view that the use of television sets and the playing of ambient music within the hotels owned by Rafael, involved communication to the public of

held that such concepts must be defined having regard to the wording and context of Article 2 of the InfoSoc Directive, where the reference to them is to be found, as well as in the light of both the overall objectives of the Directive and international law.[27] By following this principle, the CJEU provided a teleological interpretation of the InfoSoc Directive, although it did that by engaging mostly in a textual interpretation of the relevant recitals and provisions.[28]

Firstly, the Court held that, as Article 2(a) of the InfoSoc Directive states that authors have the exclusive right to authorize or prohibit reproduction, in whole or in part, of their works, the scope of the reproduction right must be intended to cover 'work'.

As a second step, the Court sought to clarify what is to be meant by 'work' and, to this end, reverted to Article 2 of the Berne Convention.[29] The CJEU thus held that it is apparent that the protection of certain subject-matter (such as artistic and literary works) presupposes that this

---

works belonging to the repertoire which it managed. Considering that those acts were carried out in breach of the intellectual property rights attached to the works, SGAE had brought an action for compensation against Rafael before the Juzgado de Primera Instancia (Court of First Instance) No 28, Barcelona (Spain). The case was eventually referred to the CJEU. This stated that (34–35) '[a]ccording to settled case-law, in interpreting a provision of Community law it is necessary to consider not only its wording, but also the context in which it occurs and the objectives pursued by the rules of which it is part [...] Moreover, Community legislation must, so far as possible, be interpreted in a manner that is consistent with international law'. The Court eventually held that the distribution of a signal by means of television sets by a hotel to customers staying in its rooms, whatever technique is used to transmit the signal, constituted communication to the public within the meaning of Article 3(1) of the InfoSoc Directive.

[27]   Case C-5/08 *Infopaq International A/S v Danske Dagblades Forening, cit,* [34].

[28]   In this sense Mireille van Eechoud, 'Along the road to uniformity – Diverse readings of the Court of Justice judgments on copyright work' (2012) 3 JIPITEC 60, 73.

[29]   Article 2 provides, *inter alia,* that 'literary and artistic works shall include every production in the literary, scientific and artistic domain, whatever may be the mode or form of its expression ... Collections of literary or artistic works such as encyclopaedias and anthologies which, by reason of the selection and arrangement of their contents, constitute intellectual creations shall be protected as such, without prejudice to the copyright in each of the works forming part of such collections ... The protection of this Convention shall not apply to news of the day or to miscellaneous facts having the character of mere items of press information ...'

amounts to being an intellectual creation. However, as pointed out by Isabella Alexander,[30] the proposition that the general scheme of the Berne Convention lays down a standard of originality which amounts to intellectual creation is not uncontroversial. In fact, even if the Berne Convention implicitly contains an originality standard, nothing prevents Berne Union countries from extending protection to works which may not be considered original in this respect. This is because the Convention merely sets minimum standards.[31]

As a final step, the CJEU had to clarify what the standard threshold for protection ought to be. In other words, the meaning of originality. Under Articles 1(3) of the Software Directive, 3(1) of the Database Directive and 6 of the Term Directive, works such as computer programs, databases and photographs are protected by copyright if they are original in the sense that they are their author's own intellectual creation. From this, the CJEU inferred that, in establishing a harmonized legal framework for copyright, the InfoSoc Directive was rooted within the same principles as these Directives. This is apparent from the reading of recitals 4,[32] 9 to 11[33] and

---

[30]   Isabella Alexander, 'The concept of reproduction and the "temporary and transient" exception' (2009) CLJ 520, 522.

[31]   *Cf supra, sub* Chapter 2, Section I, §3.

[32]   'A harmonised legal framework on copyright and related rights, through increased legal certainty and while providing for a high level of protection of intellectual property, will foster substantial investment in creativity and innovation, including network infrastructure, and lead in turn to growth and increased competitiveness of European industry, both in the area of content provision and information technology and more generally across a wide range of industrial and cultural sectors. This will safeguard employment and encourage new job creation.'

[33]   '(9) Any harmonization of copyright and related rights must take as a basis a high level of protection, since such rights are crucial to intellectual creation. Their protection helps to ensure the maintenance and development of creativity in the interests of authors, performers, producers, consumers, culture, industry and the public at large. Intellectual property has therefore been recognised as an integral part of property. (10) If authors or performers are to continue their creative and artistic work, they have to receive an appropriate reward for the use of their work, as must producers in order to be able to finance this work. The investment required to produce products such as phonograms, films or multimedia products, and services such as 'on-demand' services, is considerable. Adequate legal protection of intellectual property rights is necessary in order to guarantee the availability of such a reward and provide the opportunity for satisfactory returns on this investment. (11) A rigorous, effective system for the protection of copyright and related rights is one of the main ways of ensuring that European cultural creativity and production receive the necessary

20,[34] as well as the preamble to the InfoSoc Directive. Therefore, the Court concluded in the sense that:

> [C]opyright within the meaning of Article 2(a) of Directive 2001/29 is liable to apply only in relation to a subject-matter which is original in the sense that it is its author's own intellectual creation.

> As regards the parts of a work, it should be borne in mind that there is nothing in Directive 2001/29 or any other relevant directive indicating that those parts are to be treated any differently from the work as a whole. It follows that they are protected by copyright since, as such, they share the originality of the whole work …

> [T]he various parts of a work thus enjoy protection under Article 2(a) of Directive 2001/29, provided that they contain elements which are the expression of the intellectual creation of the author of the work.[35]

In three steps, the CJEU achieved the full harmonization of the originality requirement at the EU level.

The Court also highlighted that, since newspaper articles are considered as literary works within the meaning of the Berne Convention and the InfoSoc Directive, they qualify for copyright protection and, as a consequence, also the parts of such works (like an extract of eleven words) may be protected by copyright. Indeed, said the Court, it is through the choice of words, as well as their sequence and combination, that the author achieves a result which is an intellectual creation.[36]

As has been interestingly highlighted by Stephen Vousden,[37] the cumulative test ('choice, sequence and combination') laid down with regard to newspaper articles is not rooted within international law. Instead, a disjunctive test is set out by both Articles 2(5) of the Berne Convention and 10(2) TRIPS. This author therefore suggests that, despite

---

resources and of safeguarding the independence and dignity of artistic creators and performers.'

[34] 'This Directive is based on principles and rules already laid down in the Directives currently in force in this area, in particular Directives 91/250/EEC, 92/100/EEC, 93/83/EEC, 93/98/EEC and 96/9/EC, and it develops those principles and rules and places them in the context of the information society. The provisions of this Directive should be without prejudice to the provisions of those Directives, unless otherwise provided in this Directive.' (footnotes omitted).

[35] Case C-5/08 *Infopaq International A/S v Danske Dagblades Forening*, *cit*, [37]–[39] (emphasis added).

[36] *Ibid* [45].

[37] Stephen Vousden, 'Infopaq and the Europeanisation of copyright law' (2010) 2 WIPOJ 197, 202–03

what is stated at paragraph 34 of the decision, most of the *Infopaq* judgment gained inspiration from German copyright law, where the same cumulative test is to be found, rather than international law.

It is worth noting that, as the InfoSoc Directive has been implemented by all EU Member States,[38] the interpretation given by the Court of Justice of the originality requirement is to be followed by national courts, with consequences which, as far as certain legal systems are concerned, can be particularly relevant.

4.3   Substantial Implications of the *Infopaq* Decision

In clarifying the meaning of the originality requirement, the CJEU decided to revert to international sources and interpret them by means of a teleological approach. By pointing out that the Berne Convention extends protection to subject-matter such as artistic and literary works, the Court held that copyright protection is to encompass intellectual creations or, better, works which are their author's own intellectual creations. Furthermore, as clarified by Sam Ricketson,

> it requires some stretch of the imagination to argue that the term 'original' and 'intellectual creation' in the Berne Convention could ever extend to cover productions that are purely or almost wholly the result of 'sweat of the brow'.[39]

As already said, this meaning of originality is akin to that envisaged in continental Member States' legislations. Therefore, the effects of *Infopaq* in those legal systems are likely to be quite insubstantial, as far as copyright practice is concerned. This is true also with regard to the subject-matter for which, so far, harmonization of the originality standard has not occurred. *Vice versa*, it is in legal traditions such as the UK that the *Infopaq* ruling is to affect the scope of copyright protection.[40]

As mentioned above, in the UK the concept of originality has traditionally been intended as synonymous with 'originating' from the

---

[38]   With regard to the status of implementation of the InfoSoc Directive in the various Member States, *see* Guido Westkamp, *The Implementation of Directive 2001/19/EC in the Member States*, February 2007.

[39]   Sam Ricketson, 'Threshold requirements for copyright protection under the international convenitions' (2009) 1 WIPOJ 51.

[40]   In this sense also Tatiana-Eleni Synodinou, 'The foundations of the concept of work in European copyright law', in Tatiana-Eleni Synodinou (ed), *Codification of European copyright law* (Kluwer Law International 2012) 93, 102.

author although, as explained above *sub* Chapter 2, Section II, §2, such received wisdom is not uncontroversial. After the introduction of the requisite standard of originality into statutory copyright law in 1911, the authority consistently cited to define its meaning has been *University of London Press, Ltd v University Tutorial Press, Ltd*,[41] in which Peterson J held that a work is original if it has not been copied from another work.[42]

It is indeed in the UK that the *Infopaq* decision has been criticized from several angles. Amongst them, it has been pointed out[43] that, if the CJEU has harmonized originality in a manner which removes copyright protection from certain works or categories of works, this might conflict with the principle of respecting acquired rights and legitimate expectations. However, to counter this, it can be submitted that the CJEU case law has been always consistent with the principle laid down in *Butterfly Music*.[44] As also recently stated in the *Flos* decision:[45]

---

[41]   [1916] 2 Ch 601.

[42]   *Ibid* [608].

[43]   Alexander, 'The concept of reproduction', *cit*, 522.

[44]   Case C-60/98, *Butterfly Music Srl v Carosello Edizioni Musicali e Discografiche (CEMED)* [1999] I-3939, was a reference for a preliminary ruling from the Tribunale di Milano (Milan Court of First Instance), seeking clarification as to the interpretation of Article 10 of the Term Directive (*see* further below). The reference was made in the course of proceedings between Butterfly Music and Carosello Edizioni Musicali e Discografiche, concerning the right to reproduce and exploit recordings which, after entering the public domain under the legislation previously in force, had again become protected as a result of the provisions transposing the Directive into national law. The CJEU highlighted (25) that, despite the fact that the principle of the protection of legitimate expectations is one of the fundamental principles of the Community, 'it is settled case-law that this principle cannot be extended to the point of generally preventing new rules from applying to the future consequences of situations which arose under the earlier rules'. The Court therefore held that Article 10 of the Term Directive did not preclude a provision of national law from laying down a limited period in which sound-recording media might have been distributed by persons who, by reason of the expiry of the rights relating to those media under the previous legislation, had been able to reproduce and market them before that law entered into force.

[45]   Case C-168/09 *Flos SpA v Semeraro Casa e Famiglia SpA* [2011] I-00181. This case was another reference from the Tribunale di Milano, seeking clarification as to the meaning and scope of Article 17 of Directive 98/71/EC on the legal protection of designs, according to which a design protected by a design right registered in or in respect of a Member State in accordance with the Directive shall also be eligible for protection under the law of copyright of that State as from the date on which the design was created or fixed in any form. The reference was made in proceedings between Flos, a company manufacturing

the principle of the protection of legitimate expectations cannot be extended to the point of preventing new rules from applying to the future consequences of situations which arose under the earlier rules.[46]

Other commentators have adopted a more nuanced view of *Infopaq*. In particular, Tanya Aplin has found that the approach of the CJEU is partly consistent and partly inconsistent with UK law. On the one hand, it is consistent because the now UK Supreme Court[47] has repeatedly held that whether a substantial part of a work is copied is a qualitative assessment which is influenced by the skill, labour and judgment of the part which is copied.[48] On the other hand, the decision in *Infopaq* could be potentially problematic to the extent that it makes originality determinative of whether a substantial part of a work has been reproduced. In particular,

> UK courts, although they consider originality highly relevant to whether a substantial part has been copied, also consider other factors in determining this issue … The *Infopaq* ruling is also potentially problematic because it sets the bar of originality at 'intellectual creation' rather than 'skill, labour and judgment'. Except in relation to those works whose originality standard has been harmonised, UK courts have adopted a 'skill, labour and judgement' test

---

designer lighting, and Semeraro Casa e Famiglia, concerning breach of the copyright that Flos claimed to hold in respect of a design known as the Arco lamp. Semeraro had in fact started importing from China and marketing in Italy the Fluida lamp design, whose stylistic and aesthetic features resembled those of the Arco lamp. The Court held that Article 17 of the Directive must be interpreted as precluding legislation of a Member State which excludes from copyright protection in that Member State designs which were protected by a design right registered in or in respect of a Member State and which entered the public domain before the date of entry into force of that legislation, although they meet all the requirements to be eligible for copyright protection. Additionally, the provision must be interpreted as precluding legislation of a Member State which – either for a substantial period of ten years or completely – excludes from copyright protection designs which, although they meet all the requirements to be eligible for copyright protection, entered the public domain before the date of entry into force of that legislation, that being the case with regard to any third party who has manufactured or marketed products based on such designs in that State – irrespective of the date on which those acts were performed.

[46] *Ibid* [53].

[47] The UK Supreme Court was established by Part 3 of the Constitutional Reform Act 2005 and started work on 1 October 2009, assuming the judicial functions of the House of Lords, which were exercised by the Lords of Appeal in Ordinary.

[48] *See* above, *sub* Chapter 2, Section II, § 2.1.

of originality, rather than one of 'intellectual creation'. Therefore, a strict application of Infopaq may not only indirectly harmonize the standard of originality required for protection of all authorial works, but also curb the flexibility that UK courts have previously had when it comes to assessing whether a substantial part of work has been copied.[49]

This said, perhaps too many fears have arisen as a consequence of the *Infopaq* decision, especially in the UK, where its impact has been seen by some commentators as 'a bomb in the … copyright landscape'.[50] However, this does not mean that *Infopaq* will pass unnoticed.

In addition, recently some commentators have raised doubts as to whether the CJEU actually harmonized the originality requirement for subject-matter other than photographs, computer programs and data-bases.[51] As will be seen below *sub* Chapter 4, to this it can be objected that in case law subsequent to *Infopaq* the CJEU has not only intended that originality is now harmonized at the EU level for any copyright subject-matter, but has gone further than this and elaborated upon the meaning of originality provided in *Infopaq*.

5. APPLYING *INFOPAQ*: THE ORIGINALITY REQUIREMENT GETS A NEW SHAPE IN UK COURTS

On 26 November 2010, Proudman J handed down her judgment in *The Newspaper Licensing Agency Ltd and Others v Meltwater Holding BV and Others*,[52] in which she assessed the way EU law has been changing UK copyright.

The facts of the case were not dissimilar to *Infopaq*. Meltwater is a Dutch multi-national group that provides an online media monitoring service to business customers. Customers selected search words, in order to then receive reports of articles containing such terms (called the

---

[49]   Tanya Aplin, 'United Kingdom', in Brigitte Lindner and Ted Shapiro (eds), *Copyright in the Information Society. A guide to national implementation of the European Directive* (Edward Elgar Publishing 2011), 558, 560.

[50]   *Cf* Estelle Derclaye, 'Infopaq International A/S v Danske Dagblades Forening (C-5/08): wonderful or worrisome? The impact of the ECJ ruling in Infopaq on UK copyright law' (2010) EIPR 247, 247.

[51]   *See* Thomas Höppner, 'Reproduction in part of online articles in the aftermath of *Infopaq* (C-5/08): *Newspaper Licensing Agency Ltd v Meltwater Holding BV*' (2011) 33 EIPR 331.

[52]   [2010] EWHC 3099 (Ch).

'Meltwater news'). Each Meltwater news was composed of the title of the article – which hyperlinked to the article itself – its opening words and an extract showing the context in which the search word is to be found.

The Newspaper Licensing Agency ('NLA') is a company formed to manage the intellectual property rights of its members by licensing and collecting licensing fees for making copies of newspaper content. The other claimants in the case were publishers of national newspapers and shareholder members of NLA.[53] Due to the proliferation of online media monitoring services, NLA recently promulgated two new licensing schemes for commercial users of these services. NLA, along with UK newspaper publishers, decided to sue Meltwater, its UK subsidiary and the Public Relations Consultants Association Ltd ('PRCA')[54] for copyright infringement. In particular, the issue before the court was whether Meltwater's end-users needed a licence from newspaper publishers in order to receive and use Meltwater news. Proudman J held that, lacking a licence, end-users infringed publishers' copyright.

Among other things, the judgment is interesting because Proudman J provided a first assessment of how and to what extent the decision in *Infopaq* has affected UK copyright. With regard to the scope of the present contribution, it is important to highlight its impact on the UK concept of originality.

5.1 From a Quantitative to a Qualitative Test

As a preliminary remark, the judge stated that domestic legislation must be constructed in conformity with, and so as to achieve the results intended by, the EC directives.[55] She then identified the relevant principle of law to be applied in the case at hand, this being the test laid down in *Infopaq* and, in particular, the fact that no distinction has to be made between a work and any part thereof. Proudman J continued to point out that, unlike the CDPA 1988, Article 2 of the InfoSoc Directive contains

---

[53]   These were: MGN Ltd, Associated Newspapers Ltd, Express Newspapers Ltd, Guardian News and Media Ltd, Telegraph Media Group Ltd and Independent Print Ltd.

[54]   PRCA is an incorporated professional association which represents the interests of its members who are UK public relations providers using the Meltwater news service.

[55]   *The Newspaper Licensing Agency Ltd and Others v Meltwater Holding BV and Others, cit,* [40].

no reference to 'substantial part'.[56] This was highlighted because, as made clear by the CJEU in the *Infopaq* decision, 'originality rather than substantiality is the test to be applied to the part extracted. As a matter of principle this is now the only real test'.[57]

Proudman J stated that in the UK 'the test for quality has been re-stated but for the present purposes not significantly altered by *Infopaq*',[58] but at the same time conceded that 'the full implications of the [*Infopaq*] decision have not yet been worked out'.[59] What the judge had in mind here might be possibly explained if one looks at her later judgment in *Future Publishing*, in which she held that '[w]hat is required for artistic originality is [just] the expenditure of more than negligible or trivial effort or relevant skill in the creation of the work'.[60]

Proudman J ruled that, in some cases, headlines could be considered as independent literary works. The judge went on to and, rather bizarrely,[61] held that text extracts *could* constitute a substantial part of the articles[62] if they are tantamount to being original. Finally, the judge found that, since

---

[56] Article 16(3) CDPA 1988 makes it clear that references to doing an act restricted by copyright refer to acts done directly or indirectly and 'in relation to the work as a whole or any *substantial* part of it' (emphasis added).

[57] *The Newspaper Licensing Agency Ltd and Others v Meltwater Holding BV and Others*, cit, [69].

[58] *Ibid* [81].

[59] *Ibid*. As pointed out by Höppner, 'Reproduction in part', cit, 332, in *Meltwater* the High Court 'felt bound to incorporate into English law a new, European, test for copyright infringement. The court inferred from *Infopaq* that the copyright protection of works of literature now depends on the "expression of the intellectual creation of the author" rather than the common law criterion of the level of the author's skill, judgment, labour and capital involved in crafting the work. The court thus appears to assume that *Infopaq* harmonised the (previously purely national) conditions under which copyright protection is conferred for all types of work … [I]t is doubtful whether such an expansive conclusion can actually be drawn from *Infopaq*. The decision only clarified what constitutes a "reproduction" under the InfoSoc Directive, i.e. the infringement of a work protected by national copyright. It did not address the preliminary question of what actually constitutes a work meriting copyright protection.'

[60] *Future Publishing Limited v The Edge Interactive Media Inc and Others* [2011] EWHC 1489 (Ch), para 10.

[61] In this part of the judgment, the judge seemed to deal with the question of substantiality, for the purpose of applying the CDPA, again as a matter of quantity, rather than quality. In the same sense, *see* Andrew Hobson, 'Newspaper Licensing Agency Ltd v Meltwater Holdings BV' (2011) Ent LR 101, 102–03, who states that in assessing the issue of whether copyright was to subsist in headlines and extracts, the judge 'has gone astray in her application of *Infopaq*'.

[62] So that Article 16(3) CDPA applies.

Meltwater customers made copies of headlines and text extracts when viewing or accessing Meltwater news, this amounted to copyright infringement and no fair dealing defences were deemed to apply.

5.2 Proudman J's Views in *Meltwater* do not Melt Away before the Court of Appeal

On 27 July 2011, the Court of Appeal of England and Wales upheld the ruling of the High Court, finding that Meltwater's end-users needed a licence from newspaper publishers in order to receive and use Meltwater news. The Chancellor of the High Court, together with Jackson and Elias LJJ, dismissed PRCA's appeal and praised Proudman J's judgment as being a 'clear, careful and comprehensive' one.[63]

Interestingly enough, the Chancellor of the High Court pointed out that, although the decision of the CJEU in *Infopaq* referred to an 'intellectual creation', this is to be interpreted in relation 'to the question of origin not novelty or merit'.[64] Therefore, the test for what constitutes copyright-protectable subject-matter under UK law has not been affected by *Infopaq*, in that '[t]he word 'original' does not connote novelty but that it originated with the author'.[65] The Chancellor of the High Court also stressed that '[i]t is well established that the test of substantiality is one of quality not quantity'.[66]

The Court of Appeal did not add much to the analysis carried out by Proudman J and early responses to its decision were characterized by mixed feelings. Among those who criticized the ruling of the Court of Appeal, Lionel Bently[67] expressed his concerns in relation to the fact that granting copyright protection to titles can have negative effects on freedom of expression at large, since '[t]hose involved in all sorts of businesses which involve reproduction of titles of books, films, sound recordings and so on will now be left to wonder in what circumstances, if any, they will be infringing copyright.'[68] On the other hand, those who welcomed the outcome of the case highlighted that simply by putting

---

[63] *The Newspaper Licensing Agency Ltd and Others v Meltwater Holding BV and Others*, (EWCA), *cit*, [48].

[64] *Ibid* [20].

[65] *Ibid* [19].

[66] *Ibid* [24], citing *The Newspaper Licensing Agency Ltd v Marks & Spencer Plc, cit.*

[67] Prof Bently advised Meltwater and PRCA in these proceedings.

[68] Lionel Bently, 'Bently slams "very disappointing" ruling in Meltwater' (The IPKat, 27 July 2011) http://tinyurl.com/azecegv accessed 14 June 2013.

content on the internet without a paywall, one does not waive all copyright to it.[69] A possible implication of the ruling is that, although the *Meltwater* decision did not purport to rule on the lawfulness of browsing in general, it appears to have suggested that, lacking a clearly applicable exception, 'the mere act of browsing constitutes prima facie copyright infringement that can only be sanctioned by a web publisher's author-isation'.[70] This issue is central to the appeal currently pending before the UK Supreme Court.

5.3 The Importance of *Meltwater*

The *Meltwater* case is interesting because it shows the impact of *Infopaq* in the UK, a jurisdiction where the originality requirement has tradition-ally been intended loosely and where the test for infringement has been considered (despite the *dictum* of the Court of Appeal) as being charac-terized by more of a quantitative, rather than a merely qualitative, dimension. This is because of the wording of Article 16(3) of the CDPA 1988, as well the practical test for the finding of copyright infringement, which envisages that the part taken by the alleged infringer must be measured against the whole work of the claimant, not simply the work minus the portions which have not been copied.[71]

The Court of Appeal held that *Infopaq* did not affect the meaning of originality under UK copyright. This conclusion is also shared by Justine Pila, who observes that 'while headlines and other short strings

---

[69] Simon Clark, 'Just browsing? An analysis of the reasoning underlying the Court of Appeal's decision on the temporary copies exemption in Newspaper Licensing Agency Ltd v Meltwater Holding BV' (2011) 33 EIPR 725, 728, who adds (728): 'The fact that most churches try to keep their doors unlocked during the day in order for visitors to enter does not mean that there is an open invitation to thieves to help themselves to the valuables contained within the church. Nor should they have to lock their doors to the detriment of the majority in order to protect their valuables from the minority.' Similar views were expressed also more recently in Simon Clark, 'Why the Meltwater case won't break the internet' (The 1709 Blog, 20 September 2012) <http://tinyurl.com/asrvtz4> accessed 14 June 2013. Mr Clark is current Head of the Intellectual Property group at Berwin Leighton Paisner LLP in London, and led the team which represented the NLA and the publishers in the litigation.

[70] Ed Baden-Powell, 'Think before you link: yesterday's news – today's copyright conundrum' (2011) CTLR 25, 28. In a similar sense, also Luke Scanlon, 'Government must change copyright law to protect website browsing' (2013) 35 EIPR 63.

[71] *Cf IPC Media v Highbury-Leisure Publishing* [2004] FSR 20.

of words may in principle be original literary works, and their unauthorised reproduction thus infringing of copyright, in practice this has been consistently denied by the courts.'[72] Although this reading is in line with the findings highlighted above *sub* Chapter 2, Section II, §2, to this it can be objected that the courts taking this path did not have to cope with *Infopaq* and subsequent case law. Indeed, the impact of *Infopaq* and its progeny[73] promises to be deep. The result can be a change in the scope and meaning of protected subject-matter, in a way which, in the first place, is likely to affect low-creativity and technical subject-matter. As observed by Derclaye, following the ruling in *Infopaq*, authors of sub-creative literary works 'must feel they have been ripped of a long-established protection and left with nothing as the United Kingdom does not have an unfair competition law to fall back on'.[74] Indeed, *Infopaq* may well lead to the abandonment of traditional refrains such as 'what is worth copying is prima facie worth protecting',[75] by establishing a higher threshold to protection.[76] Secondly, and rather paradoxically, the test laid down by the CJEU might facilitate the finding of copyright infringement,[77] in that the taking of any part of a work of a third party can be sufficient to this end, if that part can be considered as its author's own intellectual creation. One may indeed wonder whether, in light of *Infopaq*, cases such as *Francis Day*,[78]

---

[72] Justine Pila, 'Copyright and internet browsing' (2012) 128 LQR 204, 205.

[73] On which, *see* below *sub* §5 and Chapter 4.

[74] Derclaye, 'Infopaq International A/S', *cit*, 249.

[75] *University of London Press Ltd v University Tutorial Press Ltd, cit*, [610] (Peterson J).

[76] For a conclusion to the contrary, *see* Ed Barker and Iona Harding, 'Copyright, the ideas/expression dichotomy and harmonization: digging deeper into *SAS*' (2012) 7(9) JIPLP 673, 678, who hold the view that the decision in *Meltwater* has not altered the traditional test of enough 'skill, labour and judgment', and therefore no real adjustment is required to comply with the 'author's own intellectual creation' standard.

[77] On which *see below sub* Chapter 5, §1.

[78] *Francis Day and Hunter v Twentieth Century Fox Corp and Others* [1939] UKPC 68. The case was brought by owners of the copyright in a song, consisting of words and music, entitled '*The Man Who Broke the Bank at Monte Carlo*', against the distributors and exhibitors at cinematograph theatres in Canada of a motion picture bearing the same title. The claimants were successful before the first instance court, but their action was reversed by the Court of Appeal of Ontario. Dismissing the appeal, the Judicial Committee of the Privy Council confirmed the decision of the Court of Appeal of Ontario and held that, although there might have been a certain amount of originality in choosing the title of a work, this could not be considered as a literary work *per se*. In fact, the

Exxon[79] or *Coffey*[80] would have had different outcomes if decided today. Although there are a few decisions by UK courts which have made it clear that, in general, short verbal texts including book and film titles, as well as advertising slogans, will not draw copyright protection, some commentators have concluded that the decisions in *Infopaq* and *Meltwater* have unsettled this traditional approach and may well lower the bar for the protection of short verbal texts.[81] In addition, as the Court of Appeal did not provide any precise guidelines for determining under what circumstances any particular headline or extract is original, this may result in uncertainties and inconsistent applications of the *Infopaq* test at the UK level.[82]

---

appellants' contention was put as high as that copyright in a title is infringed by the application of that title to a work of a different character from that of the work to which it was originally applied. Based on this reasoning, observed Lord Wright, it would be said that the title '*Adam*' applied to a work of statuary would be infringed if that title were used as that of a novel. The Privy Council thus held that these and other anomalous consequences justify the broad principle that in general a title is not by itself a proper subject-matter of copyright.

[79] *Exxon Corp v Exxon Insurance Consultants International Ltd* [1981] 1 WLR 624; [1981] 2 All ER 495 and 3 All ER 241.

[80] *Coffey v Warner/Chappell Music* [2005] EWHC 449 (Ch); [2005] ECDR 21; [2006] EMLR 2; [2005] FSR 34; (2005) 28(6) IPD 28046. The case was brought by a singer and songwriter, who claimed that vocal inflections in a single phrase of her song '*Forever After*' had been transferred into 'Nothing Really Matters', co-written and sung by Madonna and included in her album '*Ray of Light*'. In particular, it was claimed that the recording of '*Forever After*' included an original musical work comprising the combination of vocal expression, pitch contour and syncopation of or around the words 'does it really matter', which are repeated throughout the song and comprise its lyrical hook. The Court of Appeal dismissed the claim, holding that, while circumstances may exist which justify regarding a constituent part of a larger entity as in itself a copyright work, that can only be where the part in question can fairly be regarded as so separable from the material with which it is collocated as itself to constitute a copyright work. In this case, the identification of a separate copyright work in this way was not possible and so 'does it really matter' could not enjoy copyright protection.

[81] Jennifer Davis and Alan Durant, 'To protect or not to protect? The eligibility of commercially used short verbal texts for copyright and trademark protection' (2011) 4 IPQ 345, 346.

[82] According to Maryanne Stanganelli, 'Spreading the news online: a fine balance of copyright and freedom of expression in news aggregation' (2012) 34 EIPR 745, 748, '[t]he approach taken by *Meltwater* … is a dangerous one, as it does not set up a guide for determining whether any particular headline or extract is original or extracts a substantial part from an original literary work. Any future

Finally – and perhaps most importantly – the Court of Appeal, in upholding the ruling of Proudman J, referred solely to *Infopaq*, without taking into due account (*rectius*: without even mentioning) the implications of another important decision of the CJEU: *Bezpečnostní softwarová asociace*.

At the beginning of November 2011, the UK Supreme Court granted permission to PRCA to appeal against the decision of the Court of Appeal. Although the appeal (currently pending) is just on the transient copying exception within the meaning of Article 5(1) of the InfoSoc Directive as transposed into Article 17(6) CDPA 1988, the decision of the Supreme Court might clarify controversial aspects of the case, and also elaborate on the implications of the *Infopaq* ruling, not only in light of the radically different interpretations some national courts have recently given as to whether newspaper articles are subject to copyright protection,[83] but even more importantly regarding CJEU decisions which came after *Infopaq* and *Bezpečnostní softwarová asociace*.[84] On 17 April 2013 the UK Supreme Court decided to refer the *Meltwater* case to the

---

court having to rule on any particular headline will thus be ad hoc, and therefore unpredictable.'

[83]   *Ecopress as v Storin, spol sro*, 11Co 51/2010-447 IČS: 1308209396, 27 September 2011. This was a decision of the Regional Court in Bratislava, which denied copyright protection on newspaper articles. Ecopress is the publisher of Hospodárske Noviny and, along with three other publishing groups, had sued monitoring agency Storin for copyright infringement, claiming that its activities involved the unlawful reproduction of its articles. Both the District Court of Bratislava III and the Regional Court in Bratislava dismissed the action, in that copyright was held not to subsist in newspaper articles. This is because newspaper articles constitute mere information and are therefore out of the scope of copyright protection, pursuant to Article 7(3)(a) of the Slovak Copyright Act (Act No 618/2003 of 4th December 2003 on Copyright and Rights Related to Copyright). Although the case was decided after *Infopaq*, no mention was made by the Slovak courts of this CJEU decision. The defendants in this case have however pledged to file their own appeals with the country's Supreme and Constitutional courts. On this decision *see* Jeremy Phillips, 'News in Slovakia: no copyright in newspaper news' (The 1709 Blog, 5 January 2012) <http://tinyurl.com/bdjs2nj> accessed 14 June 2013; Martin Husovec, 'Newspaper articles not creative enough. An issue for the CJEU?' (Kluwer Copyright Blog, 24 January 2012) <http://tinyurl.com/av7z3fv> accessed 14 June 2013; Klára Jiřičná, 'Slovak ruling angers publishing industry' (The Prague Post, 18 January 2012) <.http://tinyurl.com/b54cvz2> accessed 14 June 2013.

[84]   *See* below *sub* Chapter 4.

CJEU.[85] Lord Sumption gave the judgment of the Court, and deemed that a reference for a preliminary ruling was necessary to seek guidance on the proper interpretation of Article 5 of the InfoSoc Directive, given the transnational dimension of the appeal and its potential implications for internet users across the EU.[86]

6. THE CJEU GOES ON: THE BEZPEČNOSTNÍ SOFTWAROVÁ ASOCIACE DECISION

This reference for a preliminary ruling was made by the Nejvyšší správní soud (Czech Supreme Administrative Court) in the context of proceedings between Bezpečnostní softwarová asociace – Svaz softwarové ochrany[87] ('BSA') and the Ministerstvo kultury[88] ('MK') concerning its refusal to grant BSA authorization to carry out collective administration of copyrights in computer programs.

6.1 Facts and Questions Referred to the CJEU

In 2001, BSA had applied to the MK, seeking to obtain the authorization for collective administration of copyrights to computer programs, pursuant to Article 98 of the Czech Copyright Law. The objective was to secure the right to the collective administration of graphic user interfaces (GUIs). The MK refused to grant such authorization and litigation ensued for the following four years, both in courts and before the MK itself. Eventually, the Ministry rejected BSA's application again, on two grounds. Firstly, that copyright law protects only the object code and the source code of a computer program, but not the result of the display of the program on the computer screen, since the graphic user interface is protected only against unfair competition. Secondly, that the collective administration of computer programs is possible in theory, but that mandatory collective administration is not an option and voluntary collective administration serves no purpose.

BSA lodged an appeal against such decision, which was dismissed both by the MK and courts.

---

[85] *Public Relations Consultants Association Limited v The Newspaper Licensing Agency Limited and Others* [2013] UKSC 18.

[86] *Ibid* [38].

[87] Security software association.

[88] Czech Ministry of Culture.

A further appeal followed before the Nejvyšší správní soud, which decided to stay the proceedings and refer two questions to the CJEU.

By its first question, the Czech court asked whether Article 1(2) of Directive 91/250/EEC[89] should be interpreted as meaning that, for the purposes of the copyright protection of a computer program as a work under that Directive, the phrase 'the expression in any form of a computer program' also includes the graphic user interface of the computer program or a part thereof.

Should the answer to that be positive, the national court also asked whether television broadcasting, whereby the public is enabled to have sensory perception of the graphic user interface of a computer program or part thereof, albeit without the possibility of exerting active control over that program, constituted making a work or part thereof available to the public within the meaning of Article 3(1) of the InfoSoc Directive.[90]

As far as the scope of the present work is concerned, attention will be limited to the answer that the CJEU provided to the first question.

6.2 Originality under the InfoSoc Directive

Article 1(2) of the Software Directive states that:

> Protection in accordance with this Directive shall apply to the expression in any form of a computer program. Ideas and principles which underlie any element of a computer program, including those which underlie its interfaces, are not protected by copyright under this Directive.

In relation to this, the CJEU observed that, as the notion of 'expression in any form of a computer program' is not defined by the Software Directive, its meaning ought to be clarified in light of both the overall objectives of the Directive and international law.[91]

The Court recalled that computer programs, whether expressed in source code or in object code, are protected by copyright as literary

---

[89] The content of Article 1(2) of Directive 91/250/EEC has been reported verbatim in its codified version, ie Directive 2009/24/EC (that in this work I am referring to as the 'Software Directive').

[90] Article 3(1) of the InfoSoc Directive states that 'Member States shall provide authors with the exclusive right to authorise or prohibit any communication to the public of their works, by wire or wireless means, including the making available to the public of their works in such a way that members of the public may access them from a place and at a time individually chosen by them.'

[91] In the same sense, *see* Case C-5/08 *Infopaq International A/S v Danske Dagblades Forening*, cit, [32].

works within the meaning of both the Berne Convention and Article 10(1) TRIPS.[92] It thus follows that the source code and the object code of a computer program are forms of expression thereof. As a consequence, they are entitled to copyright protection as computer programs. That is because the object of the protection conferred by the Software Directive is the expression in any form of a computer program (including any preparatory design work capable of leading, respectively, to the reproduction or the subsequent creation of such a program),[93] which permits reproduction in different computer languages, such as the source code and the object code.

By referring to the opinion of Advocate General Bot,[94] the CJEU pointed out that any form of expression of a computer program must be protected from the moment at which its reproduction would engender the reproduction of the computer program itself, thus enabling the computer to perform its task.

GUIs are parts of a computer program that provide for interconnection and interaction of elements of software and hardware with other software and hardware and with users in all the ways in which they are intended to function.[95] In particular, the graphic user interface is an interaction

---

[92] Article 10(1) of the TRIPS Agreeement states that '[c]omputer programs, whether in source or object code, shall be protected as literary works under the Berne Convention'.

[93] *Cf* Recital 7 in the preamble to the Software Directive, according to which, '[f]or the purpose of this Directive, the term "computer program" shall include programs in any form, including those which are incorporated into hardware. This term also includes preparatory design work leading to the development of a computer program provided that the nature of the preparatory work is such that a computer program can result from it at a later stage".

[94] Opinion of Advocate General Yves Bot, delivered on 14 October 2010, in particular [61].

[95] Recitals 10 and 11 in the preamble to the Software Directive state that '(10) The function of a computer program is to communicate and work together with other components of a computer system and with users and, for this purpose, a logical and, where appropriate, physical interconnection and interaction is required to permit all elements of software and hardware to work with other software and hardware and with users in all the ways in which they are intended to function. The parts of the program which provide for such interconnection and interaction between elements of software and hardware are generally known as "interfaces". This functional interconnection and interaction is generally known as "interoperability"; such interoperability can be defined as the ability to exchange information and mutually to use the information which has been exchanged. (11) For the avoidance of doubt, it has to be made clear that only the expression of a computer program is protected and that ideas and

interface enabling communication between the computer program and the user. However, since it does not enable the reproduction of that computer program, but merely constitutes one element of that program by way of which users make use of the features of that program, the interface does not constitute a form of expression of a computer program within the meaning of Article 1(2) of the Software Directive. Therefore, a graphic user interface cannot be protected specifically by copyright in computer programs by virtue of this Directive.[96]

The CJEU did not limit its answer to this, but went further, and deemed it appropriate to ascertain whether the graphic user interface of a computer program might be protected by the ordinary law of copyright under the InfoSoc Directive.[97] Following *Infopaq*, the CJEU held that a graphic user interface can, as a work, be protected by copyright if it is its author's own intellectual creation.[98]

Despite being a matter for the national court to decide, the CJEU clarified what criteria have to be followed in making such an assessment. It held that the national court must take account, *inter alia*, of the specific arrangement or configuration of all the components which form part of the graphic user interface, in order to determine which meet the criterion of originality. In this respect, that criterion cannot be satisfied by components of the graphic user interface, which are differentiated only by their technical function. In fact, in such a situation, the components of a graphic user interface do not permit the author to express his creativity in an original manner and achieve a result which is his own intellectual creation.[99] As noted by Tatiana-Eleni Synodinou, this finding

---

principles which underlie any element of a program, including those which underlie its interfaces, are not protected by copyright under this Directive. In accordance with this principle of copyright, to the extent that logic, algorithms and programming languages comprise ideas and principles, those ideas and principles are not protected under this Directive. In accordance with the legislation and case-law of the Member States and the international copyright conventions, the expression of those ideas and principles is to be protected by copyright.'

[96] Case C-393/09 *Bezpečnostní softwarová asociace – Svaz softwarové ochrany v Ministerstvo kultury, cit*, [42].

[97] *Ibid* [44].

[98] *Ibid* [46].

[99] *Ibid* [50].

is tantamount to recognizing the US merger doctrine in the European copyright field.[100]

6.3   A One-Size-Fits-All Rule for Originality and Copyright Assessment

As far as originality in EU copyright is concerned, the *Bezpečnostní softwarová asociace* decision is important for two reasons.

First of all, by following *Infopaq*, this judgment confirms that the originality requirement is to be considered as harmonized at the EU level.

Furthermore, it paves the way towards a different scrutiny for deciding what falls under copyright protection. While in some Member States (for instance, the UK) it is necessary that a work falls in one of the categories provided by the law to receive copyright protection; in other Member States (such as Germany, France and Italy) the list of categories is merely exemplificative. Following the reasoning of the CJEU in both *Infopaq* and *Bezpečnostní softwarová asociace*, it appears that copyright protection is to arise any time a work, which is to be meant as 'every production in the literary, scientific and artistic domain',[101] is its author's own intellectual creation. The consequences of this may be threefold.

Firstly, one can have doubts as to whether a system of exhaustive subject-matter categorization, such as the one envisaged by the CDPA 1988, is still in line with EU law.[102] That is because what the CJEU seemed to suggest in the *Bezpečnostní softwarová asociace* decision is that if a work is its author's own intellectual creation, then that work is protected by copyright.[103] As far as UK copyright is concerned, this could put an end to the need for determining *ex ante* whether a creative expression fits into any of the specific copyright subject-matter, thus

---

[100]   Synodinou, 'The foundations of the concept of work in European copyright law', in Synodinou (ed), *Codification of European copyright law, cit*, 101.

[101]   Article 2(1) of the Berne Convention.

[102]   Cf Christian Handig, 'Infopaq International A/S v Danske Dagblades Forening (C-5/08): is the term "work" of the CDPA 1988 in line with the European Directives?' (2010) EIPR 53, 55–6.

[103]   If that was the proper reading, then the *Bezpečnostní softwarová asociace* decision would go far beyond *Infopaq*, as suggested by Jonathan Griffiths, 'Infopaq, BSA, and the "Europeanisation" of United Kingdom copyright law' (2011) <http://tinyurl.com/bydchtw> accessed 14 June 2013.

avoiding the creation of unreasonable gaps in copyright protection, in particular in relation to unconventional creative works which cannot be classified as literary, dramatic, musical or artistic works.[104]

This would not be the only implication as far as UK copyright is concerned. In fact, if copyright was deemed not to subsist where the expression of a work is dictated by its technical function, this could lead to the abandonment of authorities such as *Sawkins v Hyperion Records Ltd*,[105] a case which showed 'a certain tension between what one may call a "pedestrian" approach to originality in copyright law and a "creativity" approach which resembles somewhat the principle of the continental-European protection philosophy'.[106] There, the Court of Appeal of England and Wales held that the skill and labour exerted by a musicologist in updating musical scores to recreate the music of a baroque composer was sufficient for the musicologist to be considered as the author of a musical work protected under the CDPA.[107] Contrary to the submission of Mummery LJ,[108] it may be argued that the idea that even a mere copy can qualify for copyright protection if it has required great talent and technical skill to make, is no longer sufficient to sustain a valid copyright claim.

Finally, copyright assessment is likely to become more homogeneous, as there will be no need for determining *ex ante* the subject-matter which

---

[104]　*See* Andrew Christie, 'A proposal for simplifying United Kingdom copyright law' (2001) 23 EIPR 26, 28–9 (this article is noteworthy also for anticipating problems arisen later out of the distinction in the InfoSoc Directive between tangible and intangible mediums of expression); Jeremy Phillips and Alison Firth, *Introduction to intellectual property law* (4th edn, Butterworths 2001), 138; Richard Arnold, 'Content copyrights and signal copyrights: the case for a rational scheme of protection' (2011) 1 QMJIP 272, 277.

[105]　[2005] EWCA Civ 565.

[106]　Andreas Rahmatian, 'The concepts of "musical work" and "originality" in UK copyright law – Sawkins v Hyperion as a test case' (2009) 40 IIC 560, 560.

[107]　For an argument to the contrary *see*, however, *Forensic Telecommunications Services Ltd v The Chief Constable of West Yorkshire Police Stephen Hirst* [2011] EWHC 2892 (Ch), in which Arnold J held that [94]: 'cases like *Sawkins v Hyperion* … were concerned with the reconstruction of musical and literary texts … The reconstruction required the exercise of sophisticated musical or literary judgement as well as other relevant kinds of skill and labour. In each case, it was possible to say that the later author had devised the form of expression of the work even though he was attempting to reconstruct the form of expression of the earlier author's work.'

[108]　*Ibid* [83] ff.

a work ought to belong to (as is the case with all the controversial cases that frequently give rise to copyright litigation).[109]

In any case, further clarification is certainly awaited with regards to what is to be meant by a work or production.[110] As far as this last point is concerned, a recent reference to the CJEU showed how controversial this issue remained in the UK.

7. THE *FOOTBALL DATACO* REFERENCE

On 21 December 2010, the Court of Appeal of England and Wales made a preliminary reference[111] to the CJEU in the context of proceedings concerning the alleged infringement by Brittens Pools, Yahoo! and other betting companies of the exclusive intellectual property rights in the annual fixture lists produced and published for the purposes of the English and Scottish (football) Premier Leagues and football leagues ('the fixture lists'), which they used without a licence.

In the proceedings at first instance,[112] the Chancery Division of the High Court of Justice of England and Wales was asked to decide whether any, and if so which, rights subsisted in the fixture lists. Floyd J, after

---

[109] As a very recent example, *cf Lucasfilm Ltd and Others v Andrew Ainsworth and Another* [2011] UKSC 39 in which the UK Supreme Court held – *inter alia* – that the Stormtrooper helmets from Star Wars movies cannot be intended as sculptures within the meaning of Section 4 CDPA 1988, also because [44] '[i]t would not accord with the normal use of language to apply the term "sculpture" to a 20th century military helmet used in the making of a film, whether it was the real thing or a replica made in different material, however great its contribution to the artistic effect of the finished film'. On this decision *see* below *sub* Chapter 5, §2.

[110] Before *Infopaq* was actually decided, Christian Handig, 'The copyright term "work" – European harmonization at an unknown level' (2009) IIC 665, 665 had wished that with this decision the CJEU would clarify some aspects of the term 'work', as the guidelines of Community law were deemed to be 'as imprecise as those of the copyright laws of the Member States'. However, perhaps the *Infopaq* decision did not help in this respect.

[111] Case C-604/10 *Football Dataco Ltd, Football Association Premier League Ltd, Football League Limited, Scottish Premier League Ltd, Scottish Football League and PA Sport UK Ltd v Yahoo! UK Limited, Stan James (Abingdon) Limited, Stan James PLC and Enetpulse APS*, will be discussed below *sub* Chapter 4, §3.

[112] *Football Dataco Ltd and Others v Brittens Pools Ltd and Others*, [2010] EWHC 841 (Ch).

having considered that the main candidates were copyright as a database[113] and the *sui generis* database right,[114] held that the fixture lists were the production of selection or arrangement within the meaning of Article 3(1) of the Database Directive, according to which

> databases which, by reason of the selection or arrangement of their contents, constitute the author's own intellectual creation shall be protected as such by copyright. No other criteria shall be applied to determine their eligibility for that protection.

That is because the process of selection and arrangement of the contents of a database can and often will commence before all the data is created.[115] For this reason, Floyd J held that the fixture lists were protected by copyright. However, he found no *sui generis* database right to subsist in the fixture lists, because no additional efforts had been spent in obtaining, verifying or presenting the data content.[116]

On appeal,[117] Jacob LJ, along with Hooper and Rimer LJJ, decided to stay the proceedings and make a reference to the CJEU on two questions regarding the interpretation of Article 3 of the Database Directive.

By its first question, the Court of Appeal sought clarification as to what is meant by 'databases which, by reason of the selection or arrangement of their contents, constitute the author's own intellectual creation'. In particular, the Court asked whether the intellectual effort and skill of creating data should be excluded, whether 'selection or arrangement' includes adding important significance to a pre-existing item of data (as in fixing the date of a football match), and finally whether the 'author's own intellectual creation' requires more than significant labour and skill from the author and, if so, what.

By its second question, the Court asked whether the Database Directive precludes national rights in the nature of copyright in databases other than those provided for by the Directive itself.

As it is apparent from the foregoing, in particular from the first question, the *Infopaq* decision has led to important changes in national legislations and copyright litigation. In particular, the fact that doubts

---

113   Under Articles 3 and 3A CDPA 1988.

114   Pursuant to the Copyright and Rights in Databases Regulations 1997 (SI 1997/3032), ie the legislation enacted in the UK to give effect to the Database Directive.

115   *Football Dataco Ltd and Others v Brittens Pools Ltd and Others*, EWHC, *cit*, [82].

116   *Ibid* [92].

117   *Football Dataco et al v Yahoo! UK Ltd*, [2010] EWCA Civ 1380.

persisted as to whether 'author's own intellectual creation' meant something different from the traditional UK standard of 'significant labour and skill' is indicative of the fact that the *Infopaq* ruling has also cast doubts on areas of copyright which had been apparently left untouched by it or for which (databases) harmonization had already occurred.

CONCLUSION

The debate concerning the future of copyright at the EU level has reached a peak in recent years. During 2010 alone, two important documents were published: the European Copyright Code, and the Monti Report. These two policy instruments were concerned with the actual possibility, and desirability as such (at least the Monti Report, since the Wittem Group decided not to take any position in this respect[118]), of achieving a full harmonization of copyright. However, consensus is far from being reached on whether and how the copyright laws of the Member States should be fully harmonized.

Despite this, recent decisions of the CJEU have taken a proactive approach to copyright and achieved harmonization by means of judicial interpretation of a fundamental principle of copyright, the originality requirement. The *Infopaq* decision (as confirmed by *Bezpečnostní softwarová asociace*) held that a work is original if it is its author's own intellectual creation. By providing a teleological interpretation of the rationale underlying the InfoSoc Directive, the CJEU clarified that, for subject-matter other than computer programs, databases and photographs, originality is also to be given the same meaning as provided by the Software, Database and Term Directives.

As effectively summarized by Mirelle van Eechoud,[119] from the rulings in *Infopaq* and *Bezpečnostní softwarová asociace*, three readings stand out. The first is that the CJEU recognized that copyright may exist in very short works. The second is that the Court has interpreted EU law as containing an autonomous standard of originality for copyright works. The third is that the Court of Justice did not just set an originality standard, but established that the subject-matter of copyright is equally harmonized as a domain through 'intellectual creation' as an open-ended concept covering all conceivable types of authored matter.

---

[118] Wittem Group, *European Copyright Code*, Introduction, 5. For a criticism of this choice *see below sub* Chapter 6, Section I, § 2.3.

[119] Eechoud, 'Along the road to uniformity', *cit*, 68.

This said, the implications of the *Infopaq* decision remain yet to be fully understood, as also made clear by the *Football Dataco* reference.

There is one aspect, however, where there is no doubt. As will be better explained below, the *Infopaq* judgment has finally urged the need for an exhaustive discussion on whether full copyright harmonization is to be achieved and how to go about this. With what can be properly defined as a *coup de main*, the CJEU achieved a revolutionary result. Indeed, the time has come to take a decision in this regard, at both political and institutional levels. It is felt that this cannot be further postponed, unless a continued delegation of the role of *de facto* copyright lawmaker to the EU judiciary is desired. Most importantly, any intervention in this respect, either in the form of a codification of copyright or ad hoc directives, will have to be the result of a real desire to provide an actual betterment of copyright and not a mere, even if much less inspired, replica of the famous quote from the novel *Il Gattopardo*: 'Se vogliamo che tutto rimanga come è, bisogna che tutto cambi!'[120]

---

[120] Giuseppe Tomasi di Lampedusa, *Il Gattopardo* (Feltrinelli 1958), 32 ('If we wish that everything remains the same, everything must change!').

4. The CJEU goes ahead: The decisions in *Murphy*, *Painer*, *Football Dataco* and *SAS*

1. *MURPHY*: ON TV DECODERS, FOOTBALL MATCHES AND THE INTERNAL MARKET

The decision of the CJEU in Joined Cases C-403/08 *Football Association Premier League Ltd, NetMed Hellas SA, Multichoice Hellas SA v QC Leisure, David Richardson, AV Station plc, Malcolm Chamberlain, Michael Madden, SR Leisure Ltd, Philip George Charles Houghton, Derek Owen* and C-429/08 *Karen Murphy v Media Protection Services Ltd*[1] followed two references from the High Court of Justice of England and Wales, Chancery Division,[2] and the High Court of Justice of England and Wales, Queen's Bench Division (Administrative Court),[3] respectively.

These were made in the context of proceedings concerning the marketing and use in the UK of decoding devices which gave access to the satellite broadcasting services of a broadcaster, and were manufactured and marketed with that broadcaster's authorization. They were, however, used outside the geographical area for which they had been issued, thereby disregarding the broadcaster's will (they are thus referred to as 'foreign decoding devices').

---

[1]   Joined Cases C-403/08 and C-429/08 *Football Association Premier League Ltd, NetMed Hellas SA, Multichoice Hellas SA v QC Leisure, David Richardson, AV Station plc, Malcolm Chamberlain, Michael Madden, SR Leisure Ltd, Philip George Charles Houghton, Derek Owen* and *Karen Murphy v Media Protection Services Ltd*.

[2]   *Football Association Premier League Ltd, NetMed Hellas SA, Multichoice Hellas SA v QC Leisure, David Richardson, AV Station plc, Malcolm Chamberlain, Michael Madden, SR Leisure Ltd, Philip George Charles Houghton, Derek Owen* [2008] EWHC 1411 (Ch).

[3]   *Karen Murphy v Media Protection Services Ltd* [2007] EWHC 3091 (Admin).

The UK courts had sought clarification as to the interpretation of provisions in Directive 98/84/EC of the European Parliament and of the Council of 20 November 1998 on the legal protection of services based on, or consisting of, conditional access[4] ('Conditional Access Directive'); Council Directive 93/83/EEC of 27 September 1993 on the coordination of certain rules concerning copyright and rights related to copyright applicable to satellite broadcasting and cable retransmission;[5] Council Directive 89/552/EEC on the coordination of certain provisions laid down by law, regulation or administrative action in Member States concerning the pursuit of television broadcasting activities,[6] as amended by Directive 97/36/EC;[7] the InfoSoc Directive; and Articles 34, 36, 56 and 101 TFEU.

The Grand Chamber published its decision on 4 October 2011, upholding the Opinion of Advocate General Kokott, which had been delivered on 3 February 2011.[8]

1.1 Background to the Cases: the Exclusive Licence System

The Football Association Premier League ('FAPL') runs the Premier League, which is the leading professional football league competition for football clubs in England.

Among its activities, FAPL arranges the filming of the matches, for which it exercises television broadcasting rights. These include making the audiovisual content of sporting events available to the public by means of television broadcasting.

FAPL granted exclusive licences obtained under an open competitive tender, in respect of those broadcasting rights for live transmissions. The exclusive character of such licences was aimed at realizing the optimum commercial value of all of the rights. Broadcasters were prepared to pay a premium to acquire that exclusivity, as it allowed them to differentiate their services from those of their rivals and therefore enhanced their ability to generate revenue. The licences were granted for three-year terms on a territorial basis. Indeed, such licences – as a rule – were national, as there was a limited demand from bidders for global or pan-European rights. This was because broadcasters usually operate on a

---

4   [1998] OJ L 320, 54–57.
5   [1993] OJ L 248, 15–21.
6   [1989] OJ L 298, 23–30.
7   [1997] OJ L 202, 60–70.
8   Opinion of Advocate General Juliane Kokott, 3 February 2011.

territorial basis and serve the domestic market either in their own country or in a few neighbouring countries with a common language.

To safeguard the territorial exclusivity of the various licences, broadcasters took it upon themselves to prevent the public from receiving their broadcasts outside the area for which the licence was granted. This was done, in the first place, by means of encryption of the broadcasts. In the second place, broadcasters could not supply decoding devices that allowed their broadcasts to be decrypted for the purpose of being used outside the territory of the licence.

In addition to the licensing of the broadcasting rights for Premier League matches, FAPL was responsible for the transmission of the signal to the broadcasters who had acquired the relevant rights. To this end, the images and ambient sound captured at the match were transmitted to a production facility which added logos, video sequences, on-screen graphics, music and English commentary. Afterwards, the signal was compressed and encrypted, then sent by satellite to subscribers, who were able to decrypt and decompress it thanks to a satellite decoder requiring a decoding device such as a decoder card for its operation.

1.2 Background to the Cases: the Breach to Market Segmentation of Licences

In Greece and the UK, the holders of the sub-licences to broadcast Premier League matches were, respectively, NetMed Hellas and BSkyB.

However, in the UK some restaurants and pubs had begun to use foreign decoding devices to view Premier League matches. They would buy a decoder card and box which allowed them to receive a satellite channel broadcast in another Member State, such as the NOVA channels which broadcast them in Greece, the subscription to which was cheaper than that of BSkyB.

As a result, FAPL and others had commenced different proceedings before UK courts against suppliers of equipment and satellite decoder cards which enabled the reception of programmes of foreign broadcasters, as well as licensees or operators of public houses who had screened live Premier League matches by using a foreign decoding device.

The plaintiffs had claimed infringement of the rights protected under Section 298 of the CDPA 1988,[9] and copyright infringement by creating copies of the works in the internal operation of the satellite decoder and

---

[9] Section 298 CDPA 1988 sets out 'Rights and remedies in respect of apparatus, &c. for unauthorised reception of transmissions.'

by displaying the works on screen, as well as by performing, playing or showing the works in public and communicating them to the public, and abetting infringement by third parties to whom they supplied decoder cards.

In the case of Ms Murphy, agents from MPS, a body acting on behalf of FAPL to carry out prosecutions against public house managers who used foreign decoding devices, found that her public house in Southsea (Hampshire) received broadcasts of Premier League matches transmitted by NOVA. Hence, proceedings were brought before Portsmouth Magistrates' Court, which convicted Ms Murphy of two offences under Section 297(1) CDPA,[10] on the ground that she had dishonestly received a programme included in a broadcasting service provided from a place in the UK with intent to avoid payment of any charge applicable to the reception of the programme.

Having lost her appeal before the Portsmouth Crown Court, Ms Murphy brought her case before the High Court of Justice of England and Wales, which decided to stay the proceedings and refer ten questions to the CJEU in Case C-403/08, seeking clarification as to various issues. These included: whether decoder cards purchased in Greece and imported into the UK for use in the UK were 'illicit devices' within the meaning of the Conditional Access Directive and were therefore prohibited; what the meaning of 'communication to the public' under Article 3 of the InfoSoc Directive was; questions on the interpretation of the provisions in the TFEU (Articles 34, 36 and 56) concerning free movement of goods and services in the context of the Conditional Access Directive; and a question on the interpretation of the treaty rules on competition under Article 101 TFEU.

In Case C-429/08, the High Court of Justice of England and Wales, Queen's Bench Division (Administrative Court), decided to stay the proceedings and revert to the CJEU for guidance as to eight questions, which were similar to those asked in Case C-403/08.

By order of the President of the Court of Justice of the European Union of 3 December 2008, Cases C-403/08 and C-429/08 were joined for the purposes of the written and oral procedure and the judgment.

---

[10] Section 297(1) CDPA 1988 provides that 'A person who dishonestly receives a programme included in a broadcasting service provided from a place in the United Kingdom with intent to avoid payment of any charge applicable to the reception of the programme commits an offence and is liable on summary conviction to a fine not exceeding level 5 of the standard scale'. Level 5 sets a threshold of £5,000 (Criminal Justice Act 1982, Section 37).

1.3 IP at the Crossroads with Treaty Freedoms

As far as the scope of this contribution is concerned, it is sufficient to concentrate attention on the analysis carried out by the CJEU as to whether territorial restrictions in territorial licensing carried out by FAPL were tantamount to a restriction on the freedom to provide services.

Such issues were dealt with by Advocate General Kokott in her Opinion on 3 February 2011, with a specific focus on whether the territorial exclusivity rights at issue had the effect of partitioning the internal market into separate national markets. The Advocate General found that a partitioning of the internal market for the reception of satellite broadcasts was not necessary in order to protect the specific subject-matter of the rights to live football transmissions.[11] Therefore, this was not a justified restriction of the freedom to provide services. However, the Advocate General did not determine whether sporting events were actually capable of intellectual property protection.[12]

As noted by some commentators, the main premise of AG Kokott's Opinion was based on the assumption that the various national broadcasters should be free to compete with each other, the logic of this being that parallel trade in decoder cards necessarily benefits consumers. This assumption has been criticized as ignoring the actual relationship between rightsholders such as FAPL and licensees (the broadcasters). Each broadcaster can offer its services only with the consent of the rightsholder, since this controls access to the broadcasting rights and the conditions on which access is granted. The truth is that allowing parallel trade does not necessarily create competition. Instead, this may simply result in FAPL licensing fewer broadcasters (only in the most lucrative markets in the EU)[13] or in altering licence terms to make parallel trade

---

[11] Prior to the decision of the CJEU, the Opinion of AG Kokott had been praised by Jack Anderson, 'The curious case of the Portsmouth publican: challenging the territorial exclusivity of TV rights in European professional sport' (2011) 3 ISLR 53, who pointed out (69) that genuine price competition in the broadcasting of FAPL games would be a consequence of the decision of the CJEU, should this have followed the Opinion of the AG. Not only would FAPL broadcasting rights have been lowered but, given that the FAPL model is one applied in other competitions, there would have been a reduction in value of all sports broadcasting rights in Europe.

[12] *Cf* [179] ff of the Opinion.

[13] Joel Smith and Joanna Silver, 'FA Premier League down at half-time in European Championship: Advocate General finds that territorial exclusivity agreements relating to the transmission of football matches are contrary to EU law' (2011) 33 EIPR 399, 401, who also suggest that the judgment could have

unprofitable.[14] An alternative consequence may be that FAPL begins to market its own subscription channel, effectively bypassing BSkyB and other broadcasters.[15] What seems certain is that the decision in *Murphy* will have a profound impact beyond football broadcasting, as all content owners who wish to license their rights on an exclusive basis within the EU will have to think carefully about how those licence agreements are drafted if they wish to maintain and enforce territorial exclusivity.[16]

1.4   Restrictions Imposed by IPRs: Precondition is that the Work is Protectable

In addressing the issue of whether FAPL's licensing system was tantamount to a restriction to provide services, the CJEU recalled that Article 56 TFEU[17] requires the abolition of all restrictions on the freedom to provide services, even if those restrictions apply without distinction to national providers of services and to those from other Member States, when they are liable to prohibit, impede or render less advantageous the

---

implications reaching beyond the realm of sports broadcasting, as AG Kokott drew parallels with computer software, musical works, e-books and films which are downloaded from the internet and can easily be passed on in electronic form, and noted that this shows that the question at issue has considerable importance for the functioning of the internal market beyond the scope of the cases in the main proceedings.

[14]   Pat Treacy and David George, 'Football broadcasting: Advocate General opines that internal market freedoms trump copyright' (2011) 6 JIPLP 614, 619, who also point out how the value of broadcasting FAPL games varies enormously by region, because of the existence of other more popular domestic leagues in the various countries. In such a situation, the profit-maximizing strategy is to price discriminate along territorial lines. If this is no longer possible, a rightsholder like FAPL must find an acceptable alternative means to price discriminate, or apply a uniform or near-uniform price across the entire EU.

[15]   Daniel Geey, Jessica Burns and Mitsuko Akiyama, 'Live Premier League football broadcasting rights: the CJEU judgment' (2012) 23 Ent LR 17, 19.

[16]   Mark Hyland, 'The Football Association Premier League ruling – the Bosman of exclusive broadcasting rights?' (2012) 17 Comms L 7, 12.

[17]   The provision reads as follows: '1. Within the framework of the provisions set out below, restrictions on freedom to provide services within the Union shall be prohibited in respect of nationals of Member States who are established in a Member State other than that of the person for whom the services are intended. 2. The European Parliament and the Council, acting in accordance with the ordinary legislative procedure, may extend the provisions of the Chapter to nationals of a third country who provide services and who are established within the Union.'

activities of a service provider established in another Member State where it lawfully provides similar services.

In any case, pursuant to the ruling in *Liga Portuguesa de Futebol Profissional and Bwin International*,[18] the freedom to provide services is for the benefit of both providers and recipients of services. This said, the Court acknowledged that the actual origin of the obstacle to the reception of satellite transmission services like those at issue in the main proceedings was to be found in the contracts concluded between the broadcaster and their customers, which in turn reflected the territorial restriction clauses included in contracts affecting those broadcasters and the holders of intellectual property rights. However, as the national legislation concerned prevented those services from being received by persons who resided outside the Member State of broadcast – and actually required restrictions to be complied with on pain of civil law and pecuniary sanctions – the legislation had the effect of preventing access to those services. As a consequence, such legislation constituted a restriction on the freedom to provide services. This was contrary to Article 56 TFEU, unless it could be objectively justified.

FAPL and others, along with the UK, French and Italian Governments, had submitted that the restrictions underlying the legislation at issue in the main proceedings could be justified in light of the intellectual property rights held by FAPL. Such restrictions were necessary in order to ensure that FAPL remained appropriately remunerated. In particular, it had been submitted that, should no protection of that territorial exclusivity have been available, the rightsholder would have been no longer able to get appropriate licence fees from the broadcasters, as the live broadcasts of sporting events would have in part lost their value. This was apparently because broadcasters are not interested in acquiring licences outside the territory of the Member State of broadcast, also because of the extremely high costs of such licences. They are prepared

---

[18] Case C-42/07 *Liga Portuguesa de Futebol Profissional and Bwin International Ltd v Departamento de Jogos da Santa Casa da Misericórdia de Lisboa* [2009] ECR I-7633. This was a case concerning fines imposed on the Liga and Bwin by the directors of Santa Casa on the ground that they had infringed the Portuguese legislation governing the provision of certain games of chance via the internet. At paragraph 51 of the decision, the Court of Justice pointed out that Article 56 TFEU (then Article 49 EC) 'requires the abolition of all restrictions on the freedom to provide services, even if those restrictions apply without distinction to national providers of services and to those from other Member States, when they are liable to prohibit, impede or render less advantageous the activities of a service provider established in another Member State where it lawfully provides similar services.'

to pay a substantial premium, provided that they are guaranteed territorial exclusivity.

As was made clear by the CJEU, when assessing the justification for a restriction on fundamental freedoms guaranteed by the TFEU, it is necessary to weigh this against the public interest. Such a restriction is acceptable in so far as it serves overriding reasons in the public interest, is suitable for securing the attainment of the public interest objective which it pursues and does not go beyond what is necessary in order to attain it.[19] It is settled case law that such a restriction may be justified by overriding reasons in the public interest which consist in the protection of intellectual property rights.[20]

Although the decision is noteworthy for its competition law implications, as well as its impact on rights licensing at the EU level,[21] attention will be paid here to the part of the judgment dealing with originality.

---

[19] Joined Cases C-403/08 and C-429/08 *Football Association Premier League Ltd, NetMed Hellas SA, Multichoice Hellas SA v QC Leisure, David Richardson, AV Station plc, Malcolm Chamberlain, Michael Madden, SR Leisure Ltd, Philip George Charles Houghton, Derek Owen* and C-429/08 *Karen Murphy v Media Protection Services Ltd*, cit, 93, citing Case C-222/07 *Unión de Televisiones Comerciales Asociadas (UTECA) v Administración General del Estado* [2009] ECR I-1407, in which it was (re-) affirmed (25) that 'a restriction on the fundamental freedoms guaranteed by the Treaty may be justified only where it serves overriding reasons relating to the general interest, is suitable for securing the attainment of the objective which it pursues and does not go beyond what is necessary in order to attain it'. In this sense, also Case C-250/06 *United Pan-Europe Communications Belgium SA and Others v État belge* [2007] ECR I-11135; Joined Cases C-94/04 and C-202/04 *Federico Cipolla v Rosaria Fazari, née Portolese*, and *Stefano Macrino and Claudia Capodarte v Roberto Meloni* [2006] I-11421; Case C-398/95 *Syndesmos ton en Elladi Touristikon kai Taxidiotikon Grafeion (SETTG) v Ypourgos Ergasias* [1997] ECR I-3091; Case C-6/98 *Arbeitsgemeinschaft Deutscher Rundfunkanstalten (ARD) v PRO Sieben Media AG* [1999] I-7599.
[20] *See* Case 62/79 *SA Coditel Brabant and Others v S.A. Ciné Vog Films and Others* ('*Coditel I*') [1980] ECR 881, and Case 57/80 *Musik-Vertrieb membran GmbH and K-tel International v GEMA – Gesellschaft für musikalische Aufführungs und mechanische Vervielfältigungsrechte* [1981] ECR 147.
[21] These are briefly discussed in Eleonora Rosati, 'The Hargreaves Report and copyright licensing: can national initiatives work *per se*?' (2011) 33 EIPR 673, 674–6. *See* also Adrian Wood, 'The CJEU's ruling in the Premier League pub TV cases – the final whistle beckons: Joined Cases *Football Association Premier League Ltd v QC Leisure* (C-403/08) and *Murphy v Media Protection Services Ltd* (C-429/08)' (2012) 34 EIPR 203.

1.5   Is *Murphy*'s Originality at Odds with Berne?

The CJEU deemed it necessary to determine from the outset whether FAPL could invoke such rights capable of justifying the fact that the national legislation at issue in the main proceedings established in its favour protection that was tantamount to a restriction on the freedom to provide services.

The CJEU thus considered whether sporting events *per se* might be protected by copyright. It responded to the question negatively, holding that:

> FAPL cannot claim copyright in the Premier League matches themselves, as they cannot be classified as works.

> To be so classified, the subject-matter concerned would have to be *original* in the sense that it is its author's own intellectual creation ...

> [S]porting events cannot be regarded as intellectual creations classifiable as works within the meaning of the [InfoSoc] Directive. That applies in particular to football matches, which are subject to rules of the game, leaving no room for creative freedom for the purposes of copyright.

> Accordingly, those events cannot be protected under copyright. It is, more-over, undisputed that European Union law does not protect them on any other basis in the field of intellectual property.[22]

It may be argued that the position adopted by the Court did not come as a surprise. Even under a loose UK originality standard, live sport could have hardly been considered to be a work or qualify for copyright protection as a work.[23]

However, the rationale underlying the dictum of the Court is interesting for three reasons.

---

[22]   Joined Cases C-403/08 and C-429/08 *Football Association Premier League Ltd, NetMed Hellas SA, Multichoice Hellas SA v QC Leisure, David Richardson, AV Station plc, Malcolm Chamberlain, Michael Madden, SR Leisure Ltd, Philip George Charles Houghton, Derek Owen* and *Karen Murphy v Media Protection Services* Ltd, *cit*, [96]–[99] (emphasis added).

[23]   As commented by Ben Challis, 'Murphy's law of licensing?' (The 1709 Blog, 20 October 2011) <http://tinyurl.com/a8cebry> accessed 14 June 2013, 'even accepting that football can be like ballet, I doubt if even *Infopaq* can be stretched to cover live sport. That said, at one recent seminar on *Murphy* a very amusing quip came from the audience that surely a "fixed" cricket match must have a script (hehe!). And even if logos and national anthems can be protected by copyright law, does it matter? Not really, no.'

Firstly, and quite surprisingly, the Court tackled the issue of whether sporting events are protectable by copyright by identifying 'works' with 'original', rather than with the prior requirement that a work is a 'production in the literary, scientific and artistic domain', pursuant to Article 2(1) and (2) of the Berne Convention. The Berne Convention implies that originality of a work is a subsequent assessment, undertaken only when a production is found to be in the literary, scientific and artistic domain. In other words, to constitute a work in law, the intellectual creation must fall within one of the (although merely indicative[24]) normative categories of copyright-protected subject-matter. This may be a closed list (as it is in the UK) or a non-exhaustive one (as it is in the US and in civil law traditions, such as Germany, Italy and France).[25] In looking at the issue of sporting rights in this way, the CJEU seems to have changed the order implicitly set out in Article 2 of the Berne Convention. Needless to say, should this indeed be a correct reading of this part of the judgment, then the activism of the CJEU – inaugurated by its decision in *Infopaq* – may be seen as going well beyond the borders of EU law, to the point of actually touching upon international law itself. This, though fascinating, may be worrisome, in that it urges a reflection upon the actual legitimacy of the EU judiciary in interpreting and re-assessing internationally binding instruments.

The second reason is that, as highlighted by Ted Shapiro and Brigitte Lindner, the Court created a new rule, this being that under EU law

---

[24]   As explained by Sam Ricketson and Jane C Ginsburg, *International copyright and neighbouring rights. The Berne Convention and beyond* (2nd edn, OUP 2006) Vol I, 409, 'the words "such as", which precede the enumeration, indicate that [the enumeration in Article 2(1)] is not an exhaustive list: the works enumerated are only instances of the subject-matter that fall within the ambit of the expression "literary and artistic works". Accordingly, there may be other kinds of work, not enumerated, which are still eligible for protection under the [Berne] Convention ... Nevertheless, the history of the various revisions of the Berne Convention indicates that this proposition has to be treated with considerable caution.'

[25]   As pointed out by Andreas Rahmatian, *Copyright and creativity. The making of property rights in creative works* (Edward Elgar Publishing 2011) 37, from a property theorist's perspective (which is at the basis of the rationale for copyright protection in common law countries), the existence of a non-exhaustive list of categories, or flexibility of categories constitutes a weakening of the *numerous clausus* of property rights or a blurring of the boundary between *res* and non-*res*, because the compliance with the requirement of copyright 'work' is the first step towards the creation of the legal concept of copyright-property.

sports events cannot be classified as works *per se*, and this is an area which no directive ever attempted to harmonize.[26]

Finally, this passage from the judgment further clarifies the meaning of 'intellectual creation', as adopted as the standard for originality under EU law in *Infopaq*. A creation is to be considered as an intellectual – and hence original – one, if it is the result of its author's creative freedom. By adopting such definition of originality (which is akin to that envisaged under German law[27]), the Court added something to the concept of originality in *Infopaq*. For the CJEU, originality seems to be not only about sense, but also about sensibility. This finding, as will be explained below, has also been confirmed in later decisions of the Court. In any case, such a meaning of originality is to be found in both German and French case law. French courts find originality to subsist in works which 'reflet de la personalité de l'auteur' or bear his 'empreinte personelle'.[28] Similarly, German courts hold a work to be original when the spirit of the human author is expressed in the work itself or the work shows 'creative distinctiveness'.[29]

1.6 What Protection for Sporting Events then?

Although copyright protection is not available for sporting events *per se* – in that they are not conceived as original works – the Court acknowledged that FAPL could 'assert copyright in various works contained in the broadcasts, that is to say, in particular, the opening video sequence, the Premier League anthem, pre-recorded films showing highlights of recent Premier League matches, or various graphics.'[30] This part of the

---

[26] Ted Shapiro and Brigitte Lindner, 'More football in pubs: European Union – Court of Justice (Grand Chamber) *Football Association Premier League Ltd and Others v QC Leisure and Others* (C-403/08) and *Karen Murphy v Media Protection Services Ltd* (C-429/08)' (2013) 3 QMJIP 43, 46, speak of a new EU standard having been legislated by the CJEU in the *Murphy* decision.

[27] Pursuant to Section 2(2) UrhG 1965, 'Werke im Sinne dieses Gesetzes sind nur persönliche geistige Schöpfungen' ('Personal intellectual creations alone shall constitute works within the meaning of this Law').

[28] *Cf* Cass civ 1re, 1July 1970: D 1970, 734; Cass civ 1re 13 November 1973.

[29] *Cf* BGH GRUR 1998, 916/917 – *Stadtplanwerk*; BGH GRUR 1994, 206/207f – *Alcolix*; BGH GRUR 1986, 739/740 – *Anwaltschriftsatz*; BGH GRUR 1985, 1041/1047 – *Inkassoprogramm*.

[30] Joined Cases C-403/08 and C-429/08 *Football Association Premier League Ltd, NetMed Hellas SA, Multichoice Hellas SA v QC Leisure, David Richardson, AV Station plc, Malcolm Chamberlain, Michael Madden, SR Leisure*

ruling has been interpreted as a victory for FAPL, which might decide to
integrate the Premier League branding in all live feeds transmitted to
foreign broadcasters, so as to ensure that express copyright authorization
is obtained before hosting any form of public showing of a foreign feed
of Premier League matches with English commentary.[31]

As explained by the Court, sports may have a unique and original
character which can transform them into subject-matter that is worthy of
protection, in a way comparable to the protection of other works. EU law
does not prevent *per se* a Member State from protecting sporting events
as such, when this is deemed appropriate within the legal order of the
State. Such a conclusion, according to the Court, descends from Article
165(1) TFEU, which states that:

> The Union shall contribute to the development of quality education by
> encouraging cooperation between Member States and, if necessary, by sup-
> porting and supplementing their action, while fully respecting the responsibil-
> ity of the Member States for the content of teaching and the organisation of
> education systems and their cultural and linguistic diversity.

As a consequence, nothing prevents Member States from choosing
protection under intellectual property. This may be done, explained the
Court, either by putting in place specific national legislation, or by
recognizing, in compliance with EU law, protection conferred upon those
events by agreements concluded between the persons having the right to
make the audiovisual content of the events available to the public and the
persons who wish to broadcast that content to the public of their choice.[32]
As explained by Doukas, by doing so the Court, while relying on the
specific nature of sport and recognition of the organizers' entitlement to
market the related rights, did not rule out liability in tort for managers of

---

Ltd, Philip George Charles Houghton, Derek Owen and *Karen Murphy v Media Protection Services* Ltd, *cit*, [149].

[31] Stephen Smith and Andrew Maxwell, 'Premier League football cases: linguistic tactics, non-naked match feeds and the away goals rule' (2012) 18 CTLR 33, 36.

[32] Joined Cases C-403/08 and C-429/08 *Football Association Premier League Ltd, NetMed Hellas SA, Multichoice Hellas SA v QC Leisure, David Richardson, AV Station plc, Malcolm Chamberlain, Michael Madden, SR Leisure Ltd, Philip George Charles Houghton, Derek Owen* and C-429/08 *Karen Murphy v Media Protection Services Ltd, cit,* [102].

websites which offer illegal streaming.[33] The latter point has been confirmed by the Milan prosecutor's office, which recently issued an interim injunction which prevented unauthorized websites from streaming live football matches for which Italian broadcasting corporation Mediaset was the exclusive broadcaster.[34]

In any case, the Court stressed that any restriction imposed on free movement must not go beyond what is necessary to attain the objective of protecting the intellectual property rights at issue. In particular, derogations from the free movement principle are permitted only insofar as they are justified to safeguard the rights constituting the specific subject-matter of the intellectual property right concerned.[35]

With particular regard to intellectual property, settled CJEU case law shows that specific subject-matter of an intellectual property right is intended in particular to ensure protection to rightsholders, in order to allow them to exploit commercially the marketing or the making available of the protected subject-matter, by granting licences in return for payment of remuneration.[36] This is to be intended not as the highest possible remuneration, since Recital 10 in the preamble to the InfoSoc

---

[33] Dimitrios Doukas, 'The Sky is not the (only) limit: sports broadcasting without frontiers and the Court of Justice: comment on Murphy' (2012) 37 EL Rev 605, 610.

[34] *RTI-Mediaset v dinozap.tv and Others*, Procura di Milano (Milan Prosecutor's Office), 11 January 2013.

[35] Joined Cases C-403/08 and C-429/08 *Football Association Premier League Ltd, NetMed Hellas SA, Multichoice Hellas SA v QC Leisure, David Richardson, AV Station plc, Malcolm Chamberlain, Michael Madden, SR Leisure Ltd, Philip George Charles Houghton, Derek Owen* and C-429/08 *Karen Murphy v Media Protection Services Ltd, cit,* [106], citing Case C-115/02 *Administration des douanes et droits indirects v Rioglass SA and Transremar SL* [2003] ECR I-12705 and earlier rulings (Case C-23/99 *Commission v France* [2000] I-7653; Case C-61/97 *Foreningen af danske Videogramdistributører v Laserdisken* [1998] I-5171; Case C-10/89 *SA CNL-SUCAL NV v Hag GF AG* [1990] I-3711).

[36] Joined Cases C-403/08 and C-429/08 *Football Association Premier League Ltd, NetMed Hellas SA, Multichoice Hellas SA v QC Leisure, David Richardson, AV Station plc, Malcolm Chamberlain, Michael Madden, SR Leisure Ltd, Philip George Charles Houghton, Derek Owen* and C-429/08 *Karen Murphy v Media Protection Services Ltd, cit,* [107], citing Case C-57/80 *Musik-Vertrieb membran GmbH and K-tel International v GEMA – Gesellschaft für musikalische Aufführungs und mechanische Vervielfältigungsrechte, cit,* and Joined Cases C-92/92 and C-326/92 *Phil Collins (C-92/92) v Imtrat Handelgesellschaft mbH and Patricia Im-und Export Verwaltungsgesellschaft mbH and Leif Emanuel Kraul v EMI Electrola GmbH* [1993] I-5145.

Directive[37] and Recital 5 in the preamble to Directive 2006/115/EC of the European Parliament and of the Council of 12 December 2006 on rental right and lending right and on certain rights related to copyright in the field of intellectual property (codified version)[38] envisage only *appropriate* remuneration for each use of the protected subject-matter. Such remuneration is considered to be appropriate if it is reasonable in relation to the actual or potential number of persons who enjoy or wish to enjoy the service.[39]

1.7 Is Unfair Competition the Path to Follow?

This said, it is not clear what type of intellectual property right may be suitable for protecting sport events *per se*, where no copyright protection is available.

If the originality requirement is seen as being harmonized now, as a result of the ruling in *Infopaq*, the *marge de manœuvre* is indeed tiny. It is submitted that the only form of protection intellectual property at large

---

[37]   'If authors or performers are to continue their creative and artistic work, they have to receive an appropriate reward for the use of their work, as must producers in order to be able to finance this work. The investment required to produce products such as phonograms, films or multimedia products, and services such as "on-demand" services, is considerable. Adequate legal protection of intellectual property rights is necessary in order to guarantee the availability of such a reward and provide the opportunity for satisfactory returns on this investment.'

[38]   [2006] OJ L 376, 28–35. Recital 5 provides that 'The creative and artistic work of authors and performers necessitates an adequate income as a basis for further creative and artistic work, and the investments required particularly for the production of phonograms and films are especially high and risky. The possibility of securing that income and recouping that investment can be effectively guaranteed only through adequate legal protection of the rightholders concerned.'

[39]   Joined Cases C-403/08 and C-429/08 *Football Association Premier League Ltd, NetMed Hellas SA, Multichoice Hellas SA v QC Leisure, David Richardson, AV Station plc, Malcolm Chamberlain, Michael Madden, SR Leisure Ltd, Philip George Charles Houghton, Derek Owen* and *Karen Murphy v Media Protection Services Ltd*, 109, citing *Foreningen af danske Videogramdistributører v Laserdisken, cit*, and Case C-52/07 *Kanal 5 Ltd and TV 4 AB v Föreningen Svenska Tonsättares Internationella Musikbyrå (STIM) upa* [2008] ECR I-9275. In the case of television broadcasting, as stated in Case C-192/04 *Lagardère Active Broadcast v Société pour la perception de la rémunération équitable (SPRE) and Others* [2005] ECR I-7199, such remuneration must in particular be reasonable in relation to parameters of the broadcasts concerned, such as their actual audience, their potential audience and the language version.

may offer is that provided by the law of unfair competition.[40] As correctly pointed out,

> The higher protection threshold could leave a gap, but continental European systems have separate statutes prohibiting parasitical or free-ride unfair competition, and while a certain product may not qualify for copyright protection, because it does not meet the higher originality requirements (a simple register, etc.), its copying without permission, for instance, may still constitute a violation of the Unfair Competition Acts. In this way, the economic interests of the maker of a certain product/creation are safeguarded.[41]

An unfair competition act does not exist in all the Member States. This is the case of the UK, where – quite ironically – the main proceedings were to be decided.

The result of the *dictum* of the Court might lead it to hold that no protection is actually available to sporting events in the UK. This is because passing off, due to its strict conditions of applicability, would be a harmless tool.[42] Copyright, which would have been suitable (although

---

[40] See below *sub* §3.7.

[41] Rahmatian, *Copyright and creativity, cit*, 55.

[42] The passing-off action was first developed by English courts to prevent a competitor from passing their goods off as if they were the claimant's. As incisively stated by Lord Halsbury: 'nobody has any right to represent his goods as the goods of somebody else' (*Reddaway v Banham* [1896] AC 199, 204, 13 RPC 218, 224; echoing Lord Langsdale MR in *Perry v Truefitt* (1842) 6 Beav 66, 73). It is commonly acknowledged that an action for passing off was first recognized in the Elizabethan case of *JG v Samford* (1618). In the *Jif lemon* decision (*Reckitt & Colman v Borden* [1990] RPC 340 HL) Lord Oliver (499) elaborated the three elements a claimant must show in order to make a case of passing off: 'First, he must establish a goodwill or reputation attached to the goods or services which he supplies in the mind of the purchasing public by association with the identifying "get-up" (whether it consists simply of a brand name or a trade description, or the individual features of labeling or packaging) under which his particular goods or services are offered to the public, such that the get-up is recognized by the public as distinctive specifically of the [claimant's] goods or services. Secondly, he must demonstrate a misrepresentation by the defendant to the public (whether or not intentional) leading or likely to lead the public to believe that goods or services offered by him are the goods or services of the [claimant] … Thirdly, he must demonstrate that he suffers, or in quia timet action, that he is likely to suffer damage by reason of the erroneous belief engendered by the defendant's misrepresentation that the source of the defendant's goods or services is the same as the source of those offered by the [claimant].' Frequent reference is also made in judgments to Lord Diplock's

not uncontroversial), especially under the traditionally loose originality standard, has been swept away by the firm grip of the CJEU in *Infopaq*, as then confirmed in subsequent case law.

The end result is rather paradoxical: from being a country known for having an intellectual property regime shaped with a generous harbour (also because copyright law was traditionally intended as a protection against unfair parasitical competition),[43] the UK – if it does not bring about some changes which are clearly necessary to fill out the gaps created by *Infopaq* – will end up leaving aspiring rightsholders without any actual protection. Should the UK decide to adopt a law of unfair

---

enumeration in the '*Advocaat* case' (*Erven Warnink BV v Towend (J) & Sons* [1979] AC 731 [93]), of five minimum requirements for the action: '(1) a misrepresentation (2) made by a trader in the course of trade, (3) to prospective consumers of his or ultimate consumer goods or services supplied by him, (4) which is calculated to injure the business or goodwill of another trader (in the sense that this is a reasonably foreseeable consequence) and (5) which causes actual damage to a business or goodwill of the trader by whom the action is brought or (in quia timet action) will probably do so.' On passing off, *see* William Cornish, David Llewelyn and Tanya Aplin, *Intellectual property: patents, copyright, trade marks and allied rights* (7th edn, Sweet & Maxwell 2010), 663 ff and Lionel Bently and Brad Sherman, *Intellectual property law* (3rd edn, OUP 2008), 726 ff.

[43] According to the analysis carried out by Cornish, Llewelyn and Aplin, *Intellectual Property*, *cit*, 424–5, 'An exclusive right which strikes only at copying is particularly suited to claims that a person is taking something for nothing – that he is reaping fruits sown by the creativity of others. Nonetheless UK copyright law has on the whole conformed to the prescription that new rights should not be conceded without making a reasoned case and securing legislation. Indeed, statute has increasingly been used to define not only the duration of the various copyrights, but their subject-matter, the exclusive rights to which they give rise and the exceptions that may be admitted. The refusal to allow any general principle of unfair competition that will extend to the misappropriation of ideas means, however, that no limited, short-term form of liability may be imposed upon even the most parasitic purveyor of other people's ideas and enterprise. Accordingly there is always some desire to press the existing concepts of copyright into service. Lord Devlin, for example, once said: "Free trade does not require that one should be allowed to appropriate the fruits of another's labour, whether they are tangible or intangible. The law has not found it possible to give full protection to the intangible. But it can protect the intangible in certain states, and one of them is when it is expressed in words or print. The fact that protection is of necessity limited is no argument for diminishing it further, and it is nothing to the point that either side of the protective limits a man can obtain gratis whatever his ideas of honesty permit him to pick up." (*Ladbroke (Football) Ltd v William Hill (Football) Ltd*, *cit*, [291]).'

competition, it would have then to decide what requirements this should be subject to, in particular whether actual or mere likelihood of confusion should be required, as is the case in most EU Member States' unfair competition laws.[44]

In response to the call for evidence by the Hargreaves Report, the patent judges in England and Wales[45] wished for a new UK copyright act based upon a comprehensive review to be issued, in replacement of the CDPA 1988. Their response focused on the fact that, since the entry into force of the CDPA 1988, both technology and business models have changed radically, making it inappropriate and inapt to this new environment. In particular, the process of implementation of EU directives has introduced a number of anomalies in the statute, starting with the originality standard imposed by EU law with regards to software and databases. The CDPA 1988 is said to lack clarity. This, according to the response, gives rise to uncertainty on both the side of owner and the alleged infringer. The patent judges, however, did not tackle the implications of an EU-wide harmonized concept of originality for the UK.

1.8 The Responses of the High Court and Court of Appeal

On 24 February 2012, the High Court gave a judgment allowing Ms Murphy's appeal against the dismissal by the Crown Court of Portsmouth.

Previously, on 3 February 2012 Kitchin LJ published his decision in *Football Association Premier League Ltd, NetMed Hellas SA, Multichoice Hellas SA v QC Leisure, David Richardson, AV Station plc, Malcolm Chamberlain, Michael Madden, SR Leisure Ltd, Philip George*

---

[44] For instance, under Italian law, only likelihood of confusion is required: *see*, among others, the following recent decisions: Florence Court of First Instance, *Burberry Ltd v Profumerie Frediani Snc and A L Team Srl*, No 2348, 27 June 2011; Rome Court of First Instance, *British American Tobacco Italia SpA v Oneoffcigars Ltd and Vanderwood Italia Srl*, No 25016, 20 December 2010. Mere likelihood of confusion is sufficient also under French law (Cour d'appel Paris, *Groupe Liaisons v Kavesta*, PIBD 839111720, 2 June 2006). For a comparative report on the law of unfair competition in Europe, *see* INTA European & Central Asia Legislation and Regulatory Sub-Committee, *Unfair competition reports* (2007) <http://tinyurl.com/ab84q4k> accessed 14 June 2013.

[45] The response (<http://tinyurl.com/bz4ajun> accessed 14 June 2013) was approved by Jacob LJ (who at the time was the judge in charge of the intellectual property list in the Court of Appeal), the nominated patents judges in the Patents Court and the Patents Country Court Judge.

Charles Houghton, Derek Owen.[46] Following the ruling of the CJEU, the High Court had to determine whether any of the defendants had communicated any FAPL copyright-protected works to the public, contrary to Section 20 of the CDPA 1988,[47] and, if they had, whether Section 72 of the CDPA 1988[48] provided them with a defence. Kitchin LJ found that, although FAPL's broadcasts were not copyright-protected subject-matter *per se*, they nonetheless contained an anthem, along with artistic and films works, which enjoyed copyright protection. This was said to be in line with the decision of the CJEU.[49] In addition, Kitchin LJ found that the defendants had infringed Section 20 CDPA, in that they had transmitted FAPL's relevant copyright works, including its artistic works, to a new public and by electronic means. In relation to the issue as to whether the defendants could invoke the defence pursuant to Section 72(1)(c) CDPA 1988, Kitchin LJ held that the showing or playing of a broadcast in a public house to members of the public who have not paid for admission does not infringe any copyright in any film included in the broadcast.[50]

Although the latter finding of the High Court can be said to be in line with recent CJEU case law (which has excluded that the broadcasting of copyright-protected contents which is free of charge and enjoyed by third

---

[46]   *Cit.*

[47]   '(1) The communication to the public of the work is an act restricted by the copyright in – (a) a literary, dramatic, musical or artistic work, (b) a sound recording or film, or (c) a broadcast. (2) References in this Part to communication to the public are to communication to the public by electronic transmission, and in relation to a work include – (a) the broadcasting of the work; (b) the making available to the public of the work by electronic transmission in such a way that members of the public may access it from a place and at a time individually chosen by them.'

[48]   '(1) The showing or playing in public of a broadcast to an audience who have not paid for admission to the place where the broadcast is to be seen or heard does not infringe any copyright in – (a) the broadcast; (b) any sound recording (except so far as it is an excepted sound recording) included in it; or (c) any film included in it.'

[49]   *See* Joined Cases C-403/08 and C-429/08 *Football Association Premier League Ltd, NetMed Hellas SA, Multichoice Hellas SA v QC Leisure, David Richardson, AV Station plc, Malcolm Chamberlain, Michael Madden, SR Leisure Ltd, Philip George Charles Houghton, Derek Owen* and *Karen Murphy v Media Protection Services* Ltd, *cit*, [149].

[50]   *Football Association Premier League Ltd, NetMed Hellas SA, Multichoice Hellas SA v QC Leisure, David Richardson, AV Station plc, Malcolm Chamberlain, Michael Madden, SR Leisure Ltd, Philip George Charles Houghton, Derek Owen, cit*, [78].

parties without any active choice on their part infringes the right of communication to the public),[51] it is quite disappointing that it did not deal with the issue as to the type of protection sporting events may enjoy in the UK should no copyright-protected materials be present within them. This increases uncertainties about both the current scope of copyright protection under UK law, following recent decisions of the CJEU.

On 20 December 2012 the Court of Appeal published its decision in *Football Association Premier League Ltd v QC Leisure and Others*,[52] in which it dismissed the appeal brought by FAPL. The judgment, which was delivered by Etherton LJ (with whom Munby and Lewison LJJ agreed), followed an appeal from part of an order on 3 February 2012 of Kitchin LJ,[53] ie the part of the order which had dismissed the actions insofar as they were based on a cause of action for infringement of copyright in the film works contained in the broadcasts by communication to the public by electronic transmission contrary to Section 20

---

[51]   *See* Case C-135/10 *Società Consortile Fonografici (SCF) v Marco Del Corso*, in which it was held that the concept of communication to the public for the purposes of Article 8(2) of Directive 92/100/EEC of 19 November 1992 on rental right and lending right and on certain rights related to copyright in the field of intellectual property must be interpreted as meaning that it does not cover the broadcasting, *free of charge*, of phonograms within private dental practices engaged in professional economic activity, for the benefit of patients of those practices and enjoyed by them *without any active choice* on their part. Therefore, such an act of transmission does not entitle the phonogram producers to the payment of remuneration. *See a contrario* Case C-162/10 *Phonographic Performance (Ireland) Limited v Ireland, Attorney General*, in which it was held that a hotel operator which provides in guest bedrooms televisions and/or radios to which it distributes a broadcast signal is a user making a communication to the public of a phonogram which may be played in a broadcast for the purposes of Article 8(2) of Directive 2006/115/EC of the European Parliament and of the Council of 12 December 2006 on rental right and lending right and on certain rights related to copyright in the field of intellectual property. Therefore, a hotel operator which provides in guest bedrooms televisions and/or radios to which it distributes a broadcast signal is obliged to pay equitable remuneration under Article 8(2) of Directive 2006/115 for the broadcast of a phonogram, in addition to that paid by the broadcaster.

[52]   [2012] EWCA Civ 1708.

[53]   *Football Association Premier League Ltd and Others v QC Leisure and Others* [2012] EWHC 108 (Civ).

CDPA 1988. Following the ruling of the High Court which was favour-
able to pub landlady Karen Murphy,[54] it was again the turn of QC
Leisure to see how the Court of Appeal would have applied the principles
set by the CJEU. The Court dismissed the action and held that the
defence provided under Section 72 CDPA 1988 could be invoked
successfully by QC Leisure and similar undertakings.

2. *PAINER*: NO PHOTOS DESERVE MORE PROTECTION THAN OTHERS

The CJEU decision in *Eva-Maria Painer v Standard VerlagsGmbH, Axel
Springer AG, Süddeutsche Zeitung GmbH, SPIEGEL-Verlag Rudolf
AUGSTEIN GmbH & Co KG and Verlag M. DuMont Schauberg Expedition der Kölnischen Zeitung GmbH & Co KG*[55] followed a reference
from the Handelsgericht Wien (Commercial Court, Vienna), seeking
clarification – *inter alia* – as to whether a photo-fit based on a
photograph might be published in newspapers, magazines and on the
internet without the rightholder's consent.

2.1   Facts and Questions Referred to the CJEU

The facts in the main proceedings related to the abduction of Austrian
girl Natascha Kampusch, the search measures conducted by the security
authorities in that case, and the media reporting after her escape.

The applicant in the main proceedings was freelance photographer
Eva-Marie Painer, who had taken several photographs of Natascha
Kampusch. Painer had designed the background, decided the position and
facial expression of her subject, and produced and developed the photographs. In the course of her work, Painer labelled her photographs with
her own name, by using stickers and/or impressions in decorative
portfolios or mounts. She sold the photographs she had made, but did not
confer on third parties any rights over them and did not consent to their
publication.

---

[54]   *Karen Murphy v Media Protection Services Ltd* [2012] EWHC 466
(Admin).
[55]   Case C-145/10 *Eva-Maria Painer v Standard VerlagsGmbH, Axel
Springer AG, Süddeutsche Zeitung GmbH, SPIEGEL-Verlag Rudolf AUGSTEIN
GmbH & Co KG and Verlag M. DuMont Schauberg Expedition der Kölnischen
Zeitung GmbH & Co KG.*

When Natascha Kampusch was kidnapped in 1998, aged ten, the competent security authorities launched a search appeal in which the contested photographs were used.

In 2006, the girl managed to escape from her abductor. Prior to her first public appearance, the defendants in the main proceedings (newspaper and magazine publishers established in Austria and Germany) published the photographs Painer had taken of her, without indicating the name of the photographer, or indicating a name other than Painer's as the photographer. Furthermore, several of those publications had also released a portrait (a photo-fit), created by computer from the contested photographs, which, since there was no recent photograph of Natascha until her first public appearance, represented her supposed image.

By summons before the Handelsgericht Wien in 2007, Painer had sought an order that the defendants in the main proceedings immediately cease the reproduction and/or distribution, without her consent and without indicating her as the author, of the contested photographs, as well as the photo-fit. She had also applied for an order against the defendants for accounts, payment of appropriate remuneration and damages for her loss and for an interlocutory injunction, on which a ruling had been given by the Oberster Gerichtshof (Supreme Court) before the case reached the CJEU. Interestingly enough, the Supreme Court had found that the defendants in the main proceedings did not need Ms Painer's consent to publish the contested photo-fit, in that this was to be considered a free use of her work. According to the Handelsgericht Wien, the issue of whether the photo-fit was an adaptation or a free use depended on the creative effort in the template. In particular, the greater the creative effort in the template, the less conceivable would have been a free use of her work. According to the Court, in the case of portrait photographs, the degree of individual formative freedom is small. Hence, copyright protection ought to be narrow and the contested photo-fit based on the template was to be considered as a new and autonomous work protected by copyright.

Despite this, the Austrian court decided to stay the proceedings and seek clarification from the CJEU as to four questions, regarding the correct interpretation of Article 6(1) of Council Regulation (EC) No 44/2001 of 22 December 2000 on jurisdiction and the recognition and enforcement of judgments in civil and commercial matters (also known as 'Brussels I')[56] and Articles 1(1),[57] 5(3)(d) and (e) and (5)[58] of the InfoSoc Directive.

For the purpose of this contribution, it is sufficient to limit our attention to the answer the Court of Justice provided to the fourth question, which read as follows:

> [Is] Article 1(1) of [the InfoSoc] Directive ... in conjunction with Article 5(5) thereof and Article 12 of the Berne Convention[59] ..., particularly in the light of Article 1 of the First Additional Protocol to the European Convention for the Protection of Human Rights and Fundamental Freedoms [signed at Rome on 4 November 1950] and Article 17 of the Charter of Fundamental Rights of the European Union,[60] to be interpreted as meaning that photographic works

---

[56] Article 6(1) states that: 'A person domiciled in a Member State may also be sued ... where he is one of a number of defendants, in the courts for the place where any one of them is domiciled, provided the claims are so closely connected that it is expedient to hear and determine them together to avoid the risk of irreconcilable judgments resulting from separate proceedings.'

[57] Article 1(1) states that: 'This Directive concerns the legal protection of copyright and related rights in the framework of the internal market, with particular emphasis on the information society.'

[58] Article 5(3)(d) and (e) and (5) state that: 'Member States may provide for exceptions or limitations to the rights provided for in Articles 2 and 3 in the following cases ... (d) quotations for purposes such as criticism or review, provided that they relate to a work or other subject-matter which has already been lawfully made available to the public, that, unless this turns out to be impossible, the source, including the author's name, is indicated, and that their use is in accordance with fair practice, and to the extent required by the specific purpose; (e) use for the purposes of public security or to ensure the proper performance or reporting of administrative, parliamentary or judicial proceedings; ... The exceptions and limitations provided for in paragraphs 1, 2, 3 and 4 shall only be applied in certain special cases which do not conflict with a normal exploitation of the work or other subject-matter and do not unreasonably prejudice the legitimate interests of the rightholder.'

[59] Article 12 provides that: 'Authors of literary or artistic works shall enjoy the exclusive right of authorising adaptations, arrangements and other alterations of their works.'

[60] According to Article 17, '(1) Everyone has the right to own, use, dispose of and bequeath his or her lawfully acquired possessions. No one may be deprived of his or her possessions, except in the public interest and in the cases and under the conditions provided for by law, subject to fair compensation being paid in good time for their loss. The use of property may be regulated by law in so far as is necessary for the general interest. (2) Intellectual property shall be protected.'

and/or photographs, particularly portrait photos, are afforded 'weaker' copyright protection or no copyright protection at all against adaptations because, in view of their 'realistic image', the degree of formative freedom is too minor?

2.2 The CJEU Follows *Infopaq* and goes even Further …

As pointed out by the CJEU, this question had been raised by the Austrian court in order to determine the correctness of the position which determined that the defendants in the main proceedings did not need Ms Painer's consent to publish a photo-fit worked up from a portrait photograph. This implied that the scope of the protection conferred on such a photograph was restricted, or even non-existent, because of the minimal degree of formative freedom allowed by such photographs. In other words, the referring court sought clarification as to whether the originality standard for photographs – to be found in Article 6 of the Term Directive and according to which copyright protection vests in photographs which are their 'author's own intellectual creation' – is such as to include portrait photographs. If the answer to this had been affirmative, the question which followed was whether the threshold for protection should be higher than for other categories of photographs, because of the allegedly minor degree of creative freedom such photographs display.

As regards the question whether portrait photographs deserve weaker copyright protection, the CJEU decided to address this by first recalling its earlier decision in *Infopaq*.[61] The Court pointed out that copyright protection is to arise in relation to a subject-matter which is original in the sense that it is its author's own intellectual creation: a work is original if it reflects the author's personality. According to the Court,

> That is the case if the author was able to express his creative abilities in the production of the work by making *free and creative choices* … [62]

The Court held that this was the proper interpretation of the originality requirement, by recalling *a contrario* the reasoning in *Murphy*, in which it was held that sporting events could not be regarded as intellectual

---

[61] Case C-5/08 *Infopaq International A/S v Danske Dagblades Forening* [2009] I-06569.

[62] Case C-145/10 *Eva-Maria Painer v Standard VerlagsGmbH, Axel Springer AG, Süddeutsche Zeitung GmbH, SPIEGEL-Verlag Rudolf AUGSTEIN GmbH & Co KG and Verlag M. DuMont Schauberg Expedition der Kölnischen Zeitung GmbH & Co KG, cit,* [89] (emphasis added).

creations classifiable as works within the meaning of the InfoSoc Directive. In particular, football matches, being subject to rules of the game, leave no room for creative freedom for the purposes of copyright protection.[63]

From this, held the Court, it quite easily follows that the author of a portrait photograph can also make free and creative choices in several ways and at various points in the production. So, by way of exemplification, the Court clarified that, in the pre-shooting phase, the photographer can choose the background, the subject's pose and the lighting. In particular, when taking a portrait photograph, he can choose the framing, the angle of view and the atmosphere created. Finally, when selecting the snapshot, the photographer may choose from a variety of developing techniques the one he wishes to adopt or, where appropriate, use computer software. As a consequence of such various choices, 'the author of a portrait photograph can stamp the work created with his "*personal touch*"'.[64]

This part of the judgment is reminiscent of the reasoning underlying the Opinion of Justice Miller in *Sarony*[65] and also the words of Susan Sontag in her seminal work *On photography*:

> While a painting or a prose description can never be other than a narrowly selective interpretation, a photograph can be treated as a narrowly selective transparency. But despite the presumption of veracity that gives all photographs authority, interest, seductiveness, the work that photographers do is no generic exception to the usually shady commerce between art and truth. Even when photographers are most concerned with mirroring reality, they are still haunted by tacit imperatives of taste and conscience.[66]

What results from the decision in *Painer* is that portrait photographs may not only enjoy copyright protection, but that such protection is no weaker than that granted to other types of photographs. Hence, under Article 2(a) of the InfoSoc Directive, the author of a portrait photograph is equally entitled to, amongst other things, the exclusive right to authorize or

---

[63] Joined Cases C-403/08 and C-429/08 *Football Association Premier League Ltd and Others v QC Leisure and Others* and C-429/08 *Karen Murphy v Media Protection Services Ltd, cit,* [98].

[64] Case C-145/10 *Eva-Maria Painer v Standard VerlagsGmbH, Axel Springer AG, Süddeutsche Zeitung GmbH, SPIEGEL-Verlag Rudolf AUGSTEIN GmbH & Co KG and Verlag M. DuMont Schauberg Expedition der Kölnischen Zeitung GmbH & Co KG, cit,* [92] (emphasis added).

[65] *Burrow-Giles Lithographic Co v Sarony* 111 US 53 [1884].

[66] Susan Sontag, *On photography* (Picador 1977), 6.

prohibit its direct or indirect, temporary or permanent reproduction by any means and in any form, in whole or in part.

2.3   … Clarifying the Meaning of Originality …

As far as the construction of EU copyright is concerned, the ruling in *Painer* represents another step in the clarification of what is now an EU-wide originality standard and, hence, copyright. Holding that a work is original if it shows the author's 'personal touch' makes the decision in *Painer* more akin to the notion of originality adopted in *Murphy*, rather than that of 'author's own intellectual creation' envisaged in *Infopaq* and *Bezpečnostní softwarová asociace*.

The question which arises following the judgment is whether these definitions are mere synonyms, or whether they do instead differ from the originality standard adopted in the Software, Term and Database Directives (and if so, in what respect).[67]

Drawing from the construction of the judgment, the answer seems to indicate that these definitions are synonymic. However, the recent decision of the Belgian Supreme Court in *Artetessuto*[68] might suggest the contrary. In this case, the Belgian court held that a literary or artistic work is protected by copyright on condition that it is original solely in the sense that it is the author's own intellectual creation. It is not required that the work carries the stamp of the author's personality.[69]

Despite this, the 'personal touch' requirement serves the purpose of clarifying what is to be intended by the 'author's personality' and, with it, 'intellectual creation', which is the sole criterion for copyright protection, as clarified by Recital 17 of the Term Directive.[70] In any case, this finding confirms how deeply bound the recent CJEU jurisprudence is to continental (in particular, French and German) copyright traditions.

---

[67]   *Cf* Mireille van Eechoud, 'Another piece of the puzzle, or is it? CJEU on photographs as copyright works' (Kluwer Copyright Blog, 7 December 2011) <http://tinyurl.com/bcr2d5d> accessed 14 June 2013.

[68]   Hof van Cassatie van België, *Artetessuto nv v B&T Textilia nv and Indecor-Europe nv*, arrest No C.11.0108.N, 26 January 2012.

[69]   *See* Philippe Laurent, 'Belgian Supreme Court: against the tide of CJEU's case law on "originality"?'(Kluwer Copyright Blog, 6 March 2012) <http://tinyurl.com/auq8oc5> accessed 14 June 2013.

[70]   '[A] photographic work within the meaning of the Berne Convention is to be considered original if it is the author's own intellectual creation reflecting his personality, no other criteria such as merit or purpose being taken into account'.

2.4   … Playing a Requiem for Subject-matter Categorization, and …

The decision in *Painer* is not surprising. Should the Court have decided otherwise and stated, for instance, that portrait photographs deserve narrower protection than other types of photographs, the result would have been difficult to comprehend and apply in practice. Who would think that the photographs on display at the National Portrait Gallery in London, and competing for the Taylor Wessing Photographic Portrait Prize, deserve weaker protection than other types of photographs, or are not worthy of copyright protection at all?

However, if this was the sole reason why the decision is relevant, it would be barely worth mentioning in the context of the debate at hand. Instead, what matters most for our current purposes is that, by addressing the issue posed by the Austrian court, the CJEU followed an alternative path of reasoning to a subject-matter categorization. Indeed, having recalled the standard for originality required under *Infopaq*, the Court held that, whenever the author of a work has been able to express his creative abilities in the production of the work by making free and creative choices, then that work is protected by copyright. Such a finding confirms what was only briefly touched upon in *Infopaq* and *Bezpečnostní softwarová asociace*, but was clearly implied in *Murphy*. What *Painer* suggests is indeed that subject-matter categorization is out of sight in the CJEU interpretation of copyright architecture. Therefore, not only has the Court *de facto* harmonized the originality requirement, but it appears to have also paved the way to an EU copyright architecture which, similarly to the continental model and contrary to UK copyright law, does not require that a work falls under one of the categories provided for by the law to receive protection. Getting rid of exhaustive subject-matter categorization (or reducing greatly the number of categories of protected subject-matter, as was suggested by Sam Ricketson back in 1997[71]) might help overcome the difficulties associated with it, and also favour more homogeneous copyright assessments.

2.5   Making it Clear that Copyright is not a Story of the Prince and the Pauper

In denying any *a priori* difference in the degree of protection enjoyed by portrait photographs and other types of photographs, the CJEU stressed the need to focus on the actual originality of the work at stake, rather

---

[71]   Sam Ricketson, 'The new Copyright Act 1997' (1997) 29 IPF 14.

than on the alleged subject-matter this ought to belong to. The Opinion of Advocate General Trstenjak, which was published on 12 April 2011,[72] had also adopted such a view. By relying upon a literal interpretation of Article 6 of the Term Directive, AG Trstenjak had clarified that

> The relevant factor under the first sentence of Article 6 is whether the photos are original in the sense that they are the author's own intellectual creation. The second sentence of Article 6 of that directive provides that no other criteria may be applied to determine their eligibility for protection ... According to the first sentence of Article 6 ... only human creations are therefore protected, which can also include those for which the person employs a technical aid, such as a camera ... Furthermore, the photo must be an original creation. In the case of a photo, this means that the photographer utilises available formative freedom and thus gives it originality ... Other criteria are expressly irrelevant ... [73]

So, if this is the state of the art in relation to photographs, one might argue that – after the decision in *Painer* – no distinctions ought to be made between different types of photographs. Real life reportages by Cartier-Bresson or fashion photographs by Helmut Newton are no different, as far as copyright is concerned, from portraits by Hoppé.

To decide whether a work enjoys copyright protection, what is required is not that it belongs to specific copyright subject-matter, but that it is sufficiently original.

3. *FOOTBALL DATACO*: FAREWELL TO THE ARMS (OF UK COPYRIGHT)?

Following the Opinion of AG Mengozzi on 15 December 2011,[74] on 1 March 2012 the CJEU published its judgment in *Football Dataco*,[75] another reference for a preliminary ruling from the UK, this time from the Court of Appeal of England and Wales (Civil Division).[76] The

---

[72]   Opinion of Advocate General Verica Trstenjak on 12 April 2011.

[73]   *Ibid* [119]–[123].

[74]   Opinion of Advocate General Paolo Mengozzi delivered on 15 December 2011.

[75]   Case C-604/10 *Football Dataco Ltd, Football Association Premier League Ltd, Football League Limited, Scottish Premier League Ltd, Scottish Football League and PA Sport UK Ltd v Yahoo! UK Limited, Stan James (Abingdon) Limited, Stan James PLC and Enetpulse APS.*

[76]   *Football Dataco Ltd, Football Association Premier League Ltd, Football League Limited, Scottish Premier League Ltd, Scottish Football League and PA*

reference sought clarification – *inter alia* – as to the correct reading of Article 3(1) of the Database Directive,[77] as mentioned above *sub* Chapter 3, §7.

3.1 Background to the Case

Football Dataco and the other applicants arrange the English and Scottish football leagues. In that context, they draw up and make public a list of all the fixtures to be played each year in those leagues ('the fixture lists'). The opposing parties, Yahoo! and other undertakings, used those schedules to provide news and information and/or to organize betting activities.

Football Dataco and the other applicant companies sued Yahoo! and other undertakings back in 2009, claiming the alleged infringement of exclusive IPRs in the fixture lists, which the defendants used without a licence.

In the first instance proceedings,[78] the Chancery Division of the High Court of Justice of England and Wales was asked to decide whether any (and if so which) rights subsisted in the fixture lists. As it has been correctly pointed out,[79] this represented the first judicial appraisal in the English and Welsh courts on copyright protection of databases, pursuant to Article 3 of the Database Directive.

Floyd J, after having considered that the main candidates were copyright as a database and the *sui generis* database right, found that the fixture lists involved the production of selection or arrangement within the meaning of Article 3(1) of the Database Directive. This was because the process of selection and arrangement of the contents of a database can and often will commence before all the data is created.[80] For this

---

Sport UK Ltd v Yahoo! UK Limited, Stan James (Abingdon) Limited, Stan James PLC and Enetpulse APS, [2010] EWCA Civ 1380.

[77] Article 3(1) states that: 'In accordance with this Directive, databases which, by reason of the selection or arrangement of their contents, constitute the author's own intellectual creation shall be protected as such by copyright. No other criteria shall be applied to determine their eligibility for that protection.'

[78] *Football Dataco Ltd and Others v Brittens Pools Ltd and Others*, [2010] EWHC 841 (Ch).

[79] Mark Rodgers, 'Football fixture lists and the Database Directive: Football Dataco Ltd v Brittens Pools Ltd' (2010) 32 EIPR 593. On the early stages of the case, *see* also Paul Cairns and Simone Blakeney, '1-0 to Football Dataco Ltd – the organizers of professional football matches take the lead in the battle to prevent the unauthorised use of their fixture lists' (2010) 3/4 ISLR 57.

[80] *Football Dataco Ltd and Others v Brittens Pools Ltd and Others*, (EWHC), *cit*, [82].

reason, Floyd J held that the fixture lists were protected by copyright. With particular regard to the interpretation of the 'author's own intellectual creation', Floyd J referred with approval to the following passage from *Laddie, Prescott & Vitoria*, which found that:

> More fundamentally the database must, when these two factors [selection and arrangement] are considered, constitute its author's own intellectual creation. This imposes a significant qualitative factor on the test. It would appear to exclude computer-generated databases. It is submitted that there must be something which has had the author's creativity stamped upon it. By this we mean that it must be something which could not be something which could fairly be said to be something which could have been created by many others. There must be some 'subjective' contribution. A 'sweat of the brow' collection will not do.[81]

Despite a lack of precedents from the CJEU, Floyd J drew from German case law[82] to distinguish between what parts of a database are purely deterministic and what allows sufficient room for individual creative work. Copyright protection only exists for the latter. However, the decision left some unresolved questions, such as what level of originality is required to qualify for database copyright.[83] Finally, by referring to the decision of the then ECJ in *William Hill*,[84] he held that no *sui generis* database right subsisted in the fixture lists, because no additional efforts had been spent in obtaining, verifying or presenting the data content.[85]

---

[81]   Hugh Laddie, Peter Prescott and Mary Vitoria, *The modern law of copyright and designs* (3rd edn, LexisNexis 2000), §30.27, cited at [85] of the decision.

[82]   In particular the decision of the Frankfurt Oberlandesgericht (Higher Regional Court) in *Pharma Intranet Information AG v IMS Health GmbH & Co OHG* [2005] ECC 12. This was a case concerning a database produced by the claimant for the pharmaceutical market containing figures for revenue and sales development for medicines sold in Germany, in which it asserted copyright.

[83]   *Cf* Colin Sawdy, 'High Court decision revisits protection of databases in the United Kingdom – Football Dataco Ltd v Brittens Pools Ltd' (2010) Ent LR 221, 224.

[84]   Case C-203/02 *British Horseracing Board Ltd v William Hill Organisation* [2004] ECR I-10415 was a reference from the Court of Appeal (England and Wales) (Civil Division) concerning the interpretation of Articles 7 and 10(3) of the Database Directive.

[85]   For an analysis of subsistence of *sui generis* database right in data relating to events at football matches and their timing, *see Football Dataco and Others v Sportradar GmbH and Another* and *Football Dataco and Others v Stan James Abingdon Ltd and Others* [2012] EWHC 1185 (Ch), in which Floyd J held that the *sui generis* right subsisted in such data, but accepted that there was room

On appeal, Jacob LJ, along with Hooper and Rimer LJJ ruled out any possibility of protection based on the *sui generis* right, as the Grand Chamber of the Court of Justice had made it plain that no such right subsisted in things like football fixture lists. In particular, it had done so in its 2004 decisions in *Fixtures Marketing*,[86] *William Hill*,[87] *Svenska Spel*[88] and *OPAP*.[89]

Indeed, since the introduction of the Database Directive, the CJEU has attempted to clarify the meaning of its provisions on several occasions. In its 2004 decisions, it restricted the scope of the *sui generis* right, holding that the investment in the creation of the contents of a database does not qualify as investment for obtaining, verifying or presenting the contents to prevent extraction and/or re-use of a whole or of a substantial part of the database, whether evaluated qualitatively and/or quantitatively, pursuant to Article 7(1) of the Directive. In 2008, in *Directmedia Publishing*,[90], the Court interpreted 'extraction' within the meaning of Article 7 and adopted a broad interpretation, covering the transfer of material from a protected database to another database, independent of a technical process of copying the contents of the protected database. In 2009, the decision in *Apis*[91] clarified the concept of 'permanent transfer' and 'temporary transfer' in Article 7, and held that whether there has been extraction and/or re-utilization of a substantial part of the contents of a database (evaluated quantitatively), within the meaning of such provision ought to be compared to the total contents of that module, in order to determine if the latter constitutes, in itself, a database which fulfils the conditions for protection by the *sui generis* right.[92]

---

for argument and that there had been no prior decisions on whether the recording of events could give rise to such a right.

[86]	Case C-46/02 *Fixtures Marketing Ltd v Oy Veikkaus Ab* [2004] ECR I-10365.

[87]	Case C-203/02 *The British Horseracing Board Ltd and Others v William Hill Organization Ltd, cit.*

[88]	Case C-338/02 *Fixtures Marketing Ltd v Svenska Spel AB* [2004] ECR I-10497.

[89]	Case C-444/02 *Fixtures Marketing Ltd v Organismos prognostikon agonon podosfairou AE (OPAP)* [2004] ECR I-10549.

[90]	Case C-304/07 *Directmedia Publishing GmbH v Albert-Ludwigs-Universität Freiburg* [2008] ECR I-7565.

[91]	Case C-545/07 *Apis-Hristovich EOOD v Lakorda AD* [2009] I-1627.

[92]	On this decision, *see* Stephen Vousden, 'Apis, databases and EU law' (2011) IPQ 215. As made clear by the author, with its ruling the CJEU introduced three novelties into EU database law. First, the definition of a 'temporary transfer' now appears to include a 'transient copy' exception. Second,

Despite the rich case law, as pointed out by the Court of Appeal, whether fixture lists deserve protection under copyright remained an unsolved issue. Creation of the fixture lists does involve considerable skill and judgment, as well as labour, and is not just a mechanical process. However, it was uncertain whether such skill and judgment were of the right kind for the purposes of Article 3 of the Database Directive. Therefore, as mentioned above *sub* Chapter 3, §7, the Court of Appeal decided to stay the proceedings and make a reference to the CJEU on the following questions regarding the interpretation of the Database Directive:

1. In Article 3(1) of Directive 96/9/EC on the legal protection of databases what is meant by 'databases which, by reason of the selection or arrangement of their contents, constitute the author's own intellectual creation' and in particular:

    (a) should the intellectual effort and skill of creating data be excluded?
    (b) does 'selection or arrangement' include adding important significance to a pre-existing item of data (as in fixing the date of a football match)?
    (c) does 'author's own intellectual creation' require more than significant labour and skill from the author, if so what?

2. Does the Directive preclude national rights in the nature of copyright in databases other than those provided for by the Directive?

As is apparent, particularly from the first question referred by the Court of Appeal, the impact of *Infopaq*[93] has been so substantial on national copyright laws that its implications were still to be assessed. In particular, as mentioned above *sub* Chapter 3, §7, the fact that doubts persisted as to whether 'author's own intellectual creation' meant something else than the traditional UK standard of 'significant labour and skill' stands as a demonstration of the fact that the *Infopaq* ruling cast doubts also on areas of copyright which had on the surface been left untouched by it, or for which harmonization had already occurred (such as databases).[94] In

---

there is a 'circumstantial evidence' rule to make it easier to establish that a 'transfer' has taken place. Third, the concept of a 'substantial part' has been redefined. Quantitatively assessed, a 'substantial part' may now cover 'modules' of databases. Qualitatively assessed, a 'substantial part' may protect the investment made in 'obtaining' data even if that data was already in the public domain.

[93] Case C-5/08 *Infopaq International A/S v Danske Dagblades Forening, cit.*

[94] The very meaning of 'intellectual creation' is to be considered obscure, as some commentators still write that '[t]he author's own intellectual creation should not require more than significant labor and skill from the author and of

addition, uncertainties existed as to the criteria to be used in considering whether a database is the author's own intellectual creation.[95]

The Court of Appeal's reason for seeking clarification as to the standard of originality required for obtaining copyright protection was that Article 3 of the Database Directive

> requires that the work of selecting and arranging be the 'author's own intellectual creation.' Whilst that would exclude mere mechanistic 'sweat of brow' work such as that involved in compiling a telephone book (in the old, pre-computer, days that was a lot of work), it is far from self-evident that other, truly creative but not artistic, work is excluded. Quite what the meaning and limits of 'author's own intellectual creation' is also … a question calling for an answer.[96]

---

course, originality … [I]ndependent judgment, significant skill and labor, as well as creativity, goes into the creation of the match fixture lists. If the ECJ should rule that intellectual effort and skill of creating data be included and that selection or arrangement includes adding important significance to pre-existing data, the original labor and skill that goes into this creation processes should be enough to meet a standard of author's own intellectual creation. The author's own intellectual creation standard should be nothing more than originality, stemming from the significant labor and skill from the author. It would be quite difficult for the ECJ to establish a standard above significant labor and skill of the author, under these circumstances. The ECJ should find that originality and nothing more than significant labor and skill is necessary to prove the author's own intellectual creation. Under this standard, the ECJ will know an author's own intellectual creation when they see it.' (Daniel Runge, 'Football match fixtures and European Union copyright law: answering the questions referred to the European Court of Justice in Football Dataco Ltd. v. Yahoo! UK Ltd.'<http://tinyurl.com/asyxx48> accessed 14 June 2013).

[95] As explained by Rachel Montagnon and Mark Shillito, 'Requirements for subsistence of database copyright and other national copyright in databases referred to the ECJ: Football Dataco Ltd v Yahoo!' (2011) 33 EIPR 324, 325, Jacob LJ had rejected the notion that any artistic quality was needed, as appeared to be implied from some of the comments of Floyd J on the evidence of a mixture of art and science being used to create the fixture lists. Although it must be more than the sweat of the brow and need not be 'artistic', it was far from self-evident that other, truly creative, but not artistic, work would be excluded.

[96] *Football Dataco Ltd and Others v Brittens Pools Ltd and Others*, EWCA, *cit*, [21].

3.2 Copyright in Databases: What Type of Originality? AG Mengozzi Explains

Under the Database Directive, a database may be subject to two distinct types of protection: copyright (Article 3) and the *sui generis* right (Article 7).

According to AG Mengozzi, in order to assess under what conditions a database may be protected by copyright (which in essence is the content of the first question posed by the Court of Appeal), it was necessary to first review CJEU case law on football fixture lists – in particular the 2004 decisions mentioned above – and then determine the relationship between copyright and the *sui generis* right.

In relation to CJEU case law, the Opinion states that the 2004 rulings made it clear that football fixture lists must be regarded as databases for the purposes of the Directive. Despite this, and as correctly recalled by the Court of Appeal, they cannot be protected under the *sui generis* right, in that they do not require any substantial investment in the obtaining, verification or presentation of the contents.[97]

Coming to the relationship between copyright and the *sui generis* right, clarifying that the concept of 'database' is the same in both the cases, AG Mengozzi recalled that the two types of protection must be regarded as mutually independent in all respects. This is because their very object is different. Indeed,

> protection under the copyright focuses essentially on the structure of the database, that is, the way in which it has actually been put together through the selection of the data to be included or the way in which they are presented … The 'sui generis' protection, on the other hand, is simply a right to prohibit extraction and/or re-utilisation of the data contained in the database. That right is conferred, not to protect the originality of the database in itself, but to compensate the effort expended in obtaining, verifying and/or presenting the data contained therein.[98]

---

[97] Article 7(1) of the Database Directive states that: 'Member States shall provide for a right for the maker of a database which shows that there has been qualitatively and/or quantitatively a substantial investment in either the obtaining, verification or presentation of the contents to prevent extraction and/or re-utilization of the whole or of a substantial part, evaluated qualitatively and/or quantitatively, of the contents of that database.'

[98] Opinion of Advocate General Paolo Mengozzi, *cit*, [14], recalling the DG Internal Market and Services Working Paper, *First evaluation of Directive 96/9/EC on the legal protection of databases*, Brussels, 12 December 2005.

Having clarified this, the AG further observed that the idea of using copyright to protect football fixture lists seemed peculiar, given the scope of copyright protection. In fact Yahoo! and the other defendants used the data developed by the companies which organize the leagues, in a form other than that by which those companies make the data public. In any case, should protection under copyright be available for football fixture lists, this would not be likely to impede the activities of Yahoo! and the other defendants, because such activities appeared confined to the use of raw data (the dates, times and teams for the various matches), not the structure of the database.

From the foregoing it follows that the efforts expended in the creation of the data cannot be taken into account for the purposes of assessing eligibility for protection under the copyright (these cannot be taken into account for the *sui generis* protection either).

In relation to sub-question 1(b), the Court of Appeal sought clarification as to whether the 'selection or arrangement' of the contents of the database, such as permitting protection under copyright, could also involve adding specific characteristics to an item already included in a database. According to AG Mengozzi, in abstract terms the answer would be affirmative. This is because adding important significance to pre-existing items of data may constitute an arrangement of contents, which may qualify for copyright protection. If this is the answer in general terms, in the specific case, the elements which characterize the matches of a football league are all basic data that do not qualify for copyright protection *per se*.

What matters most is in fact the answer provided to sub-question 1(c). This is because the response makes it clear, once and for all, that *Infopaq* has actually altered the meaning and scope of the originality requirement in the UK.

3.3   An Intellectual Creation in not just Labour and Skill

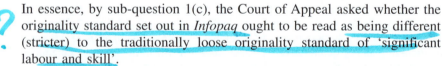

In essence, by sub-question 1(c), the Court of Appeal asked whether the originality standard set out in *Infopaq* ought to be read as being different (stricter) to the traditionally loose originality standard of 'significant labour and skill'.

According to AG Mengozzi, the answer to such a question ought to be affirmative, in that:

copyright protection is conditional upon the database being characterised by a 'creative' aspect, and it is not sufficient that the creation of the database required labour and skill.[99]

This is because the Database Directive adopted a concept of originality which requires more than a mere mechanical effort to collect the data and enter them into the database. In order to be protected by copyright, a database must be an 'intellectual creation' of its creator. What an 'intellectual creation' is depends, according to the AG, on an assessment to be undertaken by national courts in light of the circumstances of each individual case.

However, the AG indicated that the expression 'intellectual creation' adopted by the Directive echoes a formula which is typical of continental copyright laws and sets a higher threshold to protection than what is under UK copyright. Indeed, it was felt that

> a work is an intellectual creation if it reflects the personality of its author, which is the case if the author was able to *make free and creative choices* in the production of the work … [T]he necessary originality will be absent if the features of a work are predetermined by its technical function.[100]

This finding would not be surprising at all, if it was limited to the sole subject-matter of databases. In countries such as the UK, decisions such as *Football League Ltd v Littlewoods Pools*[101] no longer constitute a valid precedent which courts may rely upon.

Albeit that AG Mengozzi referred expressly to the originality standard under the sole Database Directive, it would be parochial to argue that his opinion was limited to this. This is made clear by the fact that, in explaining what meaning 'intellectual creation' ought to be given, he referred to judgments concerning not the Database Directive, but the InfoSoc Directive.

---

[99]   Opinion of Advocate General Paolo Mengozzi, *cit*, [35].
[100]   *Ibid* [40] (emphasis added).
[101]   [1959] 1 Ch 637 was a case in which the Football League had sought to enforce its rights in football fixture lists against a pools company which used the data without a licence. Upjohn J held that the chronological list qualified as literary work under the Copyright Act 1956 – which specifically included a provision for compilation – in that some labour, skill, judgment or ingenuity had been exerted in the creation of the database.

3.4   There is Little to do if Copyright cannot do

By its second question, the Court of Appeal sought clarification as to whether protection provided under the Database Directive on the basis of the copyright is the only type of protection available to a database or if, on the contrary, national law may confer similar protection on databases which do not meet the necessary conditions under the Directive.

AG Mengozzi addressed this issue by referring especially to Article 14, a provision which contains special transitional arrangements for databases formerly protected by copyright under national rules that do not meet the requirements for copyright protection under the Directive. Article 14 provides that such databases are to retain copyright protection for the remainder of the term of protection afforded under the national arrangements preceding the Directive. It is clear that this provision would make no sense if, after the entry into force of the Directive, Member States were allowed, without any limitation in time, to protect a database which does not meet the conditions set out in the Directive. Therefore, copyright cannot be vested in databases which do not meet the requirements for copyright protection as laid down in Article 3 of the Directive.

3.5   The Decision of the CJEU

On 1 March 2012, the CJEU published its decision, substantially confirming the Opinion of AG Mengozzi.

In providing its response to the first question, the Court noted that there was no controversy as to whether a football league fixture list constituted a 'database' within the meaning of Article 1(2) of the Database Directive. Indeed, in *Fixture Marketing*,[102] the Court held that the combination of the date, time and identity of the two teams playing in both home and away matches had autonomous informative value which rendered them 'independent materials' within the meaning of Article 1(2) and that the arrangement, in the form of a fixture list, of the dates, times and names of teams in the various fixtures of a football league met the conditions set out in Article 1(2) as to the systematic or methodical arrangement and individual accessibility of the data contained in the database.

This said, it was also undisputed that, from both a comparison of the terms used in Article 3(1) and Article 7(1) of the Database Directive, and from other provisions or recitals therein (in particular Article 7(4) and

---

[102]   Case C-444/02 *Fixtures Marketing Ltd v Organismos prognostikon agonon podosfairou AE (OPAP), cit,* [33]–[36].

Recital 39), copyright and the *sui generis* right are different and mutually independent rights, also with respect to their object and conditions of application. This implies that, even if a database did not meet the conditions of eligibility for protection under the *sui generis* right, it could be nonetheless protected by copyright as per Article 3 of the Database Directive. This is the case if the database, by reason of the selection or arrangement of its contents, constitutes the author's own intellectual creation.

3.5.1 The requirements for copyright protection under the Database Directive

At paragraph 30 and the subsequent paragraphs of the decision, the CJEU offered a thorough explanation of the meaning of originality within the Database Directive and, more generally, of the overall EU understanding of originality. In assessing the requirements for copyright protection pursuant to Article 3 of the Database Directive, the Court first considered the meaning of 'selection or arrangement' and then the concept of the 'author's own intellectual creation'.

First of all, the Court made it clear that Article 3(2), if read in conjunction with Recital 15[103] of the Database Directive, provides for copyright protection to vest in the structure of the database, not its contents nor, therefore, the elements constituting its contents. This reflects Article 10(2) TRIPS and Article 5 of the WIPO Copyright Treaty, which provide for copyright protection to be available to compilations of data which, by reason of the selection or arrangement of their contents, constitute intellectual creations. Protection does not extend to the data itself, although copyright may subsist in that data.

The selection and arrangement referred to in Article 3(1) of the Database Directive is the means through which the author of the database gives the database its structure. Such concepts do not extend to the creation of the data contained in that database. As a consequence, explained the Court, the intellectual effort and skill involved in creating the data is not relevant for the assessment of the eligibility of the database itself for copyright protection under the Directive. This finding is confirmed by Recitals 9, 10 and 12. The adoption of the Database Directive was justified by the objective of stimulating the creation of data storage and processing systems. This was necessary to contribute to the

---

[103] '... [T]he criteria used to determine whether a database should be protected by copyright should be defined to the fact that the selection or the arrangement of the contents of the database is the author's own intellectual creation; ... such protection should cover the structure of the database'.

development of an information market against the background of the exponential growth in the amount of information generated and processed annually in all sectors of activity,[104] *not* to protect the creation of materials to be collected in a database.

Having clarified this, the Court considered whether the fixture lists were such as to enjoy copyright protection. The Court observed that the intellectual resources in the main proceedings were deployed for the purpose of determining, in the course of arranging the leagues concerned, the date, time, and identity of teams corresponding to each fixture of those leagues. This was done in accordance with a set of rules, parameters and organizational constraints, as well as the specific requests of the clubs concerned. Those resources related to the creation of the same data that is contained in the database in question. Because of this, they were of no relevance in order to assess the eligibility of the football fixture lists for the copyright protection provided for by the Database Directive.

Having considered the meaning of 'selection or arrangement' within Article 3(1) of the Database Directive, the Court turned to consider the other requirement under that provision: whether the database was 'the author's own intellectual creation'.

Recalling Recital 16 of the Directive,[105] as well as relevant case law,[106] the CJEU held that the notion of the author's own intellectual creation refers to the criterion of originality. As regards the setting up of a database, the Court held that

---

[104]   *See* Case 46/02 *Fixtures Marketing Ltd v Oy Veikkaus Ab, cit,* [33]; Case C-203/02 *The British Horseracing Board Ltd and Others v William Hill Organization Ltd, cit,* [30]; C-338/02 *Fixtures Marketing Ltd v Svenska Spel AB, cit,* [23]; Case C-444/02 *Fixtures Marketing Ltd v Organismos prognostikon agonon podosfairou AE (OPAP), cit,* [39].

[105]   '... [N]o criterion other than originality in the sense of the author's intellectual creation should be applied to determine the eligibility of the database for copyright protection, and in particular no aesthetic or qualitative criteria should be applied'.

[106]   Case C-5/08 *Infopaq International A/S v Danske Dagblades Forening, cit,* [35], [37] and [38]; Case C-393/09 *Bezpečnostní softwarová asociace – Svaz softwarové ochrany v Ministerstvo kultury* [2010] I-13971 [45]; Joined Cases C-403/08 and C-429/08 *Football Association Premier League Ltd and Others v QC Leisure and Others* and *Karen Murphy v Media Protection Services Ltd, cit,* [97]; and Case C-145/10 *Eva-Maria Painer v Standard VerlagsGmbH and Others, cit,* [87].

that criterion of originality is satisfied when, through the selection or arrangement of the data which it contains, its author expresses his creative ability in an original manner by making free and creative choices ... and thus stamps his 'personal touch' ...

By contrast, that criterion is not satisfied when the setting up of the database is dictated by technical considerations, rules or constraints which leave no room for creative freedom ...

As is apparent from both Article 3(1) and recital 16 of Directive 96/9, no other criteria than that of originality is to be applied to determine the eligibility of a database for the copyright protection provided for by that directive.[107]

This said, the CJEU clarified two additional points.

Firstly, for the purpose of assessing whether a database is eligible for copyright protection, it is irrelevant whether the selection or arrangement of the contents includes 'adding important significance', as mentioned in Question 1(b) of the Court of Appeal. The only requirement is and ought to be that the selection or arrangement of the data is an original expression of the creativity of the author of the database.

Secondly, and most importantly as far as UK copyright is concerned,

the fact that the setting up of the database required, irrespective of the creation of the data which it contains, significant labour and skill of its author, as mentioned in [Question 1](c) ..., cannot as such justify the protection of it by copyright under Directive 96/9, if that labour and that skill do not express any originality in the selection or arrangement of that data.[108]

In light of the foregoing, the answer to the first question of the Court of Appeal is that Article 3(1) of the Database Directive is to be interpreted as meaning that a database is eligible for copyright protection, provided that the selection or arrangement of the data which it contains amounts to an original expression of the creative freedom of its author, which is a matter for national courts to determine.

3.5.2   Might there be other rights in databases?

By its second question the Court of Appeal had asked whether the Database Directive must be interpreted as precluding national legislation that grants databases copyright protection even beyond the conditions set out in Article 3(1) of the Directive.

---

[107]   Case C-604/10 *Football Dataco Ltd and Others v Yahoo! UK Ltd and Others, cit*, [38]–[40].

[108]   *Ibid* [42].

The CJEU first highlighted that the rationale underlying the Database Directive was to remove differences that existed between Member States as to the legal protection of databases, in particular with regard to the scope and conditions of copyright protection.[109]

Article 14(2) of the Directive provided that, where a database protected under copyright arrangements in a Member State on the date of publication of the Directive (27 March 1996) did not meet the eligibility criteria for copyright protection laid down in Article 3(1), the entry into force of the Directive would not have resulted in a curtailing in that Member State of the remaining term of protection afforded therein. However, subject only to that transitional provision, Article 3(1) is such as to preclude national legislation from granting databases protection under conditions which differ from those envisaged in that provision.

3.6 The Implications of the *Football Dataco* Decision

As is apparent from the foregoing, the CJEU decided to follow the Opinion of AG Mengozzi. The implications of the decision are three-fold.

First of all, it is confirmed that originality is to be considered as harmonized at the EU level and given a meaning akin to that set out in those Directives which provided a common originality standard in relation to specific subject-matter. Despite reductive interpretations of the implications descending from CJEU decisions in *Infopaq* and *Football Dataco*,[110] the stance adopted by Advocate General Mengozzi – as confirmed by the Court – demonstrates that the EU understanding of originality is rather different from the traditional UK notion.

In addition, not only has the CJEU harmonized the originality requirement and, with it, the standard protection under EU copyright for any

---

[109] *Cf* Recital 60 to the Database Directive: '... [S]ome Member States currently protect under copyright arrangements databases which do not meet the criteria for eligibility for copyright protection laid down in this Directive; ... even if the databases concerned are eligible for protection under the right laid down in this Directive to prevent unauthorized extraction and/or re-utilization of their contents, the term of protection under that right is considerably shorter than that which they enjoy under the national arrangements currently in force; ... harmonization of the criteria for determining whether a database is to be protected by copyright may not have the effect of reducing the term of protection currently enjoyed by the rightholders concerned; ... a derogation should be laid down to that effect; ... the effects of such derogation must be confined to the territories of the Member States concerned'.

[110] Andreas Rahmatian, 'Originality in UK copyright law: the old "skill and labour" doctrine under pressure' (2013) 44 IIC 4.

subject-matter other than that for which harmonization had occurred by means of ad hoc directives, but also ruled out any possible alternative protection (except for *sui generis* right where applicable).[111] This finding is likely to result in serious controversies at the national level. This is because the stance adopted by the CJEU in *Football Dataco* goes well beyond the sole category of databases and indeed implies a strict understanding of the author's own intellectual creation standard.[112] This may lead to the exclusion of sub-original (at least in the EU sense) works which have been traditionally protected also under continental copyright laws. Indeed, as explained by Andreas Rahmatian, at the national level the understanding of the originality requirement as being akin to 'the author's own intellectual creation' has been 'watered down remarkably' and accommodates very low versions of artistic creativity'.[113] Under German and other continental Member States' copyright laws, the originality requirement is in fact qualified by the principle of 'kleine Münze' or 'petite monnaie' ('small change'), ie 'the idea of a relaxed originality threshold in relation to works which constitute simple creations of daily use where only a minimum notional creative input is required for protection, such as catalogues, price lists, collection of recipes.'[114] The small change principle has been deemed applicable to information works which are of high economic significance, but irrelevant from a cultural-artistic standpoint.[115] In addition, copyright protection is said to be justified in consideration of the fact that such works would not be eligible for other types of protection, such as design law.[116]

---

[111] As also pointed out by Tatiana-Eleni Synodinou, 'Databases: sui generis protection and copyright protection' (Kluwer Copyright Blog, 20 December 2011) <http://tinyurl.com/aacyfgj> accessed 14 June 2013, '[e]ven though we can imagine copyright protection for compilations which do not meet the criteria of the definition of a database under the Directive on the basis of less stringent criteria, such as pure skill and labour, it is, however, questionable if the *Dataco* decision combined with *Infopaq* which imposes the criterion of the "author's own intellectual creation" as a threshold for all works and not only for databases, computer programs and photographs leaves any room for this option.'

[112] This will be seen in Chapter 5, §1 in relation to the recent decision of an English court which has assessed, *inter alia*, the standard of originality for photographs as resulting from CJEU case law.

[113] Rahmatian, *Copyright and creativity, cit*, 187.

[114] *Ibid*, 188.

[115] Dana Beldiman, *Functionality, information works, and copyright* (Lulu. com 2008), 71.

[116] JAL Sterling, *World copyright law*, (2nd edn, Sweet & Maxwell 2003), 345.

Following CJEU case law, it is doubtful whether such categories of works can still qualify for copyright protection or whether, instead, relief is to be sought (but this is not uncontroversial) under other types of intellectual property rights or, more generally, the law of unfair competition (where applicable).[117] Until very recently, a peculiarity of Dutch copyright law has been protection of non-original writings, the so-called 'Geschriftenbescherming'. The legal basis for this legacy of an eighteenth century printer's right was in Article 10(1)(1) of the Dutch Copyright Act of 1912, which listed 'books, brochures, newspapers, periodicals and all other writings' among the subject-matter eligible for copyright protection.[118] 'Geschriftenbescherming', whose scope has been developed through case law, was intended to grant protection against literal reprinting and forms of reproduction which showed minor changes if compared to the reproduced writing.[119] In early 2013 the Dutch Government published a draft bill that would remove the word 'all' from the text of Article 10(1), thus putting 'this relic of a distant past finally to rest'.[120]

In any case, it is not difficult to see that the conclusion of the CJEU implies that copyright is totally harmonized at the EU level. As a consequence, any discussion on the feasibility of creating an optional unitary copyright title on the basis of Article 118 TFEU should necessarily lead to the recognition that this process has been not only commenced, but is actually at a very advanced stage. An EU copyright title would then be a sort of codification of the *acquis communautaire* and, above all, of the interpretation the CJEU has given of it.

The final consideration (which will be developed further below *sub* Chapter 5) concerns the UK. From the string of decisions which have followed *Infopaq*,[121] it is apparent that precedents such as *University of London Press*[122] are no longer valid.[123] As pointed out by Trevor

---

[117] For similar considerations, *see* Gemma Minero, 'Did the Database Directive actually harmonize the database copyright? Football Dataco Ltd v Brittens Pools Ltd and the ECJ's rules against subsistence of database copyright in fixture lists' (2012) 34 EIPR 728, 730 ff. *See* also below *sub* §3.7.

[118] *See* Annemarie Beunen, '*Geschriftenbescherming*: the Dutch protection for non-original writings', in Bernt Hugenholtz, Antoon Quaedvlieg and Dirk Visser (eds), *A century of Dutch copyright law. Auteurswet 1912–2012* (deLex 2012) 57.

[119] *Ibid*, 57.

[120] Bernt Hugenholtz, 'Goodbye, Geschriftenbescherming!' (Kluwer Copyright Blog, 6 March 2013) <http://tinyurl.com/cbuhdqq> accessed 14 June 2013.

[121] Case C-5/08 *Infopaq International A/S v Danske Dagblades Forening, cit.*

[122] *University of London Press, Ltd v University Tutorial Press, Ltd* [1916] 2 Ch 601.

Cook,[124] this is because the test for a work's originality can no longer be simply a matter of degree dependent on the amount of skill, judgment, or labour involved in its making.[125] Contrary to this conclusion, a reductionist interpretation of these decisions has been advanced. According to Mireille van Eechoud, the distinction between continental Europe and UK approaches to originality is to be scaled down. This is because the distinction between the two legal traditions seems inspired by a fairly schematic view of Anglo-Saxon versus continental European notions of originality.[126]

Although some UK-based commentators have saluted the decision as 'a welcome development as there is still misinterpretation and confusion in the English courts on this point even at the appellate level',[127] uncertainty remains, amongst other things, as to the answer provided by the Court to Question 2. In particular, as mentioned, it is not clear whether databases might still enjoy protection against parasitism or slavish copying, which many national laws provide in their tort or focused unfair competition statutes. This is because the Court of Appeal of England and Wales had asked the Court more specifically whether the Directive precluded national rights in the nature of copyright in databases, other than those provided for therein. According to Estelle Derclaye, although the Court's answer is not entirely clear on this point, if anything, 'it is fair to assume that that sort of protection is also out of the window. Indeed, it would adversely affect the functioning of the

---

[123] In this sense, also David Cran and Paul Joseph, 'Football Dataco: fixture lists not protected by database copyright' (2012) 23 Ent LR 149, 151.

[124] Trevor Cook, '*Football Dataco*. Implications for copyright subsistence' (2012) April PLC 8, who notes (9) that cases such as *Sawkins v Hyperion Records Ltd* [2005] EWCA Civ 565 might be decided differently today.

[125] Contrary to what is the Canadian test for originality to be found in Giuseppina D'Agostino, *Copyright, contracts, creators. New media, new rules* (Edward Elgar Publishing 2010), 17, who in support cites *CCH v Law Society of Upper Canada* [2004] 1 SCR 339 ('What is required to attract copyright protection in the expression of an idea is an exercise of skill and judgment') and *Slumber-Magic Adjustable Bed Co v Sleep-King Adjustable Bed Co and Others* (1984) 3 CPR (3d) 81 (BCSC). The author makes it clear that 'not only must creative intellectual activity produce the right kind of work, but 'the author's input must satisfy a certain minimum standard of effort.'

[126] Mireille van Eechoud, 'Along the road to uniformity – Diverse readings of the Court of Justice judgments on copyright work' (2012) 3 JIPITEC 60, 70.

[127] Estelle Derclaye, 'Football Dataco: skill and labour is dead!' (Kluwer Copyright Blog, 1 March 2012) <http://tinyurl.com/7qgj8wm> accessed 14 June 2013.

internal market and free movement of goods and services if databases could obtain quasi-copyright protection through unfair competition law provisions.'[128]

3.7   Pre-emption and EU Copyright: Is there any *marge de manœuvre* left for Member States?

As seen in relation to the decisions of the CJEU in *Murphy* and *Football Dataco*, a question which remains unanswered is whether EU Member States can provide alternative forms of protection, eg by means of related rights, to subject-matter which may no longer qualify for copyright under EU law as interpreted by the CJEU.

Addressing this issue requires consideration of the rather obscure and unpredictable[129] doctrine of EU pre-emption, which is now (somewhat) codified in Article 2 TFEU.[130] Indeed, by providing a catalogue of EU competences and types, the Lisbon Treaty brought some clarity into the area of EU pre-emption.[131]

Although no reference to this doctrine was made in the case law of the CJEU prior to the 2009 Opinion of Advocate General Colomer in the so-called *Budweiser* case,[132] since the early 1980s[133] debate around EU pre-emption has increasingly gained momentum, and has indeed developed in parallel to (what appears a clearer) discussion around supremacy of EU law. Although difficulties in keeping the two doctrines separate arise because of their dialectical relationship, pre-emption and supremacy have distinct characters and functions. As explained by Robert Schütze,

> [T]he doctrine of pre-emption will first determine whether a conflict between two norms exists – thereby causing the supremacy doctrine to come into

---

[128]   *Ibid.*

[129]   In this sense, Amedeo Arena, 'The doctrine of Union preemption in the E.U. internal market: between *Sein* and *Sollen*' (2011) 17 Colum J Eur L 477, 477.

[130]   Damian Chalmers, Gareth Davies and Giorgio Monti, *European Union Law* (2nd edn, CUP 2010), 206–07.

[131]   For a pre-Lisbon analysis, *see* António Goucha Soares, 'Pre-emption, conflicts of powers and subsidiarity' (1998) 23 Eur L Rev 132, 133, who argued that pre-emption in the EU was essentially implied, rather than express.

[132]   Case C-478/07 *Budějovický Budvar, národní podnik v Rudolf Ammersin GmbH* [2009] I-07721, Opinion of Advocate General Ruiz-Jarabo Colomer delivered on 5 February 2009, in particular [93].

[133]   Joseph HH Weiler, 'Community, Member States and European integration: is the law relevant?' (1982) 21 J Common Mkt Stud 39.

operation. Yet, a prior clarification of what is the superior norm will be necessary to determine which rule pre-empts the other.[134]

Despite consideration of pre-emption as one of the hallmarks of the Community's normative supranationalism together with supremacy and direct effect, there remain uncertainties as to its scope, ie what room (if any) is left for national lawmaking once the EU has adopted a piece of legislation in an area of non-exclusive competence. This is probably because, as pointed out by Amedeo Arena, 'there is neither a consensus on a *doctrine* of Union Preemption nor even on its very *concept*.'[135]

As mentioned in Chapter 1, intellectual property is an area in which the EU has no exclusive internal competence. Also pursuant to Advocate General Colomer's understanding of pre-emption, the enactment of a piece of EU legislation should be such as to prevent national lawmaking in the area concerned.[136] In relation to copyright, it is thus arguable that, besides specific exceptions (such as that of Article 6 of the Term Directive in relation to sub-original photographs), following CJEU case law on originality, Member States would not be entitled to provide alternative forms of protection to sub-original (at least in the EU sense) subject-matter, with the sole exception of unfair competition, where applicable. This conclusion appears particularly supported by the decision of the CJEU in *Football Dataco* and, prior to this, the Opinion of AG Mengozzi, which stated that Member States are unable to confer quasi-copyright protection on databases that fail to meet the requirements of Article 3 of the Database Directive.

In any case clarifying the doctrine of pre-emption as applied to copyright following CJEU case law on originality is of fundamental importance, also to determine the actual degree of harmonization achieved by the Court. An area where pre-emption has been consistently recognized and applied by the CJEU has been in fact that of so-called exhaustive harmonization, eg in the context of free movement.[137] In addition, it is worth recalling that the idea that directives could not have any pre-emptive effects on national legislations due to their character of

---

[134] Robert Schütze, 'Supremacy without pre-emption? The very slowly emergent doctrine of Community pre-emption' (2006) 43 CML Rev 1023, 1023–4 (emphasis in the original text).

[135] Arena, 'The doctrine of Union preemption', *cit*, 481 (emphasis in the original text).

[136] *Ibid*, 484.

[137] *Ibid*, 501–03.

two-stage legislation has been rejected by both legislative practice and ECJ/CJEU case law.[138]

A reference for a preliminary ruling currently pending before the CJEU might help to shed some light on the relationship between pre-emption and EU copyright. In Case C-466/12 *Nils Svensson, Sten Sjögren, Madelaine Sahlman, Pia Gadd v Retreiver Sverige AB* one of the questions[139] referred by the Swedish Svea hovrätt reads as follows:

> Is it possible for a Member State to give wider protection to authors' exclusive right by enabling 'communication to the public' to cover a greater range of acts than provided for in Article 3(1) of Directive 2001/29/EC of the European Parliament and of the Council of 22 May 2001 on the harmonisation of certain aspects of copyright and related rights in the information society?

If the Court decides to address this question (which is not necessarily said), any response is likely to involve a discussion on the scope of pre-emption as applied to EU copyright law.

4. *SAS*: SHAKE-AND-STRAIN THE SCOPE OF COPYRIGHT PROTECTION

The reference for a preliminary ruling in *SAS Institute Inc v World Programming Ltd*[140] was made by the High Court of Justice of England and Wales (Chancery Division),[141] which had sought clarification, *inter alia*, as to whether the functionalities of a computer program and programming language are protected by copyright pursuant to Article 1(2) of the Software Directive. As already mentioned, this provision reads as follows:

> Protection in accordance with this Directive shall apply to the expression in any form of a computer program. Ideas and principles which underlie any

---

[138] *Ibid*, 530–1.
[139] So far this case has attracted a good deal of attention, as it also involves discussion on whether hyperlinking should be regarded as falling within the scope of the right of communication to the public as per Article 3 of the InfoSoc Directive. *See* European Copyright Society, *Opinion on the reference to the CJEU in Case C-466/12* Svensson, 15 February 2013 <http://tinyurl.com/c9qubgn> accessed 14 June 2013.
[140] Case C-406/10 *SAS Institute Inc v World Programming Ltd.*
[141] [2010] EWHC 1829 (Ch).

element of a computer program, including those which underlie its interfaces, are not protected by copyright under this Directive.

The question was therefore whether the very functionalities of a computer program may be considered as the 'expression in any form' of the computer program, or whether, instead, they are just 'ideas and principles which underlie any element of a computer program, including those which underlie its interfaces', within Article 1(2).

4.1 Background to the Case

The claimant in this case, SAS Institute, was a developer of analytical software known as SAS (also the 'SAS System'). This was an integrated set of programs which enabled users to carry out a wide range of data processing and analysis tasks, in particular statistical analysis. The core component of the SAS System was Base SAS, which permitted users to write and run application programs ('scripts') to manipulate data. Such applications were written in a language known as the SAS Language. The functionality of Base SAS could be extended by the use of additional components. Also, SAS Institute's customers wrote, or had written on their behalf, several application programs in the SAS Language. Prior to the events giving rise to this dispute, the SAS Institute's customers had no alternative but to continue to acquire a licence to use the SAS components in order to be able to run their existing application programs in SAS Language, and to create new ones. A customer wishing to change software supplier would thus need to re-write its existing application programs in a different language.

The defendant, World Programming ('WP'), created a product called World Programming System to offer alternative software which would be able to execute application programs written in the SAS Language. To do this, WPL sought to imitate many of the functionalities of the SAS components, so that the same inputs would result in identical outputs. In order to achieve this result, no evidence was produced that WPL had had access to or copied any of the text or structural designs of the source code of the SAS components.

In September 2009, SAS commenced proceedings before the High Court of England and Wales, claiming copyright infringement in its software and manuals, as well as a breach of its licence terms with regards to the learning edition of the SAS System.

4.2   The Findings of the High Court and the Reference to the CJEU

As far as the scope of the present contribution is concerned, it is sufficient to limit our analysis to the issue relating to copyright protection for programming languages, interfaces and functionality.

To address these elements, Arnold J deemed it necessary to revert to Article 1(2) of the Software Directive, which is to be read in accordance with Article 9(2) TRIPS[142] and Article 2 of the WIPO Copyright Treaty. The wording of the latter[143] is similar to Article 1(2) of the Software Directive and Section 102(b) of the 1976 US Copyright Act.[144] However, the term 'expressions' therein appears less restrictive than its counterpart ('tangible medium of expression') in Section 102(a)[145] of the US Copyright Act.[146]

By referring to the decision in *Navitaire v easyJet*,[147] Arnold J recalled that Article 1(2) of the Software Directive had been interpreted by

---

[142]   'Copyright protection shall extend to expressions and not to ideas, procedures, methods of operation or mathematical concepts as such.'

[143]   'Copyright protection extends to expressions and not to ideas, procedures, methods of operation or mathematical concepts as such.'

[144]   'In no case does copyright protection for an original work of authorship extend to any idea, procedure, process, system, method of operation, concept, principle, or discovery, regardless of the form in which it is described, explained, illustrated, or embodied in such work.'

[145]   'Copyright protection subsists, in accordance with this title, in original works of authorship fixed in any tangible medium of expression, now known or later developed, from which they can be perceived, reproduced, or otherwise communicated, either directly or with the aid of a machine or device. Works of authorship include the following categories: (1) literary works; (2) musical works, including any accompanying words; (3) dramatic works, including any accompanying music; (4) pantomimes and choreographic works; (5) pictorial, graphic, and sculptural works; (6) motion pictures and other audiovisual works; (7) sound recordings; and (8) architectural works.'

[146]   Jörg Reinbothe and Silke von Lewinski, *The WIPO Treaties 1996 – The WIPO Copyright Treaty and the WIPO Performances Treaty. Commentary and legal analysis* (LexisNexis 2002), 47.

[147]   *Navitaire Inc v easyJet Airline Company and Bulletproof Technologies Inc* [2004] EWHC 1725 (Ch); [2006] RPC 4. The airline easyJet was dissatisfied with the bookings program supplied to it by Navitaire, and so asked Bulletproof to produce its own program and make user interfaces – particularly those for day-to-day bookings and long-term changes to flight schedules and the like – as similar as possible to those of the Navitaire system. The claimant did not contend that there had been textual copying of its coding, but contested the same 'look and feel' in the resulting screens and in the output of recorded bookings. Pumfrey J partially dismissed the claim. He held that there could be infringement in

Kitchin J in *Nova v Mazooma*[148] as meaning that copyright in computer programs does not protect programming languages, interfaces or the functionality of a computer program. Such a reading of Article 1(2) was upheld by the Court of Appeal (Civil Division).[149]

Hence, in UK copyright[150] it is not an infringement of the copyright in the source code of a computer program for a competitor of the copyright holder to study how the program functions, and to subsequently write its own program and imitate such functionality.

With regard to interfaces, the Software Directive does not exclude them from copyright protection. It only excludes the ideas and principles which underlie the interfaces. Indeed, it has been observed[151] that in *Total Informatics Processing Systems Ltd v Daman Ltd*,[152] a leading case in which UK courts considered the problems of interface programs, Judge Paul Baker QC expressly referred to the distinction between ideas and their expression in refusing to treat an interface file as a separate copyright work.

Despite consistent case law in this area, Arnold J agreed with Kitchin J that the correct interpretation of Article 1(2) of the Software Directive in relation to programming languages was not an *acte clair* and that a reference to the CJEU was needed in order to receive guidance as to the proper reading of the provision. In addition, even if Kitchin J was right in holding that programming languages are not protectable *per se*, there was

---

taking an idea which is sufficiently detailed. However, relying upon Article 1(2) of the Software Directive, he found that no copyright vests in languages and the ideas which underlie interfaces. Accordingly, the judge was reluctant to find infringement in the adoption of the business logic of the program.

[148] *Nova Productions Ltd v Mazooma Games Ltd and Others* [2006] EWHC 24 (Ch). The claimant had produced a computer video game for playing pool and claimed that the defendants' game infringed copyright in the computer programs. Even if they had not copied the source code of the claimant's program, there existed some similarities in appearance and function. Both the High Court of Justice (Chancery Division) and the Court of Appeal dismissed the claim for copyright infringement, holding that the defendants had not copied the program code or architecture, but only copied ideas.

[149] [2007] EWCA Civ 219.

[150] On the evolution of UK case law in relation to copyright protection of computer programs (and a comparison with the US experience), *see* Cornish, Llewelyn and Aplin, *Intellectual Property*, *cit*, 844 ff.

[151] Henry Carr and Richard Arnold, *Computer software. Legal protection in the United Kingdom* (2nd edn, ESC Pub Ltd 1992), 17.

[152] [1992] FSR 171.

room for debate as to how broadly the concept of a programming language should be construed in this respect.[153]

Due to these points and other doubts as to the interpretation of EU law, Arnold J decided to stay the proceedings and refer nine questions to the CJEU for a preliminary ruling. Of particular interest for the present contribution are questions 1 to 3. Accordingly, analysis will be limited to the points raised therein:

1. Where a computer program ('the First Program') is protected by copyright as a literary work, is Article 1(2) [of Directive 91/250] to be interpreted as meaning that it is not an infringement of the copyright in the First Program for a competitor of the rightholder without access to the source code of the First Program, either directly or via a process such as decompilation of the object code, to create another program ('the Second Program') which replicates the functions of the First Program?

2. Is the answer to question 1 affected by any of the following factors:
    (a) the nature and/or extent of the functionality of the First Program;
    (b) the nature and/or extent of the skill, judgment and labour which has been expended by the author of the First Program in devising the functionality of the First Program;
    (c) the level of detail to which the functionality of the First Program has been reproduced in the Second Program;
    (d) if the source code for the Second Program reproduces aspects of the source code of the First Program to an extent which goes beyond that which was strictly necessary in order to produce the same functionality as the First Program?

3. Where the First Program interprets and executes application programs written by users of the First Program in a programming language devised by the author of the First Program which comprises keywords devised or selected by the author of the First Program and a syntax devised by the author of the First Program, is Article 1(2) [of Directive 91/250] to be interpreted as meaning that it is not an infringement of the copyright in the First Program for the Second Program to be written so as to interpret and execute such application programs using the same keywords and the same syntax?

As clarified by AG Bot,[154] through questions 1 to 3 the referring court was essentially asking whether Article 1(2) of the Software Directive is to be interpreted as meaning that the functionalities of a computer program and the programming language therein are to be regarded as the

---

[153]   *Nova Productions Ltd v Mazooma Games Ltd and Others, cit,* [218].
[154]   Opinion of Advocate General Yves Bot delivered on 29 November 2011 [37].

expression of that program, and thus whether they qualify for copyright protection pursuant to that Directive.

4.3 The Opinion of Advocate General Bot

Having recalled that, pursuant to Article 1(1) of the Software Directive, Member States shall protect computer programs as literary works and that protection by copyright applies to the expression in any form of a computer program and not to the ideas and principles which underlie any element therein, AG Bot referred to Recital 14 in the preamble. This states that, in accordance with that principle of copyright, to the extent that logic, algorithms and programming languages comprise ideas and principles, those ideas and principles are not protected under the Software Directive.

The Software Directive does not define the meaning of 'expression in any form of a computer program'. This was a deliberate choice in the drafting of the Directive, and was meant to avoid the risk that legislative definitions became obsolete with technological progress. In any case, it was indicated that:

> the elements of creativity, skill and inventiveness manifest themselves in the way in which the program is put together. The programmer defines the tasks to be performed by a computer program and carries out an analysis of the possible ways to achieve those results. The author of a computer program, like the author of a book, selects the steps to be taken and the way in which those steps are expressed gives the program its particular characteristics of speed, efficiency and even style.

> Consequently, protection for a computer program is conceivable only from the point at which the selection and compilation of those elements are indicative of the creativity and skill of the author and thus set his work apart from that of other authors.[155]

By referring to the ruling in *Bezpeènostní softwarová asociace*,[156] AG Bot pointed out that the protection of a computer program is not limited to the literal elements of that program, these being the source code and the object code, but extends to any other element expressing the creativity of its author.[157]

---

[155] *Ibid* [47]–[48].
[156] Case C-393/09 *Bezpečnostní softwarová asociace – Svaz softwarové ochrany v Ministerstvo kultury, cit.*
[157] Opinion of Advocate General Yves Bot, *cit*, [51].

He therefore considered whether the functionality of a computer program (this being the set of possibilities offered by a computer system, or the actions specific to that program) and the programming language might be regarded as elements which express the creativity of their author. AG Bot concluded in the sense that these cannot, as such, form the object of copyright protection under the Software Directive. In achieving this conclusion, AG Bot seemed to have in mind the factual background and reasoning of Pumfrey J in *Navitaire*.[158] However, he raised an important point of distinction in this respect, and held that copyright protection might well arise where there are many means to achieve the actual expression of those functionalities. This is because,

> creativity, skill and inventiveness manifest themselves in the way in which the program is drawn up, in its writing. The programmer uses formulae, algorithms which, as such, are excluded from copyright protection because they are the equivalent of the words by which the poet or the novelist creates his work of literature. However, the way in which all of these elements are arranged, like the style in which the computer program is written, will be likely to reflect the author's own intellectual creation and therefore be eligible for protection.[159]

So the AG, relying on the idea/expression dichotomy,[160] found that, whilst there are functionalities that have merely a technical nature and for which no copyright subsists, there are other functionalities that are indeed the expression of individual creation and are as such deserving of copyright protection.

So far, so good. However, a significant problem remains: what test is to be applied in order to distinguish the various functionalities of the computer program? This was not explained by AG Bot, who just recalled the decision of the CJEU in *Infopaq*,[161] in which it was held that the various parts of a work enjoy protection under Article 2(a) of the InfoSoc Directive, provided that they contain some elements which are the expression of the intellectual creation of the author of the work. According to Gervais and Derclaye, it may be more appropriate to say that the

---

[158] *Navitaire Inc v easyJet Airline Company and Bulletproof Technologies Inc*, cit.

[159] Opinion of Advocate General Yves Bot, *cit*, [55].

[160] *See* Sally Weston, 'Software interfaces – stuck in the middle: the relationship between the law and software interfaces in regulating and encouraging interoperability' (2012) 43 IIC 427, 442.

[161] Case C-5/08 *Infopaq International A/S v Danske Dagblades Forening*, cit.

creative choices that generate such originality are what copyright protects, but only up to a certain level of abstraction (where expression
becomes idea). The concept of 'creative choices', which the CJEU
referred to in *Painer*, is defined as follows:

> As a rule of thumb, creative choices are those that one can isolate by asking
> whether two authors in similar situations (tools, direction, budget, etc.) would
> likely have produced essentially the same thing. It is those choices that create
> protectable expression and that, at bottom, copyright is meant to incentivise
> and protect. The rule is somewhat different from the traditional skill, labour
> and judgment test, but the differences only affect a few mostly marginal
> cases. In the SAS case, one would have to find that the code (not formats or
> a language per se) which the Court of Justice found potentially protectable
> embodies such choices.[162]

In any case, the Opinion makes it clear that the nature and extent of a
functionality of a computer program reproduced in another computer
program, or the level of detail to which that functionality has been
reproduced, do not have an impact on such an analysis. This is because
Article 1(3) of the Software Directive provides that a computer program
is to be protected if it is original in the sense that it is the author's own
intellectual creation and no other criteria shall be applied in determining
its eligibility for protection. Indeed, said the Advocate General, to
establish whether a computer program is an original work, no tests as to
the qualitative or aesthetic merits of the program should be applied.
Rather, to determine whether a computer program is eligible for legal
protection under copyright, account should be taken not of the time and
work devoted to devising the program nor of the level of skill of its
author, but of the degree of originality of its writing.

The problem indeed lies therein. According to AG Bot, 'originality of
its writing' is to be intended as something which combines both the UK
standard test for infringement (which relies upon substantiality) and the
new (at least for the UK) test laid down in *Infopaq*.[163] These are
different, as was also acknowledged (although rather ambiguously) by
Proudman J in *Meltwater*.[164] For the Advocate General, instead, the two
types of scrutiny are intertwined:

---

[162]   Daniel Gervais and Estelle Derclaye, 'The scope of computer program
protection after *SAS*: are we closer to answers?' (2012) 34 EIPR 565, 567
(footnotes omitted).

[163]   *Ibid.*

[164]   '[O]riginality rather than substantiality is the test to be applied to the part
extracted. As a matter of principle this is now the only real test', said the judge

[I]t will be for the national court to examine whether, in reproducing the functionalities of the SAS components, WPL reproduced, in its WPL System, a *substantial part* of the elements of those components which are the *expression of the intellectual creation* of the author of those components.[165]

Having examined the issue concerning software functionalities, AG Bot assessed whether the programming language of a computer program may be protected by copyright under the Software Directive.

The Opinion recalls that the source code of a computer program is written in a programming language which acts as a translator between the user and the computer, enabling the user to write instructions in a language that he himself understands. Therefore, programming language is a functional element which allows instructions to be given to the computer. In other words, it is the means by which expression is given, not the expression itself. Accordingly, no copyright protection vests in the programming language.

This conclusion, according to AG Bot, is not called into question by the fact that Recital 14 of the preamble to the Software Directive states that, to the extent that logic, algorithms and programming languages comprise ideas and principles, those ideas and principles are not protected under the Directive. This is because the intention of that recital is to simply restate the principle that copyright protects the expression of ideas, rather than ideas themselves.

4.4   The Decision of the CJEU

On 2 May 2012, the Grand Chamber of the CJEU published its decision in *SAS*, which did not diverge substantially from the findings of AG Bot reported above.

By questions 1 to 3, which the Court decided to examine along with questions 4 and 5,[166] the core issue to address was whether Article 1(2)

---

at para 69 of *The Newspaper Licensing Agency, Ltd. v. Meltwater Holding BV,* EWHC, *cit.*

[165]   Opinion of Advocate General Yves Bot [67] (emphasis added).

[166]   Questions 4 and 5 read as follows: '(4) Where the First Program reads from and writes to data files in a particular format devised by the author of the First Program, is Article 1(2) [of Directive 91/250] to be interpreted as meaning that it is not an infringement of the copyright in the First Program for the Second Program to be written so as to read from and write to data files in the same format? (5) Does it make any difference to the answer to Questions 1, 3 and 4 if the author of the Second Program created the Second Program by: (a) observing, studying and testing the functioning of the First Program; or (b) reading a

of the Software Directive must be interpreted as meaning that the functionality of a computer program, the programming language and the format of data files used in a computer program in order to exploit certain of its functions, constitute a form of expression of that program and may, as such, be protected by copyright in computer programs for the purposes of that Directive. To respond to the questions asked by the referring court, the CJEU relied upon the idea/expression dichotomy. Firstly, it reverted to legislative sources, in particular Recitals 14 and 15 in the preamble to the Software Directive, Article 2 of the WIPO Copyright Treaty and Article 9(2) TRIPS. The Court then referred to the decision in *Bezpečnostní softwarová asociace*[167] and held that the object of protection under the Software Directive includes the forms of expression of a computer program and the preparatory design work capable of leading, respectively, to the reproduction or the subsequent creation of such a program. Since a GUI does not enable the reproduction of the computer program, but merely constitutes one element of that program by means of which users make use of the features of that program, the CJEU held that no protection subsists in GUIs pursuant to the Software Directive.

This said, the CJEU pointed out that protection pursuant to the InfoSoc Directive could vest in those parts of computer functionalities which are their author's own intellectual creation. In particular, though neither the functionality of a computer program *per se,* nor the programming language and the format of data files used in a computer program in order to exploit certain of its functions, constitute a form of expression of that program for the purposes of Article 1(2) of the Software Directive, this finding 'cannot affect the possibility that the SAS Language and the format of SAS Institute's data files might be protected, as works, by copyright under Directive 2001/29 if they are their author's own intellectual creation'.[168] Regrettably, the CJEU did not go into detail as to how such scrutiny should be carried out and the most authoritative source in this respect still seems to be the (ambiguous) Opinion of AG Bot. What seems, however, confirmed is that, as highlighted by Ashwin van Roojen,

---

manual created and published by the author of the First Program which describes the functions of the First Program; or (c) both (a) and (b)?'

[167]   *Bezpečnostní softwarová asociace – Svaz softwarové ochrany v Ministerstvo kultury, cit*, in particular [34]–[35], [37] and [41].

[168]   Case C-406/10 *SAS Institute Inc v World Programming Inc, cit*, [45].

the idea/expression dichotomy and the originality requirement may not be sufficient to exclude interface specifications from protection.[169]

Albeit in a much more concise manner, the CJEU also confirmed the findings of AG Bot with respect to the test for copyright infringement in the case of reproduction, in a computer program or a user manual for that program, and of certain elements described in the user manual for another computer program protected by copyright. Recalling the decision in *Infopaq*, the Court held that the various parts of a work enjoy protection under Article 2(a) of the InfoSoc Directive, provided that they contain some of the elements which are the expression of the intellectual creation of the author of the work. The CJEU found that it is for national courts 'to ascertain whether the reproduction of those elements constitutes the reproduction of the expression of the intellectual creation of the author of the user manual for the computer program at issue in the main proceedings. In this respect, the examination ... of the reproduction of those elements of the user manual for a computer program must be the same with respect to the creation of the user manual for a second program as it is with respect to the creation of that second program.'[170] It is arguable that, in devising the test for infringement, contrary to the position adopted by AG Bot, the Court did not seem to have in mind an approach which combined substantial taking and originality, but merely an approach based on whether what has been appropriate is what in a work amounts to the author's own intellectual creation.

4.5 Problems with the Interpretation of Advocate General Bot, as Confirmed by the CJEU

In relation to questions 1 to 3, the position of AG Bot, as approved by the CJEU, might give rise to problematic interpretations. This is in respect of copyright protection for functionalities, rather than the programming language. In particular, the Opinion calls for further reflection from three different angles.

The first may be perhaps the least problematic. The position of AG Bot paves the way to a distinction between the parts of the program and the program as a whole. Such a distinction, as was made clear in *Infopaq*, is to be found neither in the InfoSoc Directive nor in any other relevant

---

[169]   Ashwin van Roojen, *The software interface between copyright and competition law* (Wolters Kluwer International 2010), 53.
[170]   *SAS Institute Inc v World Programming Inc, cit,* [68]-[69].

copyright directive.[171] Albeit true that some functionalities – in the same manner as single words in newspaper articles – cannot, as such, be considered as an intellectual creation of the author of the program, it is not disputed that it is through the choice, sequence and combination of those elements that the author may express his creativity in an original manner and thus achieve a result which is an intellectual creation. Furthermore, in *Bezpečnostní softwarová asociace*,[172] the CJEU held that the object of the protection conferred by the Software Directive is the expression in any form of a computer program (including any preparatory design work capable of leading, respectively, to the reproduction or the subsequent creation of such a program) which permits reproduction in different computer languages. This criterion was not followed by AG Bot when drawing a distinction between protectable and non-protectable functionalities, although the CJEU referred to it in its decision.[173]

This leads to the second point. By distinguishing between protectable and non-protectable functionalities, it is arguable that the test for copyright protection will now focus on the functionality *per se*, rather than the way this is combined with other elements of the program. This can be seen as a rather worrisome implication of the Opinion and, now, of the judgment itself. In particular, it has been argued that competition and innovation in the software industry in the EU as a whole would be seriously undermined by this finding. This is because both the text and legislative history of the Software Directive, in line with international sources, should be understood as providing protection to the literary aspects of programs, but not to functionality, languages and data interfaces.[174] This is important to safeguard the legality of reverse engineering and interoperability of computer programs.[175] This said, the Software Directive does not require that in the process of ascertaining the existence of copyright protection in relation to computer programs, one must have complete disregard of certain elements thereof irrespective of the degree

---

[171] Case C-5/08 *Infopaq International A/S v Danske Dagblades Forening, cit,* [38].

[172] Case C-393/09 *Bezpečnostní softwarová asociace – Svaz softwarové ochrany v Ministerstvo kultury, cit.*

[173] Case C-406/10 *SAS Institute Inc v World Programming Inc, cit,* [35] ff.

[174] Pamela Samuelson, Thomas Vinje and William Cornish, 'Does copyright protection under the EU Software Directive extend to computer program behaviour, languages and interfaces?' (2012) 34 EIPR 158.

[175] *Cf* Pamela Samuelson, 'The past, present and future of software copyright: interoperability rules in the European Union and United States' (2012) 34 EIPR 229.

to which they are expressed (such as, functionality, programming languages and the format in which data files are read and written).[176]

The final angle from which *SAS* may be analyzed is the peculiar test for infringement which AG Bot envisaged therein. Neither the Software Directive nor the InfoSoc Directive contain references to a 'substantial part'. On the contrary, the *Infopaq* decision adopted a test for copyright protection (and so infringement) which is to be based on quality rather than quantity.[177] In compliance with the wordings of these directives and preceding case law, the CJEU did not uphold this part of AG Bot's Opinion.

4.6 The Response of the High Court

On 25 January 2013 Arnold J handed down his decision on *SAS*.[178] He dismissed all of SAS's claims, except that in respect of the WPS Manual. Among other things, the decision is noteworthy for Arnold J's analysis as to whether SAS Language could be considered subject to copyright protection. To advance such a case, it would have been necessary for SAS to demonstrate that the programming language was a distinct copyright work.[179] In light of recent decisions of the CJEU, no fatal objection could have been raised against the claim that copyright might subsist also in works which fall outside the list provided in Section 1(1)(a) of CDPA 1988, provided that these must be a literary or artistic work within the meaning of Article 2(1) of the Berne Convention.[180]

---

[176] Patricia Akester, '*SAS Institute Inc v World Programming Ltd*, Case C-406/10 – exploratory answers' (2012) 34 EIPR 145, 150.

[177] *Cf* Case C-5/08 *Infopaq International A/S v Danske Dagblades Forening*, *cit,* [47]–[48]: '… given the requirement of a broad interpretation of the scope of the protection conferred by Article 2 of Directive 2001/29, the possibility may not be ruled out that certain isolated sentences, or even certain parts of sentences in the text in question, may be suitable for conveying to the reader the originality of a publication such as a newspaper article, by communicating to that reader an element which is, in itself, the expression of the intellectual creation of the author of that article. Such sentences or parts of sentences are, therefore, liable to come within the scope of the protection provided for in Article 2(a) of that directive. In the light of those considerations, the reproduction of an extract of a protected work … is such as to constitute reproduction in part within the meaning of Article 2 of Directive 2001/29, if that extract contains an element of the work which, as such, expresses the author's own intellectual creation …'

[178] *SAS Institute Inc v World Programming Ltd* [2013] EWHC 69 (Ch).

[179] *Ibid* [24].

[180] *Ibid* [27].

According to Arnold J, however, this was not the case, as the SAS Language could not possibly be considered a work.

The judgment also touches upon the notion of originality, which is said to require 'something on which the author has stamped his "personal touch" through the creative choices he has made'.[181] From this descends that also the test of infringement has a qualitative dimension, in that reproduction of a substantial part of a work (this being the scrutiny to be carried out under Section 16(3) of CDPA 1988) requires that 'the defendant has reproduced something that represents the expression of the intellectual creation of the author'.[182]

It is doubtful whether Arnold J's understanding of the originality requirement can be read in the limited sense that 'the author originated it by his efforts rather than slavishly copying it from the work produced by the efforts of another person.'[183] Moreover, it seems that, by following the same approach adopted by the CJEU, Arnold J dismissed AG Bot's test of infringement, by holding that this is to be carried out under the lens of originality, rather than substantiality.

CONCLUSION

The decisions in *Murphy*, *Painer*, *Football Dataco* and *SAS* have further clarified and developed the EU concept of originality. The notion of 'author's own intellectual creation', which is to be found in the Software, Database and Term Directives and was adopted as the standard for originality in *Infopaq*, is to be understood as involving 'creative freedom' (*Murphy*), 'personal touch' (*Painer*), 'free and creative choices' (*Football Dataco*). Put differently, originality is not a matter of sense, but also sensibility, although it may be difficult to agree on this conclusion in respect of copyright protection for newspaper extracts. This last consideration raises some doubts as to the actual consistency of these decisions with *Infopaq*. In particular, it is questionable whether the 'author's own intellectual creation' requirement envisaged in *Infopaq* is reconcilable with the additions brought by *Murphy*, *Painer* and *Football Dataco*.

Furthermore, this string of cases has called into question whether a system of closed subject-matter categorization (as it is under UK law) is still in line with EU law. Following *Murphy*, *Painer* and *SAS*, EU

---

[181]   *Ibid* [41].
[182]   *Ibid* [46].
[183]   Kevin Garnett, Gillian Davies and Gwilym Harbottle, *Copinger and Skone James on copyright* (16th edn, Sweet & Maxwell 2012), Vol I, 141.

scrutiny for determining whether a work may qualify for copyright protection seems to require solely that the work is original. This may also be at odds with the Berne Convention, which appears to imply any assessment of the originality requirement (which, however, is not expressly required as a precondition of protection)[184] to follow that of the work being a production in the literary, scientific and artistic domain (while it is a matter for national legislation to prescribe that works in general or any specified categories of works shall not be protected unless they have been fixed in some material form).[185]

Finally, as was made clear in *Football Dataco*, not only has the CJEU harmonized the originality requirement and, with it, the standard protection under EU copyright, but it has also ruled out any possible alternative (quasi-copyright) protection for subject-matter such as databases. This may give rise to problematic gaps in a country (such as the UK) which lacks a law of unfair competition, but also raise controversy in those Member States which are familiar with the principle of 'small change'. Overall, this urges a reflection on the extent to which the doctrine of EU pre-emption is applicable in the area of EU copyright.

---

[184] As clarified by Sterling, *World copyright law*, cit, 337, (footnotes omitted): 'The Berne Convention does not require, as a condition of protection, that a work should be "original", or result from creative endeavour in order to be protected. However, it is generally accepted that a work must be classified as fulfilling the criterion of originality or creativity in order to fall within the categories of production which are within the scope of the Convention.'

[185] Article 2(2) of the Berne Convention. So, whilst fixation is required by Article 3(2) CDPA 1988, French and Italian copyright laws provide that, as a general rule, the author of a work of the mind shall enjoy in that work, by the mere fact of its creation, an exclusive incorporeal property right which shall be enforceable against all persons. There are however specific exceptions to such principle. For instance, Article L-112.2, paragraph 4 of the French Intellectual Property Code (Code de la Propriété Intellectuelle) provides that copyright vests in choreographic works, circus acts and feats and dumb-show works, the acting form of which is set down in writing or in other manner. In a similar manner, Article 2 No 3 of the Italian Copyright Act (Legge 22 April 1941, No 633) requires that choreographic works and pantomimes are fixed in a material (written or otherwise) manner to be eligible for copyright protection.

5. Challenging the UK understanding of copyright: Originality and subject-matter categorization at the forefront of the debate

1. THE 'RED BUS' DECISION

On 12 January 2012 Judge Birss QC (as he then was) gave judgment in *Temple Island Collections Ltd v New English Teas Ltd and Nicholas John Houghton*. This was an action for copyright infringement brought by the owner of copyright in a photograph of a red London Routemaster bus travelling across Westminster Bridge in London. Apart from the red bus, the rest of the photograph was black and white. The Houses of Parliament and the bridge itself were shown in grey, against the backdrop of a white sky, with no clouds visible.

1.1 Background to the Case

The photograph at stake in the present case was taken in 2005 by the managing director of Temple Islands.

He manipulated the photograph on his computer using Photoshop software, taking the idea of making the red bus standing against a black and white background from Steven Spielberg's 1993 film *Schindler's List*. In particular, the photograph was subject to the following manipulations: firstly, the red colour of the bus was strengthened; then, the sky was removed completely by cutting electronically around the skyline of the buildings; thirdly, some people present in the foreground of the original photograph were removed, and the rest of the image was turned to monochrome, save for the bus; finally, the whole original image was stretched somewhat to change the perspective so that the verticals in the buildings were truly vertical. The photograph was published in 2006. Since then, it has been used by the claimant on souvenirs, becoming well known in the claimant's industry.

The defendants were tea producers. Following a previous settlement with the claimant over an allegation of copyright infringement, they produced an image portraying grey scale Houses of Parliament and a red bus on the bridge, believing that the claimant's copyright did not prevent them from doing so.

The image was the result of manipulation of four different photographs by one of the defendants and an iStockphoto image of a Routemaster bus. Three of the photographs by one of the defendants were of different aspects of the Houses of Parliament and the fourth was a picture of a red Routemaster bus while it was stationary on the Strand in London. The final image was obtained by resizing the bus to fit and the road marks were changed to be consistent.

This being the background to the case, Judge Birss QC made it clear that the case involved 'a tricky area of law: i.e. copyright in photographs; and, in the end, turns on a disputed qualitative judgment.'[1]

1.2   Originality in Photographs

Having recalled that copyright subsists in original artistic works, pursuant to Section 1(1)(a) CDPA 1988, Judge Birss QC assessed the way in which EU law has affected UK copyright. In particular, he found that the decision of the CJEU in *Infopaq*,[2] as later followed with specific regard to photographs in *Painer*,[3] suggested that copyright subsists in a photograph which is its author's own intellectual creation.[4]

The counsel for the claimant referred to a 2003 decision of the Austrian Oberster Gerichtshof (Supreme Court),[5] which had tackled issues similar to those at stake before the Patents Court. In that case, it was held that photographs are protected by copyright if they are the result of the creator's own intellectual creation, with no specific measure of originality being required. What was decisive, according to the Austrian Supreme Court, was for the photographer's personality to be reflected in

---

[1]   *Temple Island Collections Ltd v New English Teas Ltd and Nicholas John Houghton* [2012] EWPCC 1 [3].

[2]   Case C-5/08 *Infopaq International A/S v Danske Dagblades Forening* [2009] I-06569.

[3]   Case C-145/10 *Eva-Maria Painer v Standard VerlagsGmbH, Axel Springer AG, Süddeutsche Zeitung GmbH, SPIEGEL-Verlag Rudolf AUGSTEIN GmbH & Co KG and Verlag M. DuMont Schauberg Expedition der Kölnischen Zeitung GmbH & Co KG.*

[4]   *Temple Island Collections Ltd v New English Teas Ltd and Nicholas John Houghton, cit,* [18].

[5]   *O (Peter) v F KG* [2006] ECDR 9.

the arrangements (motif, visual angle, illumination, etc) selected specifically for the shot.

Judge Birss QC found that there was no difference in substance between the interpretation provided by the Austrian Supreme Court and the law in the UK, in that:

> A photograph of an object found in nature or for that matter a building, which although not natural is something found by the creator and not created by him, can have the character of an artistic work in terms of copyright law if the task of taking the photograph leaves ample room for an individual arrangement. What is decisive are the arrangements (motif, visual angle, illumination, etc.) selected by the photographer himself or herself.[6]

Some commentators have observed that, since the Berne Convention only requires protection for photographic works – and not every photograph constitutes an author's work – a distinction should be made between photographs that are just the result of the pressing of a button and photographs which express the creativity of their author.[7] As is also made clear by a most influential commentary,[8] in photography there is room for originality in three respects. Firstly, originality which resides in such specialties as angle of shot, light and shade, exposure and effects achieved with filters, developing techniques, etc. Secondly, originality relating to the creation of the scene to be photographed. Finally, originality where a scene that is unlikely to recur is captured or recorded, thereby creating a worthwhile photograph.[9] As held by Judge Birss QC, the composition of a photograph may also constitute a source of originality:

---

[6] *Temple Island Collections Ltd v New English Teas Ltd and Nicholas John Houghton, cit,* [20] (emphasis added).

[7] Richard Arnold, 'Content copyrights and signal copyrights: the case for a rational scheme of protection' (2011) 1 QMJIP 272, 277. On photography and the Berne Convention, *see* Sam Ricketson, 'International conventions', in Ysolde Gendreau, Axel Nordemann and Rainer Oesch (eds), *Copyright and photographs. An international survey* (Kluwer Law International 1999), 15, 18 ff.

[8] Hugh Laddie, Peter Prescott and Mary Vitoria and Others, *The modern law of copyright and designs* (4th edn, LexisNexis 2011), 254.

[9] This aspect is supported by the dissenting judgment of Romer LJ in *Bauman v Fussell* [1978] RPC 485. This was a case in which the defendant had reproduced in a painting the scene depicted in the plaintiff's photograph of two roosters fighting, although using different colours. The plaintiff argued that, the design being a substantial part of an artistic work, reproducing the position of the birds was tantamount to taking a substantial part from his photograph. The Court of Appeal dismissed the action, holding that, whilst the relative position of

The composition of an image will certainly derive from the 'angle of shot' ... but also from the field of view, from elements which the photographer may have created and from elements arising from being at the right place at the right time. The resulting composition is capable of being the aggregate result of all these factors which will differ by degrees in different cases. Ultimately however the composition of the image can be the product of the skill and labour (or intellectual creation) of a photographer and it seems to me that skill and labour/intellectual creation directed to that end can give rise to copyright.[10]

In particular, the judge found that this case illustrated what could be a fourth category of originality as regards photography: the computerized manipulation of a photograph to the extent that this has an effect on the composition itself, since in the case at hand the images of individual persons were actually removed from the foreground.

In light of the foregoing, the judge found that copyright subsisted in the claimant's photograph. This fact a given, he then turned to consider whether the defendant had infringed such copyright.

---

objects depicted in an artistic work could be described as substantial where the work was a painting, the same could not always be said where the work was a photograph. Lord Somerville explained this point as follows [487]: 'A man takes a photograph of a procession or the laying of a foundation stone. He, of course, has chosen when and from where the photograph should be taken. The relative position of those in the procession, or their taking part in the ceremony is not, however, his work, or his design, in the sense in which the relative position of the figures on the ceiling of the Sistine chapel was the work and design of Michelangelo. The order and arrangement of the procession has been, no doubt, carefully planned and designed by someone else. It is an individual's work that the [Copyright] Act is intended to protect. I do not think that a painter who was minded to make a picture of the procession, in his own style, would be committing a breach of copyright if he used the photograph to enable him to get accurately the relative positions of those taking part. What he would be taking would not be a substantial portion of the plaintiff's work. At the other end of the photographic scale one can imagine a case where the photographer has made an original arrangement of the objects animate and inanimate which he photographs in order to create a harmonious design representing, for example, Spring. Here the design would be his work. The position of the birds here is betwixt and between. It is, I think, nearer to the former than the latter category.' Romer LJ dissented and found originality to subsist in capturing the position of the animals. For a discussion as to how one determines whether part of an image is a substantial part for infringement purposes, *see* Justine Pila, 'Compilation copyright: A matter calling for "a certain ... sobriety' (2008), *University of Oxford Legal Research Paper Series, Paper No 45/2008*, November 2008, 54–6.

[10]   *Temple Island Collections Ltd v New English Teas Ltd and Nicholas John Houghton, cit,* [27].

1.3   Reading too Much into *Infopaq* and *Painer*: Aesthetic Merit and Visual Significance as Originality?

Having recalled that, pursuant to Sections 16 and 17 CDPA 1988, copyright is infringed by reproducing the whole or a substantial part of a work in a material form and that a 'substantial part' is a matter of quality not quantity, Judge Birss QC made it clear that 'one can reproduce a substantial part without necessarily producing something that looks similar even though of course it may do so.'[11]

He then reverted to the decision of the Privy Council in *Interlego*[12] to determine the amount of skill and labour which is relevant to the originality of an artistic work and found that this is the skill and labour which is visually significant. Visual significance must also be relevant to infringement and to the question as to whether a substantial part of an artistic work has been taken. According to Judge Birss QC,

> What is visually significant in an artistic work is not the skill and labour (or intellectual creative effort) which led up to the work, it is the product of that activity. The fact that the artist may have used commonplace techniques to produce his work is not the issue. What is important is that he or she has used them under the guidance of their own aesthetic sense to create the visual effect in question.[13]

Although copyright protection for artistic works is provided under the CDPA 1988 irrespective of their artistic quality,[14] this does not mean that one ignores what such a work looks like and focuses only on the effort which went into creating it.

This said, although it is still unclear whether direct lifting of the actual image needs to be proven in order to establish infringement under UK copyright law,[15] the judge considered whether the defendants' work had derived from the claimant's photograph. He found that the defendants did not have a case of independent design at all. It was sufficient to ascertain

---

[11]   *Ibid* [30].

[12]   *Interlego v Tyco Industries* [1989] AC 217.

[13]   *Temple Island Collections Ltd v New English Teas Ltd and Nicholas John Houghton, cit,* [34].

[14]   Section 4(1)(a) CDPA 1988.

[15]   *Cf* Laddie, Prescott and Vitoria and Others, *The modern law of copyright* (4th edn), *cit,* 255 ff, who argue (255) that 'the right answer depends on whether the original scene forms a material part of the original work of the original photographer; if it does, there is no reason why its reproduction in this indirect way should not infringe.'

from what publicly available works they had derived their image. Then, from the evidence submitted, Judge Birss QC inferred the following. Firstly, that the Houses of Parliament, Big Ben, the Routemaster bus, etc, are iconic images of London; secondly, that the idea of putting such iconic images together is a common one; thirdly, that the technique of highlighting an iconic object like a bus against a black and white image was not unique to the claimant; and finally, that whether anyone had ever produced a black and white image of Big Ben and the Houses of Parliament with a red bus in it before the claimant was not clear.

To establish whether the defendant had infringed the claimant's copyright, Judge Birss QC held that the following elements needed to be taken into account. Firstly, the composition of the image: not just the Big Ben, but a substantial frontage of the Houses of Parliament and the arches of Westminster Bridge. The bus is on the central left side near a lamppost. It is framed by buildings behind it. People can be seen on the bridge and some are in front of the bus, but they are not prominent. Portcullis House is visible as well as the river itself. Secondly, the visual contrasts: one between the bright red bus and the monochrome background, and the other between the blank and white sky and the rest of the photograph. According to the judge, these elements 'derive from and are the expression of the skill and labour exercised by [the author], or in *Infopaq* terms, they are his intellectual creation.'[16]

It is apparent that for the judge the traditional requirement of sufficient skill and labour appears to be akin to the standard envisaged by the CJEU in *Infopaq*. However, in establishing infringement, he focused more on the elements that he found to constitute the claimant's intellectual creation, rather than the traditional test of substantiality. In doing so, the judge applied (quite confusingly) both the *Infopaq* qualitative test and the traditional 'substantial taking' test. He held that comparisons with other similar works are irrelevant as a matter of law in terms of originality, even if they might serve to illustrate how different choices made by different photographers lead to alternative visual effects. Judge Birss QC then addressed the issue of copying and found that the common elements between the defendants' work and the claimant's work were causally related. Indeed, according to the judge, it was apparent that it was not a coincidence that both images showed the Big Ben and the Houses of Parliament in black and white with a bright red bus driving from right to left and a blank white sky. Evidently, the reason why the defendants'

---

[16] *Temple Island Collections Ltd v New English Teas Ltd and Nicholas John Houghton, cit,* [53].

image was composed in this manner was that they had seen the claimant's work, even before having seen any other similar images.

This said, the judge considered if the reproduction from the claimant's work represented a substantial part of that work. To address that issue, he deemed it necessary to ascertain what had in fact been reproduced. He found that both elements of the composition and the visual contrast features had been copied from the claimant's image. Although some important and visually significant elements of the claimant's original artistic work had *not* been reproduced by the defendants, it is not that infringement can only be found where facsimile copying has occurred. The question was instead whether, without the parts which had been reproduced by the defendants, what was reproduced amounted to a substantial part of the claimant's work. This was because the elements which had been reproduced included the key combination of the visual contrast features alongside the basic composition of the scene itself. It was this combination which made the claimant's image visually interesting and, therefore, original in the sense of *Infopaq*. Indeed, in reaching this conclusion, the judge found it decisive that the claimant's image was not a mere photograph, ie the result of happening to click his camera in the right place at the right time. Instead, the picture was the product of deliberate choices and intentional manipulations made by the author. So, even if the image might have looked just like another photograph in that location, its appearance derived from much more than that.

1.4 Is a Cropped Portrait Version Equally Infringing?

Having held that the defendants had infringed the claimant's copyright, Judge Birss QC then considered whether a cropped version of the defendants' image which had been printed in portrait format would have been considered as infringing of the claimant's photograph. The judge recalled that the cropping (which had occurred either to fit the image onto the short side of a tea tin, with the landscape version on the long side, or else to fit it onto a smaller tin) had been carried out in such a way so as to discard only the least significant parts of the original image. So, the cropped portrait version had lost about half the riverside facade and the edge of Portcullis House, which appeared instead in the landscape version. According to Judge Birss QC, these elements were of limited importance in comparison to the elements of the claimant's work that featured in the cropped version.

Therefore, he found that the cropped portrait version still reproduced a substantial part of the claimant's work and would have been tantamount to an infringement of its copyright.

1.5   The Implications of the Decision

Although not binding on the High Court of England and Wales, the 'Red
Bus' decision has been seen as a worrisome development in UK
copyright law, not least because it may increase uncertainties regarding
the (already complicated) relationship between basic principles such as
the idea/expression dichotomy and originality.

First of all, the decision has been found[17] to mark a significant
departure from the US decision in *The Bridgeman Art Library, Ltd v
Corel Corp.* This was a case concerning whether exact photographic
reproductions of public domain images could be protected in the US.[18] In
dismissing the action, Justice Kaplan tackled the issue of whether these
would have been protectable under UK law. While finding that the
authority of the old *Graves' Case*[19] was of dubious usefulness, as recalled
above *sub* Chapter 2, Section II, §1, the judge referred to the second
edition of *Laddie*, to point out that no copyright protection would have
been available to such photographs under UK law:

> It is obvious that although a man may get a copyright by taking a photograph
> of some well-known object like Westminster Abbey, he does not get a
> monopoly in representing Westminster Abbey as such, any more than an artist
> would who painted or drew that building. What, then, is the scope of
> photographic copyright? As always with artistic works, this depends on what
> makes his photograph original. Under the [CDPA] 1988 ... the author is the
> person who made the original contribution and it will be evident that this
> person need not be he who pressed the trigger, who might be a mere assistant.
> Originality presupposes the exercise of substantial independent skill, labour,
> judgment and so forth. For this reason it is submitted that a person who makes
> a photograph merely by placing a drawing or painting on the glass of a
> photocopying machine and pressing the button gets no copyright at all; but he

---

[17]   *See* Jeremy Phillips, 'When Birss meets Bus: a study in Red and Gray'
(The 1709 Blog, 22 January 2012) <http://tinyurl.com/bhdk4vj> accessed 14
June 2013.

[18]   The Bridgeman Art Library, Ltd v Corel Corp 25 F Supp 2d 421, 36 F
Supp 2d 191 [1998]. The relevant part of this case involved an application to
cancel entries on the no longer extant Register of Proprietors of Copyright in
Paintings, Drawings and Photographs for three photographs of engravings. In
rejecting the contention that the photographs were not copyrightable because
they were copies of the engravings, Justice Blackburn held that a photograph
taken from a picture is an original photograph, in so far as that to copy it is an
infringement of the statute.

[19]   *Graves' Case* [1869] LR 4 QB 715.

might get a copyright if he employed skill and labour in assembling the thing to be photocopied, as where he made a montage.[20]

Secondly, the ruling in *Temple Islands* raises doubts as to the actual degree of protection now enjoyed by photographs in the UK.[21] In particular, if it is true that the bar to originality has been traditionally intended in the UK to be lower than in continental traditions, the fact that Judge Birss QC decided nonetheless to apply (and even go beyond) the originality standard envisaged in *Infopaq*[22] and *Painer*[23] urges a reflection as to the relationship between UK copyright and Article 6 of the Term Directive. This, while expressly providing for protection pursuant to Article 1 of the same Directive to vest in photographs which are original in the sense that they are the author's own intellectual creation, allows Member States to protect other (simple) photographs.[24] This means that the UK, despite the obiter remarks of Lord Oliver in the 1989 decision in *Interlego*,[25] could have continued to protect non-original (at least in the EU sense) photographs, as was also implied in the *Painer* judgment.[26] Apparently, following the decision by Judge Birss QC, this is no longer the case. Therefore, decisions such as *Antiquesportfolio.com*,[27] in which copyright was held to subsist in sub-original (at least in the *Painer* sense) photographs, may be considered no longer as valid precedents. This case held that copyright subsisted in simple photographs of three-dimensional objects because taking of such photographs

---

[20]   Hugh Laddie, Peter Prescott and Mary Vitoria, *The modern law of copyright and designs* (2nd edn, LexisNexis 1995), 238 (footnotes omitted).

[21]   *See* Rosie Burbidge, 'Originality or author's own intellectual creation? What is the legal test for copyright subsistence in photographs?'(Art and Artifice, 30 January 2012) <http://tinyurl.com/aaqgms3> accessed 14 June 2013.

[22]   Case C-5/08 *Infopaq International A/S v Danske Dagblades Forening*, *cit.*

[23]   Case C-145/10 *Eva-Maria Painer v Standard VerlagsGmbH, Axel Springer AG, Süddeutsche Zeitung GmbH, SPIEGEL-Verlag Rudolf AUGSTEIN GmbH & Co KG and Verlag M. DuMont Schauberg Expedition der Kölnischen Zeitung GmbH & Co KG*, *cit.*

[24]   *See* Recital 16 in the preamble to the Term Directive.

[25]   *See* above, *sub* Chapter 2, Section II, §2.1.

[26]   *See* Yin Harn Lee, 'Photographs and the standard of originality in Europe: *Eva-Maria Painer v Standard Verlags GmbH, Axel Springer AG, Suddeutsche Zeitunung GmbH, Spiegel-Verlag Rudolf Augstein GmbH & Co KG, Verlag M. DuMont Schauberg Expedition der Kolnischen Zeitung GmbH & Co KG* (C-145/10)' (2012) 34 EIPR 290, 292.

[27]   *Antiquesportfolio.com PLC v Rodney Fitch & Co Ltd*, *cit.*

involved judgment, ie the positioning of the object, the angle from which the picture is taken, the lighting, and the focus.[28]

Thirdly, doubts have been raised as to the overall merit of the analysis of Judge Birss QC. According to Andreas Rahmatian,

> The unsatisfactory aspect of this judgment is that the application of generally correct legal criteria of copyright protection (originality, taking a substantial part of the claimant's work, etc.) does not prevent an unconvincing outcome. The decision might have been different if more attention had been given to the aspect of 'composition' of the photograph and to the idea-expression dichotomy.[29]

Indeed, as was held in *Creation Records*[30] (reference to which is to be found nowhere in Judge Birss QC's decision) the recreation of a scene that is then independently photographed does not infringe the copyright in the earlier photograph.[31]

It has been argued that a case like the one at stake before the Patents Court might have had a different outcome, even if decided in continental Member States. In France, for instance, the Court of Cassation[32] has recently denied that copyright could vest in a photograph depicting two gurnards on a plate covered with saffron. These were positioned on the

---

[28] *See* Lionel Bently and Brad Sherman, *Intellectual Property Law*, (3rd edn, OUP 2008), 110 and 109-111 for an analysis of the UK position as to the protection of photographs.

[29] Andreas Rahmatian, 'Temple Islands Collections v New English Teas: an incorrect decision based on the right law?' (2012) 34 EIPR 796, 797.

[30] *Creation Records Ltd and Others v News Group Newspapers Ltd* [1997] EWHC Ch 370. The action in this case arose out of arrangements made to take photographs intended for the cover of Oasis album *Be Here Now*. The final cover had a swimming pool in the foreground with a Rolls Royce seemingly emerging from the water towards the camera. The members of the group were posed round the pool, one on a scooter, one climbing out of the pool and others with or near other objects seemingly unrelated to each other. A photographer working for *The Sun* newspaper took photographs of the shooting session. One of the photographs then published by *The Sun* showed a version of the scene that was very similar to that of the picture then chosen for the cover of the album. In dismissing the claim for copyright infringement, Lloyd J held that [8] the process of assembling disparate objects together with the members of the Oasis group could not be regarded as having anything in common with sculpture or with artistic craftsmanship and, as a result, no copyright could possibly vest in it.

[31] Rahmatian, 'Temple Islands', *cit*, 797.

[32] C Cass, civ 1re, 20 October 2011 (pourvoi No 10-21.251), as reported in Asim Singh, 'The protection of photographs in French copyright law' (The 1709 Blog, 2 February 2012) <http://tinyurl.com/auz6cat> accessed 14 June 2013.

plate with their heads and tails meeting and such as to form an arc along the edge of the plate. The Court found that the photograph did not reveal, in its various constituent elements, any aesthetic pursuit, and that it was merely the result of know-how underlying a technical service. Therefore, it did not show the personality of the author. In its judgment on 20 December 2012, the Paris High Court confirmed that:

> Une photographie n'est protégeable par le droit de la propriété intellectuelle que dans la mesure où elle procède d'un effort créatif et qu'elle ne vise pas seulement à reproduire de la manière la plus fidèle possible, un objet préexistant.[33]

Doubts have been raised also as to whether a photograph like the one discussed before Judge Birss QC would have been held to enjoy copyright protection in Germany.[34] In Italy, it is arguable that a case like the one of the 'Red Bus' would have had best chances of success on the grounds of unfair competition. This is because of the loose significance of 'unfair competition' under Article 2598 of the Italian Civil Code.[35] However, a copyright claim might also have been invoked successfully.[36]

Finally, the reasoning of Judge Birss QC shows the difficulties the UK is facing in understanding fully the implications of the string of cases following *Infopaq*.[37] According to the judge, skill and labour were tantamount to intellectual creation. This is not the case, as made clear in

---

[33] *Philippe G and Alexandra J v Paul M*, Tribunal de grande instance de Paris, 3ème ch, 4ème sec, 20 December 2012: 'A photograph is protectable under copyright only to the extent that it is the result of a creative effort and does not aim solely to reproduce, as faithfully as possible, a pre-existing object.' (English translation by Asim Singh, 'Paris court rejects photographer's copyright claim' (The 1709 Blog, 10 January 2013) <http://preview.tinyurl.com/bhzf5op> accessed 14 June 2013).

[34] *See* Rosie Burbidge, 'Would Germany and France find the red bus photo infringed?' (Art and Artifice, 27 February 2012) <http://tinyurl.com/a9wh9w6> accessed 14 June 2013.

[35] In particular, pursuant to Article 2598 No 3, whoever commits any act which is contrary to professional fairness and has the potential of damaging third parties' enterprise is liable of unfair competition.

[36] In this sense also Angela Saltarelli, 'Red bus suggests copyright law is not black and white: an Italian perspective' (Art and Artifice, 29 January 2012) <http://tinyurl.com/b5hdbj7> accessed 14 June 2013.

[37] Case C-5/08 *Infopaq International A/S v Danske Dagblades Forening*, *cit.*

Painer[38] and – even more thoroughly – in *Football Dataco*.[39] Although the judge applied the *Infopaq* test of originality quite correctly, the decision failed to follow the conceptual and logical implications of *Infopaq* consistently. Indeed, as made clear by AG Mengozzi, originality as 'intellectual creation' implies that copyright protection is conditional upon copyright subject-matter being characterized by a 'creative' aspect. In other words, it is not sufficient that the creation of the work required labour and skill,[40] nor that the author used his aesthetic sense to create certain visual effects. In addition, the *Infopaq* decision and subsequent CJEU case law do not envisage any test for substantial taking, for the sake of determining infringement.

2. THE *LUCASFILM* DECISION: A DIFFERENT OUTCOME IF DECIDED TODAY?

On 27 July 2011, the recently established UK Supreme Court published its decision in *Lucasfilm Ltd and Others v Ainsworth and Another*.[41] Lords Walker and Collins (with whom Lord Phillips and Lady Hale agreed) delivered the judgment.

2.1 Background to the Case

The case concerned intellectual property rights in various artefacts made for use in the first *Star Wars* film in 1977 (*Star Wars IV – A New Hope*), in particular the Imperial Stormtrooper helmet. The trial judge (Mann J) so described the Imperial Stormtroopers:

> One of the most abiding images in the film was that of the Imperial Stormtroopers. These were soldiers clad in white armour, including a white helmet which left no part of the face uncovered ... The purpose of the helmet was that it was to be worn as an item of costume in a film, to identify a

---

[38] Case C-145/10 *Eva-Maria Painer v Standard VerlagsGmbH, Axel Springer AG, Süddeutsche Zeitung GmbH, SPIEGEL-Verlag Rudolf AUGSTEIN GmbH & Co KG and Verlag M. DuMont Schauberg Expedition der Kölnischen Zeitung GmbH & Co KG, cit.*

[39] Case C-604/10 *Football Dataco Ltd and Others v Yahoo! UK Limited and Others*.

[40] *Cf* Opinion of Advocate General Paolo Mengozzi delivered on 15 December 2011 [35].

[41] *Lucasfilm Ltd and Others v Andrew Ainsworth and Another* [2008] EWHC 1878 (Ch); [2009] EWCA Civ 1328; [2011] UKSC 39.

character, but in addition to portray something about that character – its allegiance, force, menace, purpose and, to some extent, probably its anonymity. It was a mixture of costume and prop.[42]

The film's storyline and characters were conceived by George Lucas between 1974 and 1976. Lucas's concept of the Imperial Stormtroopers as threatening characters in fascistic white-armoured suits was given visual expression in drawings and paintings by an artist and three-dimensional form, amongst others, by Andrew Ainsworth, who was skilled in vacuum-moulding in plastic. Eventually, Ainsworth produced fifty helmets for use in the film.

In addition to the commercial success of the *Star Wars* films, over the course of the years, Lucasfilm has built up a successful licensing business, including the licensing of models of Imperial Stormtroopers and their equipment.

In 2004, Ainsworth used his original tools to make versions of the Imperial Stormtrooper helmet and armour, and other artefacts for sale to the public.

The following year Lucasfilm successfully sued Ainsworth in the US District Court, Central District of California, although the whole judgment remained unsatisfied.

In parallel to this, Lucasfilm commenced proceedings before the Chancery Division of the English High Court, claiming – amongst other things[43] – copyright infringement in the Stormtrooper helmets under the CDPA 1988. This is because the aforementioned events took place in England and because George Lucas lived in England while the film was being made at Elstree (a village north of London).

In 2008, Mann J of the Chancery Division dismissed the claim based on UK copyright infringement, holding that the helmet was not a work of sculpture as per Section 4 CDPA 1988. As a consequence, the issue of whether Ainsworth could successfully invoke defences under Sections 51[44] and 52[45] CDPA 1988 did not need to be addressed. The judge also

---

[42] [2008] EWHC 1878 (Ch), [2] and [121].

[43] The case is noteworthy also for issues pertaining to the enforcement of foreign (US) judgments in the UK.

[44] '(1) It is not an infringement of any copyright in a design document or model recording or embodying a design for anything other than an artistic work or a typeface to make an article to the design or to copy an article made to the design. (2) Nor is it an infringement of the copyright to issue to the public, or include in a film or communicate to the public, anything the making of which was, by virtue of subsection (1), not an infringement of that copyright. (3) In this section – 'design' means the design of any aspect of the shape or configuration

dismissed the defendant's counterclaim based on his own claim to copyright in the helmet.

In 2009, the Court of Appeal[46] dismissed the appeal and confirmed that any intellectual property rights in the helmet belonged to Lucasfilm. Appeal to the Supreme Court was, however, granted. The issues this had to address concerned, *inter alia,* whether the helmet was a sculpture and whether defences under Sections 51 and 52 CDPA 1988 applied.

2.2 Whether the Stormtrooper Helmet is a Sculpture

As is well known, copyright subsists in original artistic works. Among these are sculptures which, pursuant to Article 4(2) of the CDPA 1988, include 'a cast or model made for purposes of sculpture'.

The rationale underlying Sections 51 and 52 CDPA 1988 is to limit the influence of literary or artistic copyright on other persons' freedom to make and market three-dimensional objects. In particular, Section 51 applies where the end-product of a design document or model is not an artistic work. Section 52 applies where there is an artistic work, but where that work has been exploited (with the consent of the copyright owner) by the industrial production of copies to be marketed. The Copyright (Industrial Process and Excluded Articles) (No 2) Order 1989[47] provides that an article is made by an industrial process if it is one of more than fifty articles which are to be treated as copies of a particular artistic work (and are not together a set). The Order also clarifies that 'works of sculpture, other than casts or models used or intended to be

---

(whether internal or external) of the whole or part of an article, other than surface decoration; and 'design document' means any record of a design, whether in the form of a drawing, a written description, a photograph, data stored in a computer or otherwise.'

45 '(1) This section applies where an artistic work has been exploited, by or with the licence of the copyright owner, by – (a) making by an industrial process articles falling to be treated for the purposes of this Part as copies of the work, and (b) marketing such articles, in the United Kingdom or elsewhere. (2) After the end of the period of 25 years from the end of the calendar year in which such articles are first marketed, the work may be copied by making articles of any description, or doing anything for the purpose of making articles of any description, and anything may be done in relation to articles so made, without infringing copyright in the work. (3) Where only part of an artistic work is exploited as mentioned in subsection (1), subsection (2) applies only in relation to that part …'

46 [2009] EWCA Civ 1328.

47 SI 1989/1070.

used as models or patterns to be multiplied by any industrial process' are outwith the scope of Section 52.

Having recalled the legislative evolution concerning copyright protection for sculptures, the Supreme Court reverted to relevant decisions of the Court of Appeal for New Zealand[48] and the House of Lords for guidance. In *George Hensher Ltd v Restawile Upholstery (Lancs) Ltd*,[49] Lord Reid held that a work is artistic if it is genuinely admired by a section of the community on the basis of the emotional or intellectual satisfaction its appearance gives. That the author did not consciously undertake to create a work is not determinative.[50] Contrary to Mann J (who had discussed this decision at some length), the Supreme Court briefly referred to this decision, just to establish that, when interpreting statutory provisions, it is necessary to start with the ordinary meaning of the words contained therein.[51]

From such authorities, Mann J had derived what he called guidelines, not rigid requirements, as to the meaning of sculpture within the CDPA 1988.[52] These were then approved by the Court of Appeal. Before these courts, the arguments had centred on the correct approach to three-dimensional objects that have both an artistic purpose and a utilitarian function, such as the Stormtrooper helmet. Before the Supreme Court, the appellants challenged the reasoning of both the High Court and the Court of Appeal, claiming that it had been outlandish of Mann J to describe the helmet's purpose as utilitarian. They submitted that the Court of Appeal could equally have found it to have a functional purpose if they had treated it as having the same features of a real helmet, albeit for use within the confines of a film.

According to the Supreme Court, this was quite a puzzling point, as the *Star Wars* films are set in an imaginary, science-fiction world of the future, and are a mixture of costume and prop in order to contribute to the artistic effect of the film. This said,

---

[48] *Wham-O Manufacturing Co v Lincoln Industries Ltd* [1985] RPC 127 (copyright protection for frisbees); *Breville Europe Plc v Thorn EMI Domestic Appliances Ltd* [1995] FSR 77 (copyright protection for sandwich toasters); *Metix (UK) Ltd v G H Maughan (Plastics) Ltd* [1997] FSR 718 (copyright in moulds used for making cartridges used in conjunction with flow mixers); *Wildash v Klein* (2004) 61 IPR 324 (copyright in craftwork depicting wildlife).

[49] [1976] AC 64, which is discussed in detail in Laddie, Prescott and Vitoria and Others, *The modern law of copyright* (4th edn), *cit*, 214 ff.

[50] *George Hensher Ltd v Restawile Upholstery (Lancs) Ltd, cit,* [78].

[51] *Lucasfilm Ltd and Others v Ainsworth and another*, UKSC, *cit*, [30].

[52] *Lucasfilm Ltd and Others v Ainsworth and another*, EWHC, *cit*, [118].

It would not accord with the normal use of language to apply the term 'sculpture' to a 20th century military helmet used in the making of a film, whether it was the real thing or a replica made in different material, however great its contribution to the artistic effect of the finished film. The argument for applying the term to an Imperial Stormtrooper helmet is stronger, because of the imagination that went into the concept of the sinister cloned soldiers dressed in uniform white armour. But it was the Star Wars film that was the work of art that Mr Lucas and his companies created. The helmet was utilitarian in the sense that it was an element in the process of production of the film.[53]

In addition, the Supreme Court acknowledged the existence of an emerging legislative purpose of protecting three-dimensional objects in a graduated way, quite unlike the protection afforded by the indiscriminate protection of literary copyright. It found that:

> Different periods of protection are accorded to different classes of work. Artistic works of art (sculpture and works of artistic craftsmanship) have the fullest protection; then come works with 'eye appeal' …; and … a modest level of protection has been extended to purely functional objects (the exhaust system of a motor car being the familiar example). Although the periods of protection accorded to the less privileged types have been progressively extended, copyright protection has always been much more generous. There are good policy reasons for the differences in the periods of protection, and the Court should not, in our view, encourage the boundaries of full copyright protection to creep outwards.[54]

As no copyright was held to vest in the Stormtrooper helmets, Lords Walker and Collins did not deem it necessary to address whether Ainsworth had a defence under Sections 51 and 52 CDPA 1988.

2.3   Would an Originality-based Approach have Led to a Different Solution?

As is apparent from the foregoing, the UK Supreme Court rejected the idea that copyright could vest in the Stormtrooper helmet, on the (perhaps overly formalistic) assumption that this could not be considered as a sculpture pursuant to Section 4 CDPA 1988.[55] As made clear by the

---

[53] *Lucasfilm Ltd and Others v Ainsworth and another*, UKSC, *cit,* [45].
[54] *Ibid* [49].
[55] Justine Pila, 'The "Star Wars" copyright claim: an ambivalent view of the empire' (2012) 128 LQR 15, 18, holds the view that, because of heavy reliance on English copyright history, the Supreme Court adopted a too formalistic conception of artistic and literary copyright. The same author also criticizes the

Court of Appeal, legislative history is such that 'sculpture' cannot be held to encompass a work like the Stormtrooper helmet, as this cannot be intended to be a work of art. As such:

> The first point concerns the normal use of the word 'sculpture'. Most of the cases proceed on the footing that one should not stray too far from the ordinary meaning of the word but there is considerable disagreement as to what that is. One of the difficulties is that the word can be used to describe both the physical process of moulding or carving necessary to create the finished object and that object itself. Copyright has, of course, to exist in the product of one's skill and labour. Not in the skill and labour itself. In looking therefore at the finished article, it seems to us wrong to interpret the use of the word sculpture in the 1911 Act (and therefore in succeeding Copyright Acts) divorced from the earlier legislative history. The 1814 Act was clearly concerned to identify sculpture as an artistic work. Its transposition into a wider category of 'artistic work' under the 1911 Act does not mean that one can ignore that context. Although some of the items included in the list such as a map or diagram may have a high level of functionality that should not be used as a guide to the interpretation of every item which the statutory definition contains. Sculpture, like painting (however good or bad it may be), does connote the work of the artist's hand and the visual purpose attributed to it by the judge in this case. Put simply, it has, broadly speaking, to be a work at least *intended to be a work of art.*[56]

This is a somewhat odd interpretation, in that it carves out copyright with subjective connotations. Indeed, the implication of holding that a work is a sculpture if it was created with the intention to be a work of art would be difficult to prove and would be also inconsistent with relevant case law. In addition to originality, it would also be required to know what the original author's (*rectius*: artist, in a truly romantic sense moreover) intention was whilst realizing the work.[57] In addition, as also recalled more recently by Judge Birss QC (as he then was), '[a]rtistic copyright must relate to the content of the work of the artist and not the medium in which it is recorded.'[58]

CDPA 1988 subject-matter categorization, which she claims to suffer 'from the defects of formalist theory in its definitions of the categories of original works' (Justine Pila, 'Copyright and its categories of original works' (2010) 30 OJLS 229, 231).

[56] *Lucasfilm Ltd and Others v Ainsworth and another*, EWCA, *cit,* [70] (emphasis added).

[57] In a similar sense also Mark A Prinsley and Sarah Byrt, '*Lucasfilm* fails to find the force' (2011) 105 Euro Law 14, 15.

[58] *Abraham Moon & Sons Ltd v Andrew Thornber and Others* [2012] EWPCC 37, [106], referring to Arnold, 'Content copyrights', *cit.*

Above all, neither the Supreme Court nor the High Court and the Court of Appeal addressed the issue of whether the Stormtrooper helmet could have been considered as sufficiently original for copyright protection to apply. It is arguable that, should the Supreme Court have assessed the Stormtrooper helmet in light of its actual originality, copyright might have been held to vest in it. In addition, in the UK there are precedents which might have supported a result contrary to the *Lucasfilm* decision. For instance, in *Shelley Films*,[59] it was arguably held that copyright subsisted in latex prostheses, which had been designed for use in film, as sculptures.

Although the CDPA 1988 requires a subject-matter to be both original and fall within one of the categories of 'artistic work' to qualify for copyright protection,[60] it is doubtful that this part of the CDPA 1988 is still in line with EU law. Indeed, as explained above *sub* Chapters 3 and 4, it seems that following the decisions of the CJEU, especially in *Bezpečnostní softwarová asociace*,[61] *Murphy*[62] and *Painer*,[63] it is no longer necessary to scrutinize what subject-matter category a work belongs to. Originality, not subject-matter categorization, is the test for copyright protection under EU law. Under this test, copyright might well have been found to subsist in the Stormtrooper helmet.

CONCLUSION

Both the 'Red Bus' decision and the judgment in *Lucasfilm* are exemplificative of the challenges currently facing UK copyright.

---

[59] *Shelley Films Ltd v Rex Features Ltd* [1994] EMLR 134, 132, discussed in Laddie, Prescott and Vitoria and Others, *The modern law of copyright,* 4th edn, *cit,* 211–12.

[60] Laddie, Prescott and Vitoria and Others, *The modern law of copyright* (4th edn), *cit,* 190.

[61] Case C-393/09 *Bezpečnostní softwarová asociace – Svaz softwarové ochrany v Ministerstvo kultury* [2010] I-13971.

[62] Joined Cases C-403/08 and C-429/08 *Football Association Premier League Ltd, NetMed Hellas SA, Multichoice Hellas SA v QC Leisure, David Richardson, AV Station plc, Malcolm Chamberlain, Michael Madden, SR Leisure Ltd, Philip George Charles Houghton, Derek Owen* and *Karen Murphy v Media Protection Services Ltd, cit.*

[63] Case C-145/10 *Eva-Maria Painer v Standard VerlagsGmbH, Axel Springer AG, Süddeutsche Zeitung GmbH, SPIEGEL-Verlag Rudolf AUGSTEIN GmbH & Co KG and Verlag M. DuMont Schauberg Expedition der Kölnischen Zeitung GmbH & Co KG, cit.*

The recent and much criticized 'Red Bus' decision stands as a demonstration of the difficulties and the associated need to provide protection in a consistent manner, whether it be through copyright, passing off, or (in a potential future) unfair competition. In addition, an identification of labour and skill within the meaning of originality provided in *Infopaq*, as was carried out by Judge Birss QC, demonstrates that the full implications of this string of decisions of the CJEU are yet to be worked out.

Additionally, the decision in *Lucasfilm* is relevant in that it shows that UK copyright architecture requires updating in order to be in line with EU law. Above all, a closed system of subject-matter categorization does not appear to be of much assistance when it comes to determining whether copyright subsists in a work, since this implies that ambiguously teleological interpretations need to be carried out.

6. The future of copyright at the EU level: The shape of harmonization

SECTION I

1. THE US DEBATE ON THE FUTURE OF COPYRIGHT

As far as the US debate is concerned, it is sufficient to recall the proposal launched by Pamela Samuelson, directed at a radical revision of the 1976 Copyright Act, which she has defined as 'akin to an obese Frankensteinian monster'.[1] Samuelson has argued that current US copyright law is too lengthy, complex and unbalanced in many respects, and that it lacks normative heft, since it is difficult to extract rationales of protection – and corresponding limitations – from the overly detailed provisions contained in the Act. Thus, she has suggested the idea of drafting a model law or principles project, as a platform from which to launch specific copyright reforms aimed at restoring a positive and more normatively appealing vision of copyright than exists today. In the view of Samuelson, a model copyright law must include the following core elements: subject-matter, eligibility criteria for specific people and works, exclusive rights, duration, limitations and/or exceptions to those exclusive rights, infringement standards and remedies.[2]

Criticisms of the current US copyright statute have also been raised more recently by Jessica Litman,[3] who has highlighted its flaws with respect to the core objectives of any copyright system, these being production, dissemination, and enjoyment of works of authorship. In particular, she has objected to the 1976 Act, as it is said to create high entry barriers for creators, impose problematic impediments on intermediaries, and inflict burdensome conditions and hurdles on users of copyright-protected materials. Litman believes that the 1976 Act is 'old,

---

[1] Pamela Samuelson, 'Preliminary thoughts on copyright reform' (2007) 3 ULR 551, 557.
[2] *Ibid*, 558ff.
[3] Jessica Litman, 'Real copyright reform' (2010) 96 IoLR 1.

outmoded, inflexible, and beginning to display the symptoms of multiple systems failure'.[4] Similarly, she sees Title 17 of the United States Code as a 'swollen, barnacle-encrusted collection of incomprehensible prose'.[5] As a consequence, US copyright law as a whole is found to be 'long, complex, counterintuitive and packed with traps and pitfalls',[6] some of which are aimed at tripping unwary new entrants, hapless authors, or pesky potential competitors. As a consequence, copyright legislation has been used as a means to erect market barriers to block nascent competition with respect to existing players. Litman has advocated, *inter alia*, a simplification of current copyright law, so that 'most creators will not need to consult a copyright lawyer before making and exploiting works of authorship, and most readers, listeners, and viewers will not need to consult a copyright lawyer before enjoying them'.[7] Moreover, she has suggested a radical rethinking of copyright's economic rights, on the basis that:

> The law now on the books divides copyright into reproduction, derivative work, public distribution, public performance, and public display rights, and encourages authors to dispose of them separately and piecemeal. In many copyright industries, it has become conventional for different copyright rights to be separately controlled by different intermediaries. As new opportunities to exploit works have arisen, those intermediaries have insisted that the new uses impinge on the rights they control instead of or as well as the rights controlled by other intermediaries. Meanwhile, the distinctions among different exclusive copyright rights have come to seem increasingly inapposite to a networked digital world.[8]

In her view, the proposed solution to copyright over-stratification may be a unitary commercial exploitation right. She has submitted that:

> If simplicity, legitimacy, and author- and reader-empowerment were [US copyright's] only goals, untempered by past practice, vested rights, and international obligations, [the US] could do worse than to recast copyright as a single exclusive right with carefully drawn boundaries. If [the US] chose to define a single core copyright right, the most promising candidate for that

---

[4]   *Ibid*, 3.

[5]   *Ibid*, referring to 17 USC Sections 110(2), dedicated to limitations on exclusive rights for certain acts concerning performance or display of a work, and 114, tackling the scope of exclusive rights in pictorial, graphic and sculptural works.

[6]   *Ibid*, 33.

[7]   *Ibid*, 40.

[8]   *Ibid*, 42 (footnotes omitted).

right … would be a right to control commercial exploitation. Limiting the scope of copyright to commercial exploitation would be simpler than the current array of five, six, seven, or eight distinct but overlapping rights. Copyright defined as control over commercial exploitation, moreover, would accord with what [the US] know of the public's understanding of what copyright law does, and should, reserve to the author. It would also preserve for readers, listeners, and viewers the liberty to enjoy works in non-exploitative ways without seeking licenses for each.[9]

1.1   The 2010 CPP

In 2007, the Copyright Principles Project (CPP) was formed. This twenty-member group was composed of leading US academics (including Samuelson and Litman), legal practitioners and industry executives (comprising companies such as Walt Disney, IBM and Warner Bros) alike. The formation of the CPP was the result 'of a collective sense among its members that although copyright law today works reasonably well in some domains, it can be improved and should be refined in light of dramatic technological advances'.[10] Given the growth of user-generated content and its copyright implications,[11] the widespread use of peer-to-peer file-sharing technologies to exchange copyright-protected materials, and technological advancements could not have been anticipated in the mid-1970s (when the current Copyright Act was adopted). As such,

> The goal of the CPP was to explore whether it was possible to reach some consensus about how current copyright law could be improved and how the law's current problems could be mitigated.

> Copyright law is, for many reasons, under considerable stress today. The most obvious and perhaps most significant source of this stress is the radical transformation of public access to information that has been brought about by changes in computing and communications technologies and accessibility of information through global digital networks. The Internet and World Wide Web, in particular, have destabilized many copyright industry sectors as the economics of creating, publishing, and disseminating information-rich works have dramatically changed. New business models have not always proven

---

[9]   *Ibid*, 43 (footnotes omitted).

[10]   Pamela Samuelson and Members of The CPP, 'The Copyright Principles Project: directions for reform' (2010) 25 Berkeley Tech LJ 1.

[11]   *Cf* Nobuko Kawashima, 'The rise of "user creativity" – Web 2.0 and a new challenge for copyright law and cultural policy', presentation at the annual congress of the Society for Economic Research on Copyright Issues (SERCI), Berkeley, 9–10 July 2009.

successful. It may take some time and patience to allow disrupted copyright sectors to consider, experiment with, and develop other or more refined models and approaches with which they will be reasonably comfortable.[12]

Although the CPP does not offer a comprehensive and detailed set of reform proposals to ameliorate US copyright, it articulates some principles of what is called a 'good' copyright law, in order to appreciate whether and to what extent current US copyright law conforms to such principles. The CPP therefore seeks to recommend changes to US copyright law, which would bring it into greater conformity with the principles set out therein.

Highlighting that discourse about copyright in the past fifteen years has been burdened by rhetorical excesses and an unwillingness of those with opposing viewpoints to engage in rational discourse,[13] the very existence of the CPP was meant to prove that it is indeed possible for persons from different backgrounds and with diverse perspectives and economic interests to engage in a thoughtful, civil, discourse concerning even the toughest and most controversial copyright issues.

Reaffirming the core objective of copyright, ie enhancing the creation and dissemination of new works, the CPP contains a series of principles aspiring to such an overarching aim. Further, the Project assesses various aspects of US copyright in light of this aim.

1.2 Originality and Fixation as Pre-requisites to Protection. Reinvigorating the Role of Formalities

With particular regard to the subject-matter of copyright, the CPP praises

> the simplicity and elegance of that part of U.S. copyright law that extends copyright protection to authors of newly created works of authorship that have been fixed in a tangible medium of expression. These works must be 'original' not only in the sense that they owe their origin to the person claiming to be the author, but also in the sense that they exhibit some creativity in the expression of whatever ideas or information the works embody.[14]

---

[12] Samuelson and Members of The CPP, *The Copyright Principles Project*, *cit*, 2.

[13] *Ibid*, 4.

[14] *Ibid*, 8 (emphasis added).

With this said, the CPP then considers the role of formalities[15] following an assessment of copyright duration.[16] In particular, it highlights how the current lack of obligations upon authors to give notice to the world about their claim to copyright – either by placing notices on individual copies of their works or by registering their claims of copyright with a government office – has contributed to substantial difficulties in tracking down who owns which rights in what works. These difficulties have been impeding many socially desirable uses, including some that would be licensed if it were easier to find the appropriate rightsholder.

The abolition of formalities occurred quite recently in the US. For two hundred years previously, US law had required authors to give public notice of their claims of copyright, register those claims and deposit copies of their works with a centralized government office. It was only in 1908, at the Berlin revision conference of the 1886 Berne Convention, that formalities were prohibited in international copyright law. Indeed, it was at that time that the following provision, which was then incorporated in Article 5(2) of the Berne Convention, was adopted:

> The enjoyment and the exercise of [the rights specially granted by the Berne Convention] shall not be subject to any formality …

When the US joined the Berne Convention in 1989, the US formalities had to be adapted, at least in so far as they affected the protection of foreign works. However, the US lawmaker chose to employ a minimalist approach.[17]

---

[15]   *Ibid*, 10–12.

[16]   *Ibid*, 9–10.

[17]   As recalled by Stef van Gompel, *Formalities in copyright law. An analysis of their history, rationales and possible future* (Kluwer Law International 2011), 97, although copyright notices as prerequisites for protection were abolished following access to Berne, the US awarded evidentiary weight to their use to preclude innocent intent defences in the mitigation of damages. The US legislator limited the requirement of registration as a prerequisite to infringement suits to works of US origin and eliminated the requirement to record assignments before instituting a copyright infringement action. As pointed out also recently, 'copyright registration, while not jurisdictional, is a substantive requirement of infringement litigation' (*per* Justice Kendall, *Peters v West and Others*, 7th Cir, 11-1708 (2012), I, citing *Reed-Elsevier v Muchnick*, 130 S Ct 1237, 1241 (2010)). The remainder of formalities (such as voluntary copyright notices and deposit, registration and recordation formalities) were unaltered: *cf* 17 USC Section 205, and Sections 401 to 412.

Even today, as pointed out by the CPP, the fact that many creators continue to employ some form of copyright notice despite its optional nature indicates that it is important for authors and owners to give practical signals to the world about their claims of ownership.

Therefore, the CPP suggests that registration, notice, and similar opt-in features to US copyright law should be reinvigorated. This would also help to make US law more compatible with good copyright principles, since deposit requirements are held to be consistent with the preservation of cultural heritage and with copyright's constitutional purpose to 'promote the progress of science'.

Other commentators[18] have also recently argued in favour of the reintroduction of some formalities. They have observed that while the public's exposure to copyright infringement was in the past limited, due to the short copyright term coupled with formalities and the supply chain restraints which arose in the hard-copy world (eg, the costs associated with production and distribution of works), nowadays contravention is facilitated by the increased duration of copyright protection, the absence of formalities and instant global distribution. It is argued that formalities are necessary to ensure copyright owners can protect their investment for a reasonable period of time and to make sure that the public does not inadvertently partake in copyright infringement.[19]

1.3 Difficulties in Assessing Infringement Cases: The Idea/Expression Dichotomy, Exceptions And Limitation, Safe Harbour Reform

After considering exclusive and moral rights (the latter are deemed to be worthy of wider protection),[20] the CPP highlights how the idea/expression dichotomy offers little help in assessing infringement cases.[21]

Although it is a basic principle that copyright protects the way in which authors express themselves in their works, but not the ideas, facts, or functional designs depicted therein, the concept of 'expression' has

---

[18]   William Patry, *How to fix copyright* (OUP 2011), 203 ff.

[19]   *Ibid*, 204. In a similar sense, also Takeshi Hishinuma, 'The scope of formalities in international copyright law in a digital context', in Lionel Bently, Uma Suthersanen and Paul Torremans (eds), *Global copyright. Three hundred years since the Statute of Anne, from 1709 to cyberspace* (Edward Elgar Publishing 2010), 460, who highlights (475) how global registration of copyrights would be beneficial not only to users but also other stakeholders such as creditors and insolvency administrators.

[20]   Samuelson and Members of The CPP, *The Copyright Principles Project*, *cit*, 12–14.

[21]   *Ibid*, 15–16.

expanded through strands of case law that may be deemed incoherent and somewhat confusing. US courts use several different tests for determining when a work is similar enough to a prior creation to constitute an infringement.

If we turn now to the fair use doctrine,[22] the CPP finds that this is generally consistent with good copyright principles,[23] although some fine-tuning of fair use might be warranted to ensure that courts recognize fair use as serving a broader array of policy purposes than those which are currently acknowledged. This is also because the existing set of exceptions and limitations to US copyright is deemed to be more a product of legislative compromise than that of a principled assessment of how far the law should extend to regulate certain uses of copyright-protected materials.

With particular regard to Section 512 of the Digital Millennium Copyright Act (DMCA)'s safe harbours, it is asserted that these are an important legal device, which can be used both to limit liability in an appropriate manner and to encourage service providers to help reduce widespread infringement.[24] The US Supreme Court created the first safe harbour in the *Sony Betamax* case, concerning the manufacturers of technologies having substantial non-infringing uses.[25] The Online Copyright Infringement Liability Limitation Act (OCILLA), as part of the DMCA, introduced four other safe harbours specifically concerning ISPs into US copyright law in 1998.[26] While holding that current safe harbours

---

[22]   *Ibid*, 16–17.

[23]   A view supporting the livelihood of fair use in US copyright, also in relation to specific works such as diagnostic tests, is presented in Eleonora Rosati and Carlo Maria Rosati, 'Copyright in diagnostic tests: not death time for fair use yet' (2012) 7 JIPLP 510.

[24]   Samuelson and Members of The CPP, *The Copyright Principles Project, cit*, 19.

[25]   *Sony Corp of Am v Universal City Studios, Inc*, 464 US 417 (1984), in which the US Supreme Court ruled that the making of individual copies of complete television shows for the purpose of time-shifting did not constitute copyright infringement and that the manufacturers of home video recording devices which have substantial non-infringing uses, such as Betamax, were not liable for infringement by third parties.

[26]   As recalled by Samuelson and Members of The CPP, *The Copyright Principles Project, cit*, 20, these safe harbours allow ISPs: (1) to transmit digital content from one user to another free from concern about whether the transmitted material is or is not infringing; (2) to store digital content on behalf of customers; (3) to cache digital content to make it more accessible to customers; and (4) to facilitate users' queries to locate information of interest to them. The

are generally consistent with good copyright principles, the CPP advocates that US Congress considers creating a new safe harbour aimed at
insulating firms which undertake reasonable measures to prevent copyright infringement from copyright liability. In any case, no duty should be
imposed on technology developers or service providers to adopt such
measures.[27] In support of this argument, the CPP shows awareness that
since the enactment of the DMCA, technological progress has proceeded
speedily. This means that filtering tools capable of assessing how much
of copyright-protected material is contained in a given online file are now
possible.[28]

---

latter three safe harbours are subject to 'notice and take down' rules, which
provide that upon receiving notice from a copyright owner that specific infringing materials exist on the ISP's site, or that a search engine is linking to
infringing materials, the ISP or search engine has an obligation, to remove the
infringing materials or not link to them. These safe harbours are also contingent
on ISPs having rules to prevent abuse by restricting access to the internet by
repeat infringers.

[27] *Ibid*, 20.

[28] For instance, in summer 2011 a voluntary 'Memorandum of Understanding' was achieved between a large number of the major US ISPs and music and
film industries to introduce a new system of 'copyright alerts'. These are
warnings which, with escalating urgency, aim to nudge broadband users from
piracy downloading and streaming music from legitimate sources. The idea is to
overcome some of the major arguments against disconnecting accounts which are
being used for piracy, ie that often the person who pays the internet bill is not
aware that illegal activity is occurring or that the accused infringer is unaware of
the applicable copyright laws. On this agreement, *see* Ben Challis, 'US content
industry and ISPs to inform and alert' (The 1709 Blog, 8 July 2011) <http://
tinyurl.com/bd852pj> accessed 14 June 2013, Paul McGuinness, 'Digital downloads: the "age of free" is coming to an end' (*The Telegraph*, 8 July 2011)
<http://tinyurl.com/3lw5tmy> accessed 14 June 2013, Eleonora Rosati, 'ISPs' six
strikes enforcement plan in force next July' (The 1709 Blog, 15 March 2012)
<http://tinyurl.com/axkr82g> accessed 14 June 2013, Eleonora Rosati, 'ISPs' six
strikes enforcement plan delayed' (The 1709 Blog, 20 May 2012) <http://
tinyurl.com/axkr82g> accessed 14 June 2013, Iona Harding, 'Verizon, six strikes
and piracy' (The 1709 Blog, 11 January 2013) <http://tinyurl.com/b8eoksa>
accessed 14 June 2013, and Ben Challis, 'Six strikes launches in the US' (The
1709 Blog, 26 February 2013) <http://tinyurl.com/cvv3ra9> accessed 14 June
2013.

1.4 CPP's Proposals. Reforming Section 102(b) of the Copyright Act but Neglecting Originality

Following the assessment of the current copyright scenario, the CPP sets forth twenty-five proposals to reform and improve US copyright. Among them, and in addition to the issues highlighted above, CPP's Proposal No 16 is worthy of attention, insofar as it concerns the present contribution.

The proposal reads as follows:

> More elements in copyrighted works than just ideas and information should be excluded from the scope of copyright's protection for original works of authorship.

To achieve this, the CPP does not suggest raising the bar to copyright protection by making the originality requirement more stringent. Instead, it advocates a rewriting of Section 102(b) of the 1976 Copyright Act on copyright-protected subject-matter. The provision, currently provides that copyright protection '[i]n no case … extend[s] to any idea, procedure, process, system, method of operation, concept, principle, or discovery, regardless of the form in which it is described, explained, illustrated, or embodied in such work.' The CPP deems it to a be a partial embodiment of good copyright principles, insofar as it characterizes ideas, concepts, and principles, along with procedures, processes, and methods of operation, as unprotectable elements of copyright-protected works. However, it should be amended so as to reflect the many elements of works that copyright law does not, and indeed should not, protect.

It is suggested by the CPP that a revised version of Section 102(b) should read as follows:

> Copyright protection extends to an author's expression, but not to any (a) ideas, concepts, or principles; (b) facts, data, know-how, or knowledge; (c) stock elements typical in works of that kind; (d) laws, regulations, or rules; (e) systems, processes, procedures, methods of operation, or functions, regardless of how any of these elements may be embodied in protected works. Nor is copyright protection available to a work or an element of a work if there is only one or a very small number of ways to express that idea or other unprotectable element. Elements identified in (a) through (d) should be regarded as in the public domain and available for free copying and reuse when the work has been made available to the public such that it cannot be claimed as a trade secret. The elements identified in (e) may also be in the

public domain after publication of a work in which they are explained or embodied unless protected by a utility patent.[29]

In this proposed revised formulation of Section 102(b), there is no mention of the requirement for a work to be original in order for it to be protected by copyright. Certainly, the originality requirement cannot be identified with protection being excluded from works or an element of a work where 'there is only one or a very small number of ways to express that idea or other unprotectable element'.

In other words, there is something missing in the CPP's proposed amendment of Section 102. As acknowledged by the CPP elsewhere in its set of proposals, the policy role that originality plays, as discussed above *sub* Chapter 2, cannot be neglected. Indeed, it may be argued that an even more suitable revision to the wording of Section 102(b) should include the following additional clarification:

> A work is original not only if it owes its origin to the person claiming to be the author, but also in the sense that it exhibits some creativity in the expression of whatever ideas or information the work embodies.[30]

1.5   The Next Great Copyright Act

In March 2013 US Register of Copyrights Maria Pallante delivered a lecture at Columbia Law School entitled 'The next great copyright act',[31] in which she called for reform of US copyright, with particular regard to – among other things – licensing, 17 USC Section 109's first sale doctrine (including the introduction of a digital first sale), exception and limitations, enforcement (including the revision of the DMCA safe harbour provisions), orphan works and the role of formalities.

On 24 April 2013 US House Judiciary Committee Chairman Bob Goodlatte announced that the Judiciary Committee would conduct a comprehensive review of US copyright law over the course of 2013.[32]

---

[29]   Samuelson and Members of The CPP, *The Copyright Principles Project, cit*, 52.

[30]   This definition of originality is indeed provided by the CPP at 8.

[31]   Maria Pallante, 'The next great copyright act' (2013) 36(3) Colum JL & Arts 315.

[32]   *See* <http://tinyurl.com/d5fwzp3> accessed 14 June 2013.

2. HOW TO REFORM COPYRIGHT: A VIEW FROM THE EU[33]

The protection of intellectual property rights has also been at the centre of attention in the EU context in recent years, as laid out above, especially *sub* Chapter 1. In particular, interest in copyright has grown through an increased emphasis on its fundamental role as a legal tool to protect and enhance creativity. Additionally, the importance of copyright for realizing the goal of internal market integration has only gained prominence relatively recently, although this has been a fundamental objective since the signing of the Treaty of Rome in 1957.

Having a strong harmonization law is said to enhance legal security and transparency, as well as reduce transaction costs. If construed as taking precedence over national titles, an EU copyright would remove the inherent territoriality that comes with state-made copyright rules, thus contributing to the full integration of the internal market. As pointed out by Viviane Reding, former EU Commissioner for information society and media and current Commission's Vice-President, it would be a means to enhance the IT skills and expertise of European businesses and societies.[34] Also William Hague, appointed Foreign Secretary and First Secretary of State by UK Prime Minister David Cameron, used unusually positive language about the European Union with respect to copyright. Although the UK conservative party has traditionally adopted rather sceptical views on the advantages of European integration, in an article published in *Europe's World*, Hague linked the growth of the European economy to further integration of the internal market, highlighting in particular the role that innovation and copyright play in such a process.[35]

---

[33]   Some parts of this paragraph represent an extended and updated version of the following contribution: Eleonora Rosati, 'The Wittem Group and the Project of a European Copyright Code' (2010) 5(12) JIPLP 862–868.

[34]   *Cf* the speeches given at IDATE Conference (Montpellier, 21 November 2005) and at Visby Agenda: Creating an Impact for an eUnion 2015 (Visby, 9 and 10 November 2009).

[35]   'With the rise of new economic powers in many industries, Europe has already lost its cost advantage. If we also lose our knowledge advantage our future could be very bleak … EU's internal market needs to evolve further … [I]nnovation is almost universally understood to be crucial to our economic future, but our economies are being held back by fragmented licensing and copyright regimes.' (William Hague, 'How the UK's New Tory-led Government sees its EU Policy' (17 May 2010) Europe's World).

Despite the positive remarks about harmonization in theory, thus far the unitary protection of copyright across the EU is viewed as being less viable than for trademarks and patents. As pointed out by Trevor Cook,[36] this is because copyright and related rights subsist automatically in all EU Member States, independent of registration and by virtue of the membership of such States to various international conventions. The result is that there exists no mechanism for choosing whether to seek protection on an EU-wide rather than, or in addition to, a national basis.

2.1 The Wittem Group and the Project of a European Copyright Code

As previously mentioned, the issue of further harmonization of the copyright laws of the Member States has also received attention in academic circles. In 2002, leading copyright scholars from across Europe assembled in the so-called Wittem Group and launched a Project aimed at drafting and proposing a European Copyright Code.

On 26 April 2010, the long-awaited European Copyright Code was published.

Insofar as the drafting procedure was concerned, each chapter was drawn up by one or two members of the Drafting Committee, acting as rapporteurs. The draft chapters were then discussed in plenary with the members of the Wittem Advisory Board and other experts invited ad hoc. As a last step, the Code was finalized by a Drafting Committee. As also recently recalled by Bernt Hugenholtz, the Code took account of the relevant legislative framework, both internationally (the Berne Convention and the TRIPS Agreement) and regionally. As regards the latter, although the members of the Group found it difficult to depart from the *acquis communautaire*, the Code does on occasion deviate from the *acquis*.[37]

Certainly, what can be said for the Wittem Group Project and the resulting code is that the goals it aimed at realizing were both numerous and ambitious.

---

[36] Trevor Cook, *EU intellectual property law* (OUP 2010), 69.

[37] P Bernt Hugenholtz, 'The Wittem Group's European Copyright Code', in Tatiana-Eleni Synodinou (ed), *Codification of European copyright law* (Kluwer Law International 2012), 339, 342.

2.2   The Objectives of the Project

The Preamble to the Code recognizes the importance of copyright in the process of market-building at the European level. It states that:

> [T]he establishment of a fully functioning market for copyright protected works in the European Union, as necessitated in particular by the Internet as the primary means of providing information and entertainment services across the Member States, requires common rules on copyright in the EU that reflect and integrate both civil and common law traditions of copyright and authors' right respectively.[38]

The Wittem Project was clearly aimed at promoting transparency and consistency in European copyright law.[39] This was because the members of the Group shared a serious concern, ie that 'the process of copyright lawmaking at the European level lacks transparency and that the voice of academia all too often remains unheard'.[40] Indeed, numerous legislative choices endorsed by EC Directives have been criticized by both legal academics and economists as either being contrary to the rationale of copyright protection, or for departing from the criteria of economic efficiency. However, it would seem that EU legislators have never attempted to address such criticisms nor provide solutions that could resolve them. Therefore, doubts may arise as to the effective impact that this European Copyright Code will ever have on the future of EU copyright policy, despite the belief that a code 'drafted by legal scholars might serve as a model or reference tool for future harmonization or unification of copyright at the European level'.[41]

This observation, as discussed below, is not the only one which questions the actual importance and influence this Code will have on copyright lawmaking at the European level.

2.3   Congenital Weaknesses ...

The European Copyright Code is drafted in the form of a legislative instrument, thus exceeding the level of detail normally associated with the drafting of simple common principles of law. So, from this point of

---

[38] Wittem Group, *European Copyright Code*, 26 April 2010, available at copyrightcode.eu, *Preamble*, 7.
[39] *Ibid, Introduction*, 5.
[40] *Ibid.*
[41] *Ibid.*

view, the Project is valuable, as it may serve as a framework for an actual codification of copyright at the EU level. However, the Code is far from being complete. This is due to a variety of reasons, although two criticisms in particular are worth highlighting.

The first criticism concerns what can be defined as the 'original sin' of the Code itself, which diminishes the overall value such a project could have had. From reading the legal solutions provided by the Code, one has the impression that there is a gap between the Project's ambitious objectives and the actual positions ensued therein, which are somewhat weakly endorsed. The most serious example of this dichotomy can be found in the Introduction. After having pointed out that the aim of the Wittem Project and the Code is to promote transparency and consistency in European copyright law, it is clarified that the members of the Wittem Group shared a concern that the process of copyright lawmaking at the European level lacks transparency and that the voice of academia often remains unheard. Thereof, the belief that a copyright code drafted by academics might serve as a reference tool for future legislative action. So far, so good. However, directly after laying out these beliefs and objectives, the following disclaimer is expressed: '[T]he Group does not take a position on the desirability as such of introducing a unified European legal framework'.[42]

It is arguable that such an attitude diminishes the importance and the political value of this work, as the current problem is really whether or not the process of harmonization of the copyright laws of the Member States should go further and realize the objective of the unification of European copyright laws. Providing an answer to such a question would really have made the Wittem Project invaluable, as having a definitive position of leading European academics in this respect would not only have given the entire project a stronger impact, but would also certainly have made it more capable of influencing and orientating European lawmaking in the field of copyright.

Moving to a closely related second criticism of the Wittem Project, the structure of the Code itself is not as comprehensive as one might have hoped. In fact, attention is paid only to the main elements of copyright. The Code is composed of five chapters, respectively dedicated to the subject-matter of copyright (Chapter 1), authorship and ownership (Chapter 2), moral rights (Chapter 3), economic rights (Chapter 4), and limitations (Chapter 5). It may well be interesting to compare the structure of the European Copyright Code with the model copyright law

[42]   *Ibid.*

proposed by Pamela Samuelson,[43] as she considered the elements included in her proposal to be core components which cannot be omitted from any model copyright law. As mentioned above *sub* Section I, §I, these elements are: subject-matter, eligibility criteria for specific people and works, exclusive rights, duration, limitations and/or exceptions to those exclusive rights, infringement standards and remedies. Indeed, it seems that topical and highly controversial issues have been left outwith the Code. In particular, it does not provide an answer to either the problem of the legal protection of technical measures, or to the issue of copyright liability or enforcement.[44] Relating to this point, it is worth recalling that the Enforcement Directive was prompted not only by the awareness of the importance of providing effective enforcement to intellectual property rights,[45] but also by the fact that

> the disparities between the systems of the Member States as regards the means of enforcing intellectual property rights are prejudicial to the proper functioning of the Internal Market and make it impossible to ensure that intellectual property rights enjoy an equivalent level of protection throughout the Community.[46]

The exclusion from the Project of such relevant themes is even more problematic if one takes into account the duties imposed, at an international level, by the WIPO Internet Treaties,[47] as well as the criticisms which have been raised with regard to the implementation of their provisions into domestic laws.[48] Therefore, it is difficult to understand the reasons for *not* including such important market integration issues in the Code. This gap is especially puzzling in light of the Preamble of the Code itself, which expressly links the need for common rules on copyright in the EU to the project of market-building, 'as necessitated in particular by the Internet as the primary means of providing information

---

[43]   Samuelson, 'Preliminary thoughts', *cit.*

[44]   As clarified in Wittem Group, *European Copyright Code*, *cit*, *Introduction*, 6, other issues have been left untreated, such as public lending right, *droit de suite*, neighbouring rights and database right.

[45]   Enforcement Directive, Recital 3.

[46]   *Ibid*, Recital 8.

[47]   *Cf* Article 11 WIPO Copyright Treaty and Article 19 WIPO Performances and Phonograms Treaty.

[48]   *Cf* Jerome H Reichman, Graeme B Dinwoodie and Pamela Samuelson, 'A reverse notice and takedown regime to enable public interest uses of technically protected copyrighted works', in Alain Strowel (ed), *Peer-to-Peer file sharing and secondary liability in copyright law* (Edward Elgar Publishing 2009), 229.

and entertainment services across the Members States'.[49] It goes without saying that providing for the sound regulation of the means through which access and enjoyment of protected works may be granted is a matter of fundamental importance. This should go alongside a clarification of the conditions under which direct and, moreover, indirect, liability for copyright infringement arise. Thus far, no satisfactory legal framework has been provided. Furthermore, the coupled issues of legal protection of technical measures and secondary liability call for a rethinking of the very basics of copyright, such as the territoriality principle. Including provisions on these two issues within the Code would perhaps have provided some clarification of the meaning and scope of the territoriality principle, which is at the core of the copyright unification project at the European level, but which, paradoxically, has not yet been fully explored.[50]

Finally, it is worth mentioning that the Code does not provide a precise duration for economic rights.[51] This is because '[i]t was generally felt by the members of the Group that the current term of protection of the economic rights is too long. However views diverged as to the appropriate term'.[52] There is no need to recall that the term of copyright protection has been of topical interest in recent years, and has attracted a series of criticisms.[53] Such criticisms have been revamped recently in the context of the EU discussion on extending the term of protection for sound recordings, which eventually led to the adoption of Directive 2011/77/EU. As previously mentioned, this has extended the term of protection over sound recordings from fifty to seventy years, despite widespread concerns in the form of academic critiques,[54] policy recommendations and the Hargreaves Report

---

[49]   *Cf* van Eechoud, Hugenholtz, Gompel, Guibault and Helberger, *Harmonizing European copyright law, cit*, 308.

[50]   *Cf* Mireille van Eechoud, P Bernt Hugenholtz, Stef van Gompel, Lucie Guibault and Natali Helberger, *Harmonizing European copyright law. The challenges of better law making* (Kluwer Law International 2009), 308.

[51]   *See* Wittem Group, *European Copyright Code*, Article 4.1(2).

[52]   Note 40 to Wittem Group, *European Copyright Code, cit*, Article 4.1(2).

[53]   *See, ex multis*, Silke von Lewinski, 'EC Proposal for Council Directive Harmonizing the Term of Protection of Copyright' (1992) 23 IIC 785.

[54]   *See, inter alia*, the criticisms raised by Natali Helberger, Nicole Dufft, Stef van Gompel and P Bernt Hugenholtz, 'Never forever: why extending the term of protection for sound recordings is a bad idea' (2008) EIPR 174 and Christophe Geiger, 'The extension of the term of copyright and certain neighbouring rights – a never-ending story?' (2009) IIC 78. *See* also the Joint Academic Statement by the Centre for Intellectual Property Policy and Management (CIPPM, Bournemouth University) – Centre for Intellectual Property and

in the UK,[55] which all questioned the desirability of such an extension. The latter in particular highlighted the influence of lobbying on copyright reforms, finding that much of the data needed to develop empirical evidence on copyright is privately held and enters the public domain chiefly in the form of evidence supporting the arguments of lobbyists, rather than as independently verified research conclusions. Hargreaves called such *état de*

Information Law (CIPIL, Cambridge University) – Institute for Information Law (IViR, University of Amsterdam) – Max Planck Institute for Intellectual Property, Competition and Tax Law (Munich), *The proposed directive for a copyright term extension – A backward-looking package* (2008), 3, which argued that the then proposed Sound Recordings Term Extension Directive should not be aimed at performers, but rather at record companies. This is because performers on existing recordings have assigned their rights to record companies, and the proposal applies the terms of such agreements to the proposed extension of term. So, the chief beneficiaries of extension were said to be the owners of large back-catalogues of rights, going back more than fifty years. Moreover, says the joint academic statement, if the Commission's proposal had been truly aimed at performers, it would have linked the term to the performer's life (or a close proxy) and it would have not granted the extended term to the producers of sound recordings. These arguments are shared by Benjamin Farrand, 'Too much is never enough? The 2011 Copyright in Sound Recordings Extension Directive' (2012) 34 EIPR 297, who highlights how the main beneficiaries of the increased duration of protection are not the artists but their publishers. This is because a vast share of the additional revenue gained thanks to the increased term of protection would go directly to record labels which, however, may not be likely to use it to invest in new musicians or works. *See* also above, *sub* Chapter 1, Section II.

[55]   Ian Hargreaves, *Digital opportunity. A review of intellectual property and growth* (2011) <http://tinyurl.com/6bxcerw> accessed 14 June 2013. In November 2010 UK Prime Minister David Cameron asked Prof Hargreaves of Cardiff University to prepare a review of current intellectual property framework, with a special focus on how this could be designed to promote innovation and growth in the UK economy. One of the reasons behind the commissioning of the review was the fact that the founders of Google said that they could have never started their company in the UK, because the UK copyright system was not perceived as being as welcoming of their sort of innovation as in the US (David Cameron, November 2010, announcing the review of IP and growth). The review therefore contains a series of recommendations to improve the quality of UK copyright law and make it fit for the digital age. However, it may be questioned whether most of Prof Hargreaves's recommendations can actually be implemented successfully in the UK alone, ie in the absence of related legislative reforms at the EU level. The author of the present work has argued that this can be hardly the case in relation to copyright licensing (this being rather at the centre of the review): *see* Eleonora Rosati, 'The Hargreaves Report and copyright licensing: can national initiatives work *per se*?' (2011) 33 EIPR 673.

fait 'lobbynomics'.[56] This phenomenon is said to have played a consistent role in extending copyright duration, the most recent example being the UK decision to support the EU process to extend the rights of owners of sound recordings from fifty to seventy years,[57] despite contrary recommendations such as those contained in the 2006 Gowers Review.[58]

In light of the foregoing, it is apparent that the debate over the ideal duration of copyright is far from settled. Hence, a contribution from leading academics in this respect would have been useful and would have indeed strengthened the value of the Code.

2.4 ... But a Sensible Approach

Despite the criticisms raised above, the Code is the product of sound drafting techniques and the provisions contained therein do achieve a fair balance between common and civil law approaches to copyright. This was not an easy task, as

> Any endeavour to meld civilian and common law approaches to copyright may inevitably dissatisfy all sides at least sometimes ... [T]he drafters therefore deserve applause for persevering in an attempt some might consider quixotic and others (from both ends of property rights/users' rights spectrum) might view with some suspicion.[59]

As highlighted, the Code pays due regard to the legacy of the legislative choices of the Directives which have, to date, harmonized specific aspects of copyright. As mentioned above, many of the provisions of those Directives have been subject to criticism, standing accused of providing legal solutions which were (and are) unable to maintain a proper balance between the protection of the interests of authors and

---

[56] Hargreaves, *Digital Opportunity, cit*, 18.
[57] *Ibid*, 93–94.
[58] Andrew Gowers, *Gowers review of intellectual property*, December 2006, <http://tinyurl.com/af3gyqc> accessed 14 June 2013, 56, 52: 'Evidence suggests that most sound recordings sell in the ten years after release, and only a very small percentage continue to generate income, both from sales and royalty payments, for the entire duration of copyright ... In a system where all works receive protection for the maximum term, the vast majority of works remain in copyright despite not being economically viable for the rights holder ... Therefore, extension would only raise revenue for a small minority of sound recordings, keeping the vast majority locked up.'
[59] Jane C Ginsburg, 'European Copyright Code – Back to first principles (with some additional details)' (2011) *Columbia Public Law Research Paper No 11-261*, 3.

owners, and the interests of the public at large to access, build upon, and use copyright-protected works. This fundamental objective of copyright protection, which finds its roots historically in the first legal instruments regulating copyright (such as the 1709 Statute of Anne and the Copyright Clause of the US Constitution), is strongly reaffirmed in the European Copyright Code. Indeed, and notwithstanding the final outcomes achieved by EU Directives, the legal solutions of the Code have been reformulated in this well-balanced legal framework, which manages to reconcile authors' rights with the public interest.

2.5 Integrating Copyright and *droit d'auteur* Traditions

Coming to specific topics, it is of particular relevance to analyze issues which, so far, have been left outside the *acquis communautaire*. The originality requirement, in particular, has been subject to only limited harmonization with regard to specific categories of works (computer programs, photographs and databases), with full harmonization being deemed unnecessary, since differences in the meaning of originality across Member States do not impair the proper functioning of the internal market. The same conclusion has been reached with regard to differences in the scope and duration of moral rights. We will now consider these issues in turn.

It is interesting to note that, as far as originality is concerned, the meaning given by directives which dealt expressly with the issue of originality and adopted its continental meaning (an 'authorial standard', in the words of Jane Ginsburg[60]), have been endorsed by the Code. In fact, despite the fact that the Code does not use or define the term 'original', Article 1.1(1) expressly states that 'Copyright subsists in a work, that is to say, any expression within the field of literature, art or science in so far as it constitutes its author's own intellectual creation'. It is also pointed out that this

> can be interpreted as the 'average' European threshold, presuming it is set somewhat higher than skill and labour. This is possible if emphasis is put on the element of creation. For factual and functional works, the focus will be more on a certain level of skill (judgment) and labour, whereas for productions in the artistic field the focus will be more on personal expression.[61]

In any case, as clarified by Bernt Hugenholtz,

---

[60] *Ibid*, 5.
[61] Wittem Group, *European Copyright Code, cit*, note 7 to Article 1.1(1).

the Code does not rule out works based (largely) on expended skill and labour. In this respect, the Wittem Code appears to be less rigorous than the originality standard recently established by the [CJEU]. In *Football Dataco Ltd [and Others] v. Yahoo! UK Ltd [and Others]* the Court held that the 'author's own intellectual creation' standard rules out copyright protection merely based on expended skill and labour.[62]

Contrary to the InfoSoc Directive[63] and the subsequent Commission review of the *acquis communautaire*,[64] the Code sets forth a specific and interesting regulation of moral rights. In particular, in contrast to dualistic *droit d'auteur* regimes,[65] the Code provides for their duration to be limited in time. Indeed, not only are moral rights to last for a limited number of years, but the Code provides that their duration should differ depending on which right is at stake. So, for example, the right of divulgation is said to last for the life of the author,[66] while the rights of attribution and integrity are said to last 'for the life of the author and until

---

[62] Hugenholtz, 'The Wittem Group's European Copyright Code', in Synodinou (ed), *Codification of European copyright law*, *cit*, 344 (footnotes omitted).

[63] Recital 19 to the directive states that '[t]he moral rights of rightholders should be exercised according to the legislation of the Member States and the provisions of the Berne Convention for the Protection of Literary and Artistic Works, of the WIPO Copyright Treaty and of the WIPO Performances and Phonograms Treaty. Such moral rights remain outside the scope of this Directive'.

[64] Commission Staff Working Paper on the review of the EC legal framework in the field of copyright and related rights, 19 July 2004, SEC (2004), §3.5.

[65] In monistic regimes moral rights exist alongside economic rights and expire at the same time: *see*, for instance, Article 60 Austrian Copyright Law (Bundesgesetz über das Urheberrecht an Werken der Literatur und der Kunst und über verwandte Schutzrechte (Urheberrechtsgesetz) (zuletzt geändert durch das Bundesgesetz BGBl I No 58/2010) and Article 64 German Copyright Law (Urheberrechsgestetz, UrhG 1965 as last amended on 8 May 1998). In dualistic systems, moral and economic rights are subject to different regimes and may be perpetual: *see*, for instance, Article L121-1, paragraph 3, French Intellectual Property Code (Code de la Propriété Intellectuelle) and Article 23 Italian Copyright Act (Legge 22 April 1941, No 633). For an analysis of the disparities in the legislation and case law of EU Member States concerning the protection of moral rights, *see* Marjut Salokannel and Alain Strowel, 'Study contract concerning moral rights in the context of the exploitation of works through digital technology' (2000), final report, <http://tinyurl.com/2fqbd8> accessed 14 June 2013.

[66] Wittem Group, *European Copyright Code*, *cit*, Article 3.2(2).

... years after his death'.[67] This is because '[i]t was generally felt by the members of the group that not all the moral rights merit the same term of protection, and that the right of divulgation might expire following the death of the author, whereas other moral rights could remain protected for a certain period post mortem'.[68] This approach to moral rights departs greatly from dualistic *droit d'auteur* traditions and, if adopted in the future by EU legislation, may be likely to face criticism and resistance. In fact, unlike concepts whose meanings have always been fairly vague (such as the originality requirement itself), moral rights have traditionally been considered as the true foundations of any copyright structure realized in a dualistic *droit d'auteur* fashion. In other words, moral rights in continental countries have never (or have very seldom) been subject to discussion or criticism, thus greatly differing from copyright debates in Anglo-Saxon environments.[69]

2.6   Copyright Limitations: An Inspiration for Reform

With regard to copyright limitations (Chapter 5), the European Copyright Code sets forth its own provisions. These achieve a sensible balance between a US style open-ended system of limitations and a civil law style exhaustive enumeration. In fact, copyright limitations are divided into several categories, according to which interest is given primacy over normal copyright protection. However, it is made clear that:

> [T]he categories do not ... prejudice as to the questions, what interests do, or should, in a particular case or even in general, underlie the limitation. In practice, this might be a mixture of several of the interests indicated. The weakness in a particular case of the interest which the applicable limitation has been categorized does not prejudice as to the (non-)applicability of the limitation. However, the concrete examples enumerated under those categories do have a normative effect, since art. 5.5 extends the scope of the specifically enumerated limitations by permitting other uses that are similar to any of the uses enumerated, subject to the operation of the three-step test.[70]

---

[67]   *Ibid*, Article 3.3., paragraph 2 (right of attribution) and Article 3.4, paragraph 2 (right of integrity).

[68]   *Ibid*, note 22 to Article 3.2, paragraph 2.

[69]   *See*, for instance, Roberta Rosenthal Kwall, 'Originality in context' (2007) Hous LR 871, who argues for the granting of moral rights only to works displaying a significant amount of originality intended as substantial creativity. For a criticism of this view, *see* Joseph Scott Miller, 'Hoisting originality' (2009) Cardozo L Rev 459.

[70]   Wittem Group, *European Copyright Code*, *cit*, note 48 to Article 5.1.

Thus, the Code contains an open clause: Article 5.5 extends the scope of the limitations listed in specific provisions, by allowing other uses which are comparable to any of the uses enumerated. It stipulates that:

> [P]rovided that the corresponding requirements of the relevant limitation are met and the use does not conflict with the normal exploitation of the work and does not unreasonably prejudice the legitimate interests of the author or rightholder, taking account of the legitimate interests of third parties.

As observed by Jonathan Griffiths,[71] this proposed provision seems to be directed at national legislators, permitting the creation of new exceptions where these would: (i) be compatible with existing statutory exceptions; and (ii) comply with a redrafted, less restrictive version of the Berne three-step test.[72] Moreover, if such a provision was to be adopted, the added flexibility which it bestows might allow for a rapid and proportionate response to be provided in case of altered circumstances.

As far as UK copyright is concerned, it is worth highlighting that the set of limitations introduced by the Code is in line with the recommendations contained in the 2006 Gowers Review of Intellectual Property. The Gowers Review expressed the concern that the UK system of exceptions was too narrow and that this might have stunted new creators from producing work and generating new value.[73] UK copyright law provides for a limited set of exceptions, meaning that it is only disapplied in specific situations provided for in legislation. To address this, the Gowers Review suggested the introduction of new exceptions in order to bring the UK system up to date and make it more flexible.

However, despite the opportunity provided by the passage of the Digital Economy Act in 2010 (as recently upheld by the Court of Appeal

---

[71] Jonathan Griffiths, 'Unsticking the centre-piece – The liberation of European copyright law?' (2010) 1 JIPITEC 87, 89–90.

[72] The three-step test was first adopted by Article 9(2) of the Berne Convention in relation to the right of reproduction ('It shall be a matter for legislation in the countries of the Union to permit the reproduction of such works in certain special cases, provided that such reproduction does not conflict with a normal exploitation of the work and does not unreasonably prejudice the legitimate interests of the author.') and then – *inter alia* – by Article 26(2) TRIPS ('Members may provide limited exceptions to the protection of industrial designs, provided that such exceptions do not unreasonably conflict with the normal exploitation of protected industrial designs and do not unreasonably prejudice the legitimate interests of the owner of the protected design, taking account of the legitimate interests of third parties.') and Article 5(5) of the InfoSoc Directive.

[73] Gowers, *Gowers Review*, *cit*, 61 ff.

of England and Wales),[74] the British Parliament has addressed neither the
concerns of the Gowers Review, nor the problems that can arise (or have
already arisen) with respect to the competitiveness of UK copyright
internationally. At the end of 2012, however, HM Government announced
its intention to introduce new exceptions into UK copyright[75] and in June
2013 the UK Intellectual Property Office published its technical review
of draft legislation on new copyright exceptions for private copying,
parody, quotation, and amendments to exception for public administration.[76]

As mentioned, the European Copyright Code seems to have, in
contrast, welcomed the analysis carried out by the Gowers Review.
Indeed, it sets forth a system of exceptions which is in line with the
recommendations contained therein. For instance, Article 5.1 expressly
allows the making of a back-up copy of a work by a person having a
right to use it and insofar as it is necessary for that use;[77] Article 5.2
creates an exception for the purpose of caricature, parody or pastiche;[78]
Article 5.3 expressly allows use for the purpose of non-commercial
archiving by publicly accessible libraries, educational establishments or
museums, and archives.[79]

In light of the foregoing, the set of exceptions provided by the Code is
worthy of praise. In fact, the final result is not only a balanced
compromise between open-ended and exhaustive systems of copyright
limitations, but can actually serve as a valuable model for reforming the
CDPA 1988 in compliance with the recommendations contained in the
Gowers Review.

Thus, it can be seen that despite its flaws, the Code has indeed some
positive features that are worthy of praise. In particular, from a thorough
reading of the provisions, one gets the impression that the drafters have
actually managed to combine common and civil copyright traditions in a
fair way. Furthermore, the traditional view of copyright as a mechanism

---

[74] *The Queen on the application of British Telecommunication Plc and
TalkTalk Telecom Group Plc v Secretary of State for Culture, Olympics, Media
and Sports and Others* [2012] EWCA Civ 232.

[75] HM Government, *Modernising copyright: A modern, robust and flexible
framework. Government response to consultation on copyright exceptions and
clarifying copyright law* (2012) http://tinyurl.com/mgy4y5f accessed 14 June
2013.

[76] See http://tinyurl.com/kal2ld9 (accessed 14 June 2013).

[77] *Cf* Gowers, *Gowers Review*, *cit*, Recommendations 8 and 9.

[78] *Ibid*, Recommendation 12.

[79] *Ibid*, Recommendations 10a and 10b.

for balancing authors' and the public's rights is respected within the general architecture of the Code. Indeed, the choices made in relation to issues such as the originality requirement and moral rights are certainly to be applauded. Above all, the meaning given to the originality requirement has the potential to create an effective boundary to the currently over-extended scope of copyright protection. Furthermore, the Code serves as a model for reform of domestic copyright laws, particularly with respect to the legal regulation of limitations to copyright.

In light of the foregoing, the Code can be a staging post in the debate which focuses, on the one hand, on the need to balance authors' and the public's rights and, on the other, to integrate common and civil law traditions. Paradoxically, this need has often been left to one side in EU lawmaking. Beyond being a simple legislative instrument, the Code is moreover noteworthy for being the first document of its kind at European level to provide for such a balance. It can be hoped that, as such, it might well furnish fresh motivation to bring together debates in this respect.

SECTION II

1. EU COPYRIGHT HARMONIZATION: HOW?

As seen above *sub* Chapter 1, EU intervention in the field of copyright has gone through different phases and has been characterized by different intensities. However, over the past couple of years, it could well be said that discourse around full harmonization has been revived in both political and academic circles. In particular, not only is the desirability of such unification now openly discussed, but debates on how this is to be best achieved are also at the centre of attention.

After the entry into force of the Lisbon Reform Treaty, there may be finally both the political will and legal instruments to achieve the full harmonization of the copyright laws of the Member States. As already mentioned, new Article 118(1) TFEU could provide the legal basis for the full harmonization of the copyright laws of the Member States. This provision stipulates that:

> In the context of the establishment and functioning of the internal market, the European Parliament and the Council, acting in accordance with the ordinary legislative procedure, shall establish measures for the creation of European intellectual property rights to provide uniform protection of intellectual property rights throughout the Union and for the setting up of centralised Union-wide authorisation, coordination and supervision arrangements.

However, reliance on Article 118 as a legal basis to harmonize copyright fully at the EU level might prove problematic, especially considering that culture is an area in which the EU has a limited role. Pursuant to Article 167(1) TFEU,

> The Union shall contribute to the flowering of the cultures of the Member States, while respecting their national and regional diversity and at the same time bringing the common cultural heritage to the fore.

Nonetheless, as illustrated by Cook and Derclaye,[80] there may be four viable options for tackling further (full) copyright harmonization at the EU level: unification, through a regulation pursuant to Article 118 TFEU; further harmonization, through ad hoc directives; guidance, through non-binding recommendations; or, simply doing nothing.

Considering the first option (a copyright regulation), this would have the primary merit of overcoming problems relating to the issue of territoriality. This peculiar feature of copyright, which the then ECJ expressly acknowledged in the *Lagardère* ruling,[81] has impaired the process of EU harmonization. This, amongst others, was also highlighted by Hugenholtz, who also recently defined territoriality as 'the real Achilles heel of harmonization'.[82] He observed that:

---

[80]   Trevor Cook and Estelle Derclaye, 'An EU Copyright Code: what and how, if ever?' (2011) 3 IPQ 259, 260 ff.

[81]   Case C-192/04 *Lagardère Active Broadcast v Société pour la perception de la rémunération équitable (SPRE), Gesellschaft zur Verwertung von Leistungsschutzrechten mbH (GVL), Compagnie européenne de radiodiffusion et de télévision Europe 1 SA (CERT)* [2005] I-07199. This case was a reference for a preliminary ruling from the French *Cour de cassation* on the interpretation of Council Directive 92/100/EEC on rental and lending rights and on certain rights related to copyright in the field of intellectual property, and of Council Directive 93/83/EEC of 27 September 1993 on the coordination of certain rules concerning copyright and rights related to copyright applicable to satellite broadcasting and cable retransmission in the context of proceeding concerning the obligation to pay equitable remuneration for the broadcasting of phonograms to the public by satellite and terrestrial repeater stations in France and Germany. At [46], the Court of Justice pointed out that the principle of the territoriality of copyright and related rights, which is recognized in international law and also in the EC Treaty, is not affected by Directive 92/100, as '[t]hose rights are ... of a territorial nature and, moreover, domestic law can only penalise conduct engaged in within national territory.'

[82]   P Bernt Hugenholtz, 'Harmonization or unification of EU copyright law', in Johan Axhamn (ed), *Copyright in a borderless online environment* (Kluwer Law International 2012), 189, 194.

Basing its harmonization agenda primarily on disparities between national laws, the European legislature has been aiming, as it would seem, at the wrong target. Disparities between national laws by themselves hardly amount to impediments of the free movement of goods or services, given that copyrights and related rights that reflect these disparities are drawn along national borders. Indeed, for as long as the territorial nature of copyright and related rights is left intact, harmonization can achieve relatively little.[83]

Furthermore, an EU regulation may help in solving issues concerning applicable law, as well as reducing costs and lengthy procedures associated with the implementation of EU directives by Member States.[84] Additionally, a regulation pursuant to Article 118 TFEU would no longer require unanimity to be adopted (as it was before the amendments brought about by the Lisbon Treaty), but just a qualified majority.

It is therefore apparent that a copyright regulation might be a feasible and desirable option, if not a mandatory one, in that:

> it is permissible to think that the Union is even obliged to adopt such a Regulation, at least if adopting such a copyright Regulation is necessary for the functioning of the internal market, as … [a]rticle [118 TFEU] uses the term 'shall'.[85]

With specific regard to Article 118 TFEU as a legal basis to adopt an EU copyright title, Bernt Hugenholtz has highlighted how this provision 'would allow not only for the introduction of Union-wide copyright titles, but also for the simultaneous abolishment of national titles, which would be necessary for such an initiative to take its full effect and remove territorial restrictions'.[86] Reto Hilty appears to share similar views, by saying that

> at least within Europe it is inconceivable why 2[8] different national legislations should apply, particularly in view of the fact that comprehensive harmonization based on Directive 2001/29 (explicitly directed at the 'harmonization of certain aspects of copyright and related rights in the information

---

[83]   P Bernt Hugenholtz, 'Copyright without frontiers: the problem of territoriality in European copyright law', in Estelle Derclaye (ed), *Research handbook on the future of EU copyright* (Edward Elgar Publishing 2009), 12, 18.

[84]   Cook and Derclaye, 'An EU Copyright Code', *cit*, 263. The problems of the costs associated with the implementation of directives have been included also by Hugenholtz, 'Harmonization or unification of copyright in the EU?', *cit*, among the 'bad' features of EU harmonization so far.

[85]   Cook and Derclaye, 'An EU Copyright Code', *cit*, 263–4.

[86]   Hugenholtz, 'The Wittem Group's European Copyright Code', in Synodinou (ed), *Codification of European copyright law*, *cit*, 352.

society' …) in truth failed, and that no initiative to remedy this imperfection has been taken during the last decade.[87]

However, the peculiarities of copyright, in particular the fact that – unlike patents and trademarks – copyright is not a registered right, may make a unitary EU copyright difficult to establish. This is also because the introduction of an EU copyright would make it necessary to determine whether national copyrights are to continue to exist alongside the EU one (as this is currently the case with trademarks), or not. Indeed, 'it is hard to envisage how a unitary EU copyright could subsist in parallel with national copyrights, with the two rights coming into effect simultaneously and in parallel every time a new work is created and then enduring for life plus 70 years.'[88]

In addition, it is not clear what standards a hypothetical EU copyright regulation should try to adhere to. Probably neither complex legislative techniques, nor over-stratified legislations should be endorsed at the EU level. As was suggested by Dietz back in 1978, a model European copyright regulation could rest just on three more or less independent sections: firstly, copyright law itself; secondly, law on copyright contracts, and thirdly the law of the collecting societies.[89] As to the latter, it is worth recalling that the EU is currently committed to adopting measures aimed at harmonizing and, possibly, improving their structure and governance.[90] So, at the moment, it seems that the EU is interested in implementing the second[91] and third part of Dietz's proposed European copyright, while leaving behind the first and most important part:

---

[87]   Reto Hilty, 'Reflections on a European copyright codification', in Tatiana-Eleni Synodinou (ed), *Codification of European copyright law* (Kluwer Law International 2012), 355, 357–8, who also provides (362–3) the contents of a hypothetical European copyright codification.

[88]   Cook and Derclaye, 'An EU Copyright Code', *cit*, 262. In the same sense, also Hans Ullrich, 'Harmony and unity of European intellectual property protection', in David Vaver and Lionel Bently (eds), *Intellectual property in the new millennium. Essays in honour of William R Cornish* (CUP 2004), 20, 36–7.

[89]   Adolf Dietz, *Copyright law in the European Community* (Sijthoff & Noordhoff 1978), 11 and 246 ff.

[90]   Proposal for a Directive of the European Parliament and of the Council on collective management of copyright and related rights and multi-territorial licensing of rights, in musical works for online uses in the internal market, Brussels, 11 July 2012, COM (2012) 372 final, 2012/0180 (COD).

[91]   For critical considerations as to the opportunity of unifying all aspects of authors' rights and related rights including copyright contracts, *see* Silke von Lewinski, 'Copyright contracts', in Tatiana-Eleni Synodinou (ed), *Codification of European copyright law* (Kluwer Law International 2012), 241.

substantial copyright law. As regards the main issue this contribution has dealt with, ie the notion of originality, a model EU copyright law should make it clear that the 'author's own intellectual creation' threshold to protection applies to any subject-matter and is to be intended in compliance with relevant CJEU decisions. In relation to subject-matter categorization, which has been a topic incidental to the discourse around originality, a good solution might be that proposed by Andrew Christie more than a decade ago in relation to UK copyright. While recognizing that the purpose of categorization of protected subject-matter is to allow the differential application of subsistence requirements and exclusive rights, he supported a minimalistic approach to subject-matter differentiation. In particular, he proposed that

> there be two categories of protected subject-matter – one for creative material (which is protected at a high level) and another for productive material (which is given a lower level of protection). The maintenance of the distinction between creative and productive material requires the maintenance of different innovation thresholds based on the degree of creativity which is reflected in the subject-matter.[92]

Should an EU copyright regulation not be considered as a feasible option, alternatives would be to enact directives (ie continue with ad hoc harmonization of Member States' copyright laws), or adopt recommendations. As soft law instruments and not binding as such, the latter would have limited importance, but may still be a good starting point for harmonization.

Nonetheless, it is to be noted that further copyright harmonization may well be obtained without legislative input, whether this is due to the activity of the EU judiciary or by way of national courts following each others' decisions. This would signal a continuation of the evolutions brought about by the activism of the CJEU over the past few years, as explained above. However, it is observed that:

> While this is welcome, this 'do nothing' approach is the most minimalist and probably the least satisfactory in terms of cost and legal certainty. Indeed, one needs to wait for litigation to occur and for the willingness of national courts to refer questions. Until then, the law is unclear and it is costly for those litigating. It is also in some way discriminatory because private parties bear the cost which should be borne by all.[93]

---

[92] Andrew Christie, 'A proposal for simplifying United Kingdom copyright law' (2001) 23 EIPR 26, 33.

[93] Cook and Derclaye, 'An EU Copyright Code', *cit*, 264.

In light of the issues highlighted for each of the three alternative instruments for bringing about EU copyright harmonization, and the fourth *laissez faire* approach, it seems that the first option, ie an EU copyright regulation, remains the most preferable. This conclusion is reached by looking at the increased legal certainty and overall increased competitiveness that it provides, even despite there being a risk that an EU regulation would undermine the benefits arising from competition in lawmaking by EU Member States. Indeed, it has been argued that a system of centralized EU-wide authorization, coordination and super-vision arrangements may deprive the EU of the value of legislators and civil servants in EU Member States trying to develop new laws to facilitate innovation.[94]

2. EU COPYRIGHT HARMONIZATION: WHEN IF EVER?

This contribution, while being concerned primarily with the process of EU harmonization, has attempted to highlight the fundamental role the CJEU has had recently in harmonizing the aspects of copyright law which the EU legislator has not considered worthy of address. This has been the case, in particular, with regard to the originality requirement. However, the CJEU case law has not only harmonized originality. Indeed, as explained by Lionel Bently, the Court has provided a harmonized meaning of other fundamental concepts, such as 'work', 'public' and 'part'. Bently has incisively defined this process 'harmonization by stealth'.[95]

When discussing harmonization through CJEU case law, concerns may certainly arise relating to the need for democratic lawmaking and legitimacy. However, to address these would be outwith the scope of this present work. To an extent, we can lay these to one side. What matters most is the fact that the harmonization effect of the CJEU has been achieved through references for preliminary ruling, referred by the national courts of Member States. In other words, this shows that the CJEU *needed* to

---

[94]   *See* William Kingston, 'Intellectual property in the Lisbon Treaty' (2008) 30 EIPR 439.

[95]   Lionel Bently, 'Harmonization by stealth: the role of the ECJ', present-ation at InfoSoc @ Ten. Ten years under the EU Directive on Copyright in the Information Society: looking back and looking forward, CRIDS – IViR confer-ence, hosted by Marielle Gallo (Member of the European Parliament), European Parliament, Brussels, 13 January 2012.

intervene, in order to provide guidance in relation to aspects which were either unclear, or for which no legislative guidance was available. Thus, in areas such as originality, a certain level of judicial appreciation has been required to address concepts left outwith the EU legislative plan because harmonization was deemed unnecessary in light of major EU objectives (such as the internal market).

This contribution has attempted to demonstrate that this attitude of EU legislative policy is parochial, also in light of the difficulties and doubts which some Member States (notably the UK insofar as originality is concerned) have been experiencing following CJEU decisions. Michel Barnier, current European Commissioner for Internal Market and Services has recently written about the need to develop the digital single market, by addressing four main copyright-related challenges in the years to come. These pertain to collective rights management, orphan works, online dissemination of audiovisual works, and enforcement of rights. However, no full copyright harmonization should be pursued, in that the single market in creative works should be 'a Single Market but not a uniform one'.[96]

Contrary to the belief of Commissioner Barnier, it is submitted that the time is apt for the EU to approach the issue of full copyright harmonization. A properly integrated and fully functioning market at the European level requires a common framework for copyright protection, particularly considering the massive digitalization of goods and the parallel development of digital distribution channels. What was for a long time a distinctive feature of intellectual property rights, ie their territorial nature, has been challenged by a series of phenomena. With regard to copyright, these relate not only to the cross-fertilization of different legal solutions and theories, but also the supranational reach of judicial decisions,[97] all of which result from the intangibility of channels through which works are exchanged and enjoyed. As highlighted by André Lucas, opposition to an EU copyright codification might be rooted within three types of arguments. Firstly, it might be said that a European copyright code is unnecessary for the completion of the internal market. Secondly, it might be argued that such an objective is impossible because the

---

[96] Michel Barnier, 'To be or not to be: Copyright makes all the difference', in L'Ingénieur Conseil – Intellectual Property (ICIP) (ed), *The future prospects for intellectual property in the EU: 2012–2022* (Gevers 2011), 13, 18.

[97] *See* Graeme W Austin, 'Global networks and domestic laws: some private international law issues arising from Australian and US liability theories', in Alain Strowel (ed), *Peer-to-Peer file sharing and secondary liability in copyright law* (Edward Elgar Publishing 2009), 124.

differences that remain among the various Member States could not be overcome. Thirdly, the idea of a code could be said to be undesirable because countries that enjoy a high level of protection would inevitably see it reduced. Together with Lucas, it is submitted that none of these objections are decisive.[98] Indeed, as also recently highlighted by the Max Planck Institute for Intellectual Property and Competition Law, the current level of harmonization is not enough, especially as far as 'online rights' are concerned.[99] Among other things, this is because, as recently highlighted also by Advocate General Mengozzi, the degree of harmonization resulting from the InfoSoc Directive is not sufficient to ensure that Europe has a modern legislative framework in the area of copyright.[100]

Even if those academics united under the Wittem Project preferred not to take a position on the opportunity to harmonize copyright fully at the European level, the drafting of a codification of copyright seems to recognize implicitly the desirability of going down this route. In addition, Article 118 TFEU might be a good legal basis for the issuing of an EU copyright regulation.

However, what matters most is that a full harmonization project is discussed in detail as soon as possible. EU legislators cannot leave the task of shaping EU copyright policy to the CJEU. This is also on account of the fact that the Court appears more interested in harmonization as an end in itself, rather than in matters of policy.[101] In any case, pursuing an EU copyright policy is not within the competence of the Court, nor should it be.

Europe as a continent is a powerful producer of cultural goods and services, and yet its market for digital content still lags behind. In the

---

[98]   André Lucas, 'European copyright codification', in Tatiana-Eleni Synodinou (ed), *Codification of European copyright law* (Kluwer Law International 2012), 373, 373–5.

[99]   Joscf Drexl, Sylvie Nérisson, Felix Trumpke and Reto M Hilty, *Comments of the Max Planck Institute for Intellectual Property and Competition Law on the Proposal for a Directive of the European Parliament and of the Council on collective management of copyright and related rights and multi-territorial licensing of rights in musical works for online uses in the internal market COM (2012)372*, February 2013 <http://tinyurl.com/bbwfbdu> accessed 14 June 2013, 10.

[100]   Opinion of Advocate General Paolo Mengozzi, Case C-521/11 *Amazon. com and Others v Austro-Mechana Gesellschaft zur Wahrnehmung mechanisch-musikalischer Urheberrechte Gesellschaft mbH*, 7 March 2013, [5]–[6].

[101]   In this sense, Lionel Bently, 'The return of industrial copyright?' (2012) 34 EIPR 654, 672.

words of Neelie Kroes, this is a tragedy,[102] but also an opportunity to commence a political and legal project which relies on an efficient system of EU copyright. EU copyright can no longer be subject to ad hoc harmonizing interventions. What is needed now is an EU copyright title, no matter whether this is an optional or a compulsory one (at least at this stage of the discussion). This is necessary to not only ensure the competitiveness of the European economic and legal model, but also the very survival of copyright itself. In the age of digital production and dissemination of works, good, well drafted, law is required in order to keep the pace with technological progress. Within the concept of good law, there is an EU-wide copyright. This is necessary to safeguard the proprietary interests of creators, support sustainable industries and acknowledge the needs and demands of users of copyright-protected materials which are no longer drawn along national borders. Since there exist EU consumers of goods and services, there must also be EU consumers of copyright-protected content. What is missing is an EU copyright that is fit for the digital age.

As suggested by John Howkins, copyright material is best protected by a mixture of two factors: good law, and bad technology. The meaning assigned to 'good law' is law which is fair and effective, and whose remedies are proportionate to the injury. 'Bad technology' refers to the inability of technology to make good copies. As such, whilst 'it is much easier, and more fun, to make new technology than new law, the whole point of a property contract is to reconcile these two forces.'[103] As things currently stand, we have bad law and good technology: a perfect combination to accelerate the decline of copyright.

In conclusion, we cannot look backwards. We must instead (and as quickly as possible) move forwards to ensure technological, cultural and economic investments are combined with effective, EU-wide legal rules. Although an air of nostalgia is sometimes unavoidable, this should not be given credence when it comes to providing a legal shape for technologically driven sectors, as is the case for copyright law. In short, it seems appropriate to conclude with a literary quotation, which manages to sum up this very sentiment. We can learn from and cherish the past, but at the same time we must also embrace a new future. In order to do

---

[102] Neelie Kroes, 'Good for artists, good for consumers, good for the economy', speech at CISAC World Copyright Summit, Brussels, 7 June 2011, SPEECH/11/413.

[103] John Howkins, *The creative economy. How people make money from ideas* (updated edn, Penguin 2007), 67.

so, it is important that we do not get caught up with something, somewhere, which is instead lost for good:

> And as I sat there brooding on the old, unknown world, I thought of Gatsby's wonder when he first picked out the green light at the end of Daisy's dock. He had come a long way to this blue lawn, and his dream must have seemed so close that he could hardly fail to grasp it. He did not know that it was already behind him, somewhere back in that vast obscurity beyond the city, where the dark fields of the republic rolled under the night.
>
> Gatsby believed in the green light, the orgiastic future that year by year recedes before us. It eluded us then, but that's no matter – tomorrow we will run faster, stretch out our arms further … And one fine morning –
>
> So we beat on, boats against the current, borne back ceaselessly into the past.[104]

---

[104]　These are the closing paragraphs from Francis Scott Fitzgerald, *The Great Gatsby* (first published 1926, Penguin Books 2010), 192.

Bibliography

Abbott, FM, Cottier, T and Gurry, F, *International intellectual property in an integrated world economy* (2nd edn, Wolters Kluwer Law & Business 2011)

Abrams, HB, 'Originality and creativity in copyright law' (1992) Law and Contemp Probs 3

Akester, P, '*SAS Institute Inc v World Programming Ltd*, Case C-406/10 – exploratory answers' (2012) 34 EIPR 145

Alexander, I, 'The concept of reproduction and the "temporary and transient" exception' (2009) CLJ 520

Anderson, D, *References to the European Court* (1st edn, Sweet & Maxwell 1995)

Anderson, J, 'The curious case of the Portsmouth publican: challenging the territorial exclusivity of TV rights in European professional sport' (2011) 3 ISLR 53

Aplin, T, *Copyright law in the digital society. The challenges of multimedia* (Hart Publishing 2005)

Aplin, T, 'United Kingdom', in Lindner, B and Shapiro, T (eds), *Copyright in the Information Society. A guide to national implementation of the European Directive* (Edward Elgar Publishing 2011) 558

Aplin, T and Davis, J, *Intellectual property law. Text, cases, and materials* (1st edn, OUP 2009)

Arena, A, 'The doctrine of Union preemption in the E.U. internal market: between *Sein* and *Sollen*' (2011) 17 Colum J Eur L 477

Arnold, R, 'Are performers authors?' (1999) 21 EIPR 464

Arnold, R, 'Content copyrights and signal copyrights: the case for a rational scheme of protection' (2011) 1 QMJIP 272

Arnull, A, *The European Union and its Court of Justice* (OUP 1999)

Austin, GW, 'Global networks and domestic laws: some private international law issues arising from Australian and US liability theories', in Strowel, A (ed), *Peer-to-Peer file sharing and secondary liability in copyright law* (Edward Elgar Publishing 2009) 124

Baden-Powell, E, 'Think before you link: yesterday's news – today's copyright conundrum' (2011) CTLR 25

Barker, E and Harding, I, 'Copyright, the ideas/expression dichotomy and harmonization: digging deeper into *SAS*' (2012) 7(9) JIPLP 673

Barnier, M 'To be or not to be: Copyright makes all the difference', in L'Ingénieur Conseil – Intellectual Property (ICIP) (ed), *The future prospects for intellectual property in the EU: 2012–2022* (Gevers 2011) 13

Barroso, JM, *Political Guidelines for the Next Commission*, 3 September 2009

Barthes, R, *Image Music Text* (first published 1977, Noonday Press edition 1988)

Beldiman, D, *Functionality, information works, and copyright* (Lulu.com 2008)

Bently, L, 'Copyright and the death of the author in literature and law' (1994) 57 MLR 973

Bently, L, 'Bently slams "very disappointing" ruling in Meltwater' (The IPKat, 27 July 2011) <http://tinyurl.com/azecegv> accessed 14 June 2013.

Bently, L, 'Harmonization by stealth: the role of the ECJ', presentation at InfoSoc @ Ten. Ten years after the EU Directive on Copyright in the Information Society: looking back and looking forward, CRIDS – IviR conference, hosted by Marielle Gallo (Member of the European Parliament), European Parliament, Brussels, 13 January 2012

Bently, L, 'The return of industrial copyright?' (2012) 34 EIPR 654

Bently, L and Sherman, B, *Intellectual property law* (3rd edn, OUP 2008)

Bergé, JS, *La protection internationale et communautaire du droit d'auteur. Essai d'une analyse conflictuelle* (L.G.D.J. 1996)

Beunen, AC, *Protection for databases: the European Database Directive and its effects in the Netherlands, France and the United Kingdom* (Wolf Legal Publishers 2007)

Beunen, AC, '*Geschriftenbescherming*: the Dutch protection for non-original writings', in Hugenholtz, PB, Quaedvlieg, A and Visser, D (eds), *A century of Dutch copyright law. Auteurswet 1912–2012* (deLex 2012) 57

Bitton, M, 'Protection for informational works after Feist Publications Inc. v. Rural Telephone Service' (2011) 21 Fordham Intell Prop Media & Ent LJ 611

Bleakley, A, Baden-Powell, E and Eneberi, J, *Intellectual property and media law companion* (4th edn, Bloomsbury Professional 2010)

Bloom, H, *The anxiety of influence. A theory of poetry* (2nd edn, OUP 1973)

Bracha, O, 'The ideology of authorship revisited: authors, markets, and liberal values in early American copyright' (2008) 118 Yale LJ 186

Brauneis, R, 'The transformation of originality in the progressive-era debate over copyright in news' (2009) *The George Washington Law*

School Public Law and Legal Theory Working Paper No 463 – Legal Studies Research Paper No 463

Brinkley, I and Lee, N, The Work Foundation, *The knowledge economy in Europe. A report prepared for the 2007 EU Spring Council* (2007)

Burbidge, R, 'Originality or author's own intellectual creation? What is the legal test for copyright subsistence in photographs?' (Art and Artifice, 30 January 2012) <http://tinyurl.com/aaqgms3> accessed 14 June 2013.

Burbidge, R, 'Would Germany and France find the red bus photo infringed?' (Art and Artifice, 27 February 2012) <http://tinyurl.com/a9wh9w6> accessed 14 June 2013

Burkitt, D, 'Copyrighting culture – the history and cultural specificity of the Western model of copyright' (2001) 2 IPQ 146

Cairns, P and Blakeney, S, '1-0 to Football Dataco Ltd – the organizers of professional football matches take the lead in the battle to prevent the unauthorised use of their fixture lists' (2010) 3/4 ISLR 57

Carr, H and Arnold, R, *Computer software. Legal protection in the United Kingdom* (2nd edn, ESC Pub Ltd 1992)

Casas Vallés, R, 'The requirement of originality', in Derclaye, E (ed), *Research handbook on the future of EU copyright* (Edward Elgar Publishing 2009) 102

Challis, B, 'US content industry and ISPs to inform and alert' (The 1709 Blog, 8 July 2011) <http://tinyurl.com/bd852pj> accessed 14 June 2013

Challis, B, 'Murphy's law of licensing?' (The 1709 Blog, 20 October 2011) <http://tinyurl.com/a8cebry> accessed 14 June 2013

Challis, B, 'Six strikes launches in the US' (The 1709 Blog, 26 February 2013) <http://tinyurl.com/cvv3ra9> accessed 14 June 2013

Chalmers, D, Davies, G and Monti, G, *European Union Law* (2nd edn, CUP 2010)

Christie, A, 'A proposal for simplifying United Kingdom copyright law' (2001) 23 EIPR 26

Clark, S, 'Just browsing? An analysis of the reasoning underlying the Court of Appeal's decision on the temporary copies exemption in Newspaper Licensing Agency Ltd v Meltwater Holding BV' (2011) 33 EIPR 725

Clark, S, 'Why the Meltwater case won't break the internet' (The 1709 Blog, 20 September 2012) <http://tinyurl.com/asrvtz4> accessed 14 June 2013

Colston, C and Middleton, K, *Modern intellectual property law* (2nd edn, Cavendish 2005)

Cook, T, *EU intellectual property law* (OUP 2010)

Cook, T, '*Football Dataco*. Implications for copyright subsistence' (2012) April PLC 8

Cook, T and Derclaye, E, 'An EU Copyright Code: what and how, if ever?' (2011) 3 IPQ 259

Copenhagen Economics – European Policy Centre (EPC), *The Economic Impact of a European Digital Single Market*, final report, March 2010

Cornish, WR, 'Sound recordings and copyright' (1993) 24 IIC 306

Cornish, W, Llewelyn, D and Aplin, T, *Intellectual property: patents, copyright, trade marks and allied rights* (7th edn, Sweet & Maxwell 2010)

Craig, P and Búrca, G de, *EU law. Text, cases and materials* (5th edn, OUP 2011)

Cran, D and Joseph, P, 'Football Dataco: fixture lists not protected by database copyright' (2012) 23 Ent LR 149

Czarnota, B and Hart, RJ, *Legal protection of computer programs in Europe: a guide to the EC Directive* (LexisNexis 1991)

D'Agostino, G, *Copyright, contracts, creators. New media, new rules* (Edward Elgar Publishing 2010)

Danaher, B, Dhanasobhon, S, Smith, MD and Telang, R, 'Converting pirates without cannibalizing purchasers: the impact of digital distribution on physical sales and internet piracy', presentation at the annual congress of the Society for Economic Research on Copyright Issues (SERCI), Berkeley, 9–10 July 2009

Davies, G, *Copyright and the public interest* (2nd edn, Sweet & Maxwell 2002)

Davies, G and Garnett, K, *Moral rights* (Sweet & Maxwell 2010)

Davis, J and Durant, A, 'To protect or not to protect? The eligibility of commercially used short verbal texts for copyright and trademark protection' (2011) 4 IPQ 345

Davison, MJ, *The legal protection of databases* (CUP 2003)

Derclaye, E, 'Infopaq International A/S v Danske Dagblades Forening (C-5/08): wonderful or worrisome? The impact of the ECJ ruling in Infopaq on UK copyright law' (2010) EIPR 247

Derclaye, E, 'Football Dataco: skill and labour is dead!' (Kluwer Copyright Blog, 1 March 2012) <http://tinyurl.com/7qgj8wm> accessed 14 June 2013

De Sanctis, VM, *Il diritto d'autore* (Giuffré 2012)

Dietz, A, *Copyright law in the European Community* (Sijthoff & Noordhoff 1978)

Doukas, D, 'The Sky is not the (only) limit: sports broadcasting without frontiers and the Court of Justice: comment on Murphy' (2012) 37 EL Rev 605

Drexl, J, Nérisson, S, Trumpke, F and Hilty, RM, *Comments of the Max Planck Institute for Intellectual Property and Competition Law on the Proposal for a Directive of the European Parliament and of the Council on collective management of copyright and related rights and multi-territorial licensing of rights in musical works for online uses in the internal market COM (2012)372*, February 2013 <http://tinyurl.com/bbwfbdu> accessed 14 June 2013

Eechoud, M van, 'Another piece of the puzzle, or is it? CJEU on photographs as copyright works' (Kluwer Copyright Blog, 7 December 2011) <http://tinyurl.com/bcr2d5d> accessed 14 June 2013

Eechoud, M van, 'Along the road to uniformity – Diverse readings of the Court of Justice judgments on copyright work' (2012) 3 JIPITEC 60

Eechoud, M van, Hugenholtz, PB, Gompel, S van, Guibault, L and Helberger, N, *Harmonizing European copyright law. The challenges of better law making* (Kluwer Law International 2009)

Emilianides, AC, 'The author revived: harmonisation without justification' (2004) 26 EIPR 538

European Copyright Society, *Opinion on the reference to the CJEU in Case C-466/12*, Svensson, 15 February 2013 <http://tinyurl.com/c9qubgn>, accessed 14 June 2013

Farley, CH, 'The lingering effects of copyright's response to the invention of photography' (2004) 65 U Pitt L Rev 385

Farrand, B, 'Too much is never enough? The 2011 Copyright in Sound Recordings Extension Directive' (2012) 34 EIPR 297

Fichte, JG, 'Beweis der Unrechtmäßigkeit der Büchernachdruckes: Ein Räsonment und eine Parabel' (1791), Italian Translation: 'Dimostrazione dell'illegittimità dell'editoria pirata: un ragionamento e una parabola', in Pozzo, R (ed), *L'autore e i suoi diritti. Scritti polemici sulla proprietà intellettuale* (Biblioteca di Via Senato Edizioni 2005) 73

Flint, MF, Thorne, CD and Williams, AP, *Intellectual property – The new law. A guide to the Copyright, Designs and Patents Act 1988* (Butterworths 1989)

Foster, NG, *EU law directions* (OUP 2008)

Foucault, M, 'What is an author?' in Bouchard, DF (ed), *Language, counter-memory, practice: selected essays and interviews* (first published 1969, Cornell University Press 1977) 113

Fromer, JC, 'A psychology of intellectual property' (2010) 104 NW L Rev 1441

Galli, P, 'Commento all'articolo 1 della Legge 22 aprile 1941 n. 633', in Ubertazzi, LC (ed), *Commentario breve alle leggi su proprietà intellettuale e concorrenza* (4th edn, CEDAM 2007) 1487

Garnett, K, Davies, G and Harbottle, G, *Copinger and Skone James on Copyright* (16th edn, Sweet & Maxwell 2012)

Geey, D, Burns, J and Akiyama, M, 'Live Premier League football broadcasting rights: the CJEU judgment' (2012) 23 Ent LR 17

Geiger, C, 'The extension of the term of copyright and certain neighbouring rights – a never-ending story?' (2009) IIC 78

Geiger, C, 'Intellectual "property" after the Treaty of Lisbon: towards a different approach in the new European legal order?' (2010) 32 EIPR 255

Gendreau, Y, 'United Kingdom', in Gendreau, Y, Nordemann, A and Oesch, R (eds), *Copyright and photographs. An international survey* (Kluwer Law International 1999) 283

Georgopoulos, T, 'The legal foundations of European copyright law', in Synodinou, TE (ed), *Codification of European copyright law. Challenges and perspectives* (Kluwer Law International 2012) 31

Gervais, DJ, '*Feist* goes global: a comparative analysis of the notion of originality in copyright law' (2002) J Copyr Socy 949

Gervais, DJ, *The TRIPS Agreement. Drafting history and analysis* (2nd edn, Sweet & Maxwell 2003)

Gervais, DJ, 'The compatibility of the skill and labour standard with the Berne Convention and the TRIPs Agreement' (2004) 26 EIPR 75

Gervais, DJ and Derclaye, E, 'The scope of computer program protection after *SAS*: are we closer to answers?' (2012) 34 EIPR 565

Ginsburg, JC, 'No "sweat"? Copyright and other protection of works of information after *Feist v. Rural Telephone*' (1992) Colum L Rev 338

Ginsburg, JC, 'A tale of two copyrights: literary property in revolutionary France and America', in Sherman, B and Strowel, A (eds), *Of authors and origins. Essays on copyright law* (Clarendon Press 1994) 131

Ginsburg, JC, 'The concept of authorship in comparative copyright law' (2003) *Columbia Law School Public Law & Legal Theory Research Paper Group – Paper No 03-51*

Ginsburg, JC, 'European Copyright Code – Back to first principles (with some additional details)' (2011) *Columbia Public Law Research Paper No 11-261*

Goldstein, P and Hugenholtz, PB, *International copyright. Principles, law and practice* (2nd edn, OUP 2010)

Gompel, S von, *Formalities in copyright law. An analysis of their history, rationales and possible future* (Kluwer Law International 2011)

Goucha Soares, A, 'Pre-emption, conflicts of powers and subsidiarity' (1998) 23 Eur L Rev 132

Gowers, A, *Gowers Review of Intellectual Property*, December 2006, <http://tinyurl.com/af3gyqc> accessed 14 June 2013

Griffiths, J, 'Unsticking the centre-piece – The liberation of European copyright law?' (2010) 1 JIPITEC 87

Griffiths, J, 'Infopaq, BSA, and the "Europeanisation" of United Kingdom copyright law' (2011), <http://tinyurl.com/bydchtw> accessed 14 June 2013

Grosheide, FW 'Paradigms in copyright law', in Sherman, B and Strowel, A (eds), *Of authors and origins. Essays on copyright law* (Clarendon Press 1994) 203

Grosheide, FW, 'Moral rights', in Derclaye, E (ed), *Research handbook on the future of EU copyright* (Edward Elgar Publishing 2009) 242

Guibault, L, 'Has the directive achieved its goals of harmonisation and greater legal certainty?', presentation at InfoSoc @ Ten. Ten years after the EU Directive on Copyright in the Information Society: looking back and looking forward, CRIDS – IViR conference, hosted by Marielle Gallo (Member of the European Parliament), European Parliament, Brussels, 13 January 2012

Hague, W, 'How the UK's New Tory-led Government sees its EU Policy' (17 May 2010) Europe's World

Handig, C, 'The copyright term "work" – European harmonisation at an unknown level' (2009) IIC 665

Handig, C, 'Infopaq International A/S v Danske Dagblades Forening (C-5/08): is the term "work" of the CDPA 1988 in line with the European Directives?' (2010) EIPR 53

Harding, I, 'Verizon, six strikes and piracy' (The 1709 Blog, 11 January 2013) <http://tinyurl.com/b8eoksa> accessed 14 June 2013

Hargreaves, I, *Digital Opportunity. A review of intellectual property and growth* (2011) <http://tinyurl.com/6bxcerw> accessed 14 June 2013

Hart, M, 'The Copyright in the Information Society Directive: an overview' (2002) 24 EIPR 58

Hegel, GWF, *Grundlinien der Philosophie des Rechts* (1820), English Translation, in Wood, AW (ed), *Elements of philosophy of right* (CUP 1991)

Helberger, N, Dufft, N, Gompel, S van and Hugenholtz, PB, 'Never forever: why extending the term of protection for sound recordings is a bad idea' (2008) EIPR 174

Hilty, R, 'Reflections on a European copyright codification', in Synodinou, TE (ed), *Codification of European copyright law* (Kluwer Law International 2012) 355

Hilty, RM, Krujatz, S, Bajon, B, Früh, A, Kur, A, Drexl, J, Geiger, C and Klass, N, 'European Commission – Green Paper. Copyright in the Knowledge Economy – Comments by the Max Planck Institute for Intellectual Property, Competition and Tax Law' (2008) *Max Planck*

Institute for Intellectual Property, Competition & Tax Law Research Paper Series No 08/05

Hishinuma, T, 'The scope of formalities in international copyright law in a digital context', in Bently, L, Suthersanen, U and Torremans, P (eds), *Global copyright. Three hundred years since the Statute of Anne, from 1709 to cyberspace* (Edward Elgar Publishing 2010) 460

Hobson, A, 'Newspaper Licensing Agency Ltd v Meltwater Holdings BV' (2011) Ent LR 101

Höppner, T, 'Reproduction in part of online articles in the aftermath of *Infopaq* (C-5/08): *Newspaper Licensing Agency Ltd v Meltwater Holding BV*' (2011) 33 EIPR 331

Howkins, J, *The creative economy. How people make money from ideas* (updated edn, Penguin 2007)

Hugenholtz, PB, 'Why the Copyright Directive is unimportant, and possibly invalid' (2000) 22 EIPR 499

Hugenholtz, PB, 'Copyright without frontiers: the problem of territoriality in European copyright law', in Derclaye, E (ed), *Research handbook on the future of EU copyright* (Edward Elgar Publishing 2009) 12

Hugenholtz, PB, 'Harmonization or unification of copyright in the EU?', presentation at InfoSoc @ Ten. Ten years after the EU Directive on Copyright in the Information Society: looking back and looking forward, CRIDS – IviR conference, hosted by Marielle Gallo (Member of the European Parliament), European Parliament, Brussels, 13 January 2012

Hugenholtz, PB, 'Harmonization or unification of EU copyright law' in Axhamn, J (ed), *Copyright in a borderless online environment* (Kluwer Law International 2012) 189

Hugenholtz, PB, 'The Wittem Group's European Copyright Code', in Synodinou, TE (ed), *Codification of European copyright law* (Kluwer Law International 2012) 339

Hugenholtz, PB, 'Goodbye, Geschriftenbescherming!' (Kluwer Copyright Blog, 6 March 2013) <http://tinyurl.com/cbuhdqq> accessed 14 June 2013

Hugenholtz, PB, Eechoud, M van, Gompel, S van, Guibault, L, Helberger, N, Rossini, M, Steijger, L, Dufft, N and Bohn, P, *The recasting of copyright and related rights for the knowledge economy*, final report, November 2006 <http://tinyurl.com/ab9vlwy> accessed 14 June 2013

Hugenholtz, PB and Senftleben, MRF, 'Fair use in Europe. In search of flexibilities' (2012) *Amsterdam Law School Research Paper No 2012-39*

Hughes, J, 'The photographer's copyright – photograph as art, photograph as database' (2011) Benjamin N Cardozo School of Law, Yeshiva

University, Jacob Burns Institute for Advanced Legal Studies, *Faculty Research Paper No 347*, November 2011

Husovec, M, 'Newspaper articles not creative enough. An issue for the CJEU?', Kluwer Copyright Blog (Kluwer Copyright Blog, 24 January 2012) <http://tinyurl.com/av7z3fv> accessed 14 June 2013

Hyland, M, 'The Football Association Premier League ruling – the Bosman of exclusive broadcasting rights?' (2012) 17 Comms L 7

INTA European & Central Asia Legislation and Regulatory Sub-Committee, *Unfair competition reports* (2007) <http://tinyurl.com/ab84q4k> accessed 14 June 2013

Jaszi, P, 'Toward a theory of copyright: the metamorphoses of "authorship"'(1991) 40 Duke LJ 455

Jaszi, P, 'On the author effect: contemporary copyright and collective creativity', in Woodmansee, M and Jaszi, P, (eds), *The construction of authorship. Textual appropriation in law and literature* (Duke University Press 1994) 29

Jiřičná, K, 'Slovak ruling angers publishing industry' (The Prague Post, 18 January 2012) <http://tinyurl.com/b54cvz2> accessed 14 June 2013

Joint Academic Statement by the Centre for Intellectual Property Policy and Management (CIPPM, Bournemouth University) – Centre for Intellectual Property and Information Law (CIPIL, Cambridge University) – Institute for Information Law (IViR, University of Amsterdam) – Max Planck Institute for Intellectual Property, Competition and Tax Law (Munich), *The proposed directive for a copyright term extension – A backward-looking package* (2008)

Jougleux, P, 'The plurality of legal systems in copyright law: an obstacle to European Codification?', in Synodinou, TE (ed), *Codification of European copyright law* (Kluwer Law International 2012) 55

Judge, EF and Gervais, D, 'Of silos and constellations: comparing notions of originality in copyright law' (2009) 27 Cardozo Arts & Ent LJ 375

Kant, I, 'Von der Unrechtmässigkeit des Büchernachdruckes' (1785), Italian Translation: 'Dell'illegittimità dell'editoria pirata', in Pozzo, R (ed), *L'autore e i suoi diritti. Scritti polemici sulla proprietà intellettuale* (Biblioteca di Via Senato Edizioni 2005) 39

Kaplan, B, *An unhurried view of copyright* (Columbia University Press 1967)

Karnell, GWG, 'European originality: a copyright chimera', in Kabel, JJC and Alexander, W (eds), *Intellectual property and information law: essays in honour of Herman Cohen Jehoram* (Kluwer Law International 1998)

Kawashima, N, 'The rise of "user creativity" – Web 2.0 and a new challenge for copyright law and cultural policy', presentation at the annual congress of the Society for Economic Research on Copyright Issues (SERCI), Berkeley, 9–10 July 2009

Keeling, DT, *Intellectual property rights in EU law* (OUP 2003)

Kingston, W, 'Intellectual property in the Lisbon Treaty' (2008) 30 EIPR 439

Komárek, J, 'Judicial lawmaking and precedent in supreme courts' (2011), *LSE Law, Society and Economy Working Papers 4/2011*

Kretschmer, M. 'Digital copyright: the end of an era' (2003) 25 EIPR 333

Kroes, N, 'A digital world of opportunities', speech at the Forum d'Avignon, *Les rencontres internationals del de la culture, de l'économie et des medias*, Avignon, 5 November 2010, SPEECH/10/619

Kroes, N, 'Addressing the orphan works challenge', speech at IFRRO (The International Federation of Reproduction Rights Organisations) launch of ARROW+ (Accessible Registries of Rights Information and Orphan Works towards Europeana), Brussels, 10 March 2011, SPEECH/11/163

Kroes, N, 'Good for artists, good for consumers, good for the economy', speech at CISAC World Copyright Summit, Brussels, 7 June 2011, SPEECH/11/413

Kroes, N, 'Investing in the future: meeting the internet's astonishing promise', speech at "Talk in Brussels" – Deutsche Telekom Annual Reception, Brussels, 29 November 2011, SPEECH/11/857

Kroes, N, 'Creativity for the creative sector: entertaining Europe in the electronic age', speech at European Parliament Intellectual Property Forum, European Parliament, Brussels, 24 January 2012, SPEECH/12/30

Kroes, N, 'What does it mean to be open online?', speech at World Wide Web Conference 2012, Lyon, 19 April 2012, SPEECH/12/275

Kroes, N, 'Copyright and innovation in the creative industries', speech at *The 2012 intellectual property and innovation summit*, The Lisbon Council Brussels, 10 September 2012, SPEECH/12/592

Kroes, N, 'Digital technology and copyright can fit together', Brussels, 4 February 2013, SPEECH/13/96

Kwall, RR, 'Originality in context' (2007) Hous LR 871

Laddie, H, 'Copyright: over-strength, over-regulated, over-rated?' (1996) 5 EIPR 253

Laddie, H, Prescott, P and Vitoria, M, *The modern law of copyright and designs* (2nd edn, LexisNexis 1995)

Laddie, H, Prescott, P and Vitoria, M, *The modern law of copyright and designs* (3rd edn, LexisNexis 2000)

Laddie, H, Prescott, P, Vitoria, M et al., *The modern law of copyright and designs* (4th edn, LexisNexis 2011)

Lai, S, *The copyright protection of computer software in the United Kingdom* (Hart Publishing 2000)

Landes, WM and Posner, RA, *The economic structure of intellectual property* (Belknap Press of Harvard University Press 2003)

Laurent, P, 'Belgian Supreme Court: against the tide of CJEU's case law on "originality"?' (Kluwer Copyright Blog, 6 March 2012) <http://tinyurl.com/auq8oc5> accessed 14 June 2013

Lee, YH, 'Photographs and the standard of originality in Europe: *Eva-Maria Painer v Standard Verlags GmbH, Axel Springer AG, Suddeutsche Zeitunung GmbH, Spiegel-Verlag Rudolf Augstein GmbH & Co KG, Verlag M. DuMont Schauberg Expedition der Kolnischen Zeitung GmbH & Co KG* (C-145/10)' (2012) 34 EIPR 290

Leenheer Zimmerman, D, 'It's an original!(?): in pursuit of copyright's elusive essence' (2005) 28 Colum J L & Arts 187

Lewinski, S von, 'EC proposal for Council directive harmonizing the term of protection of copyright' (1992) 23 IIC 785

Lewinski, S von, *International copyright law and policy* (OUP 2008)

Lewinski, S von, 'Copyright contracts', in Synodinou, TE (ed), *Codification of European copyright law* (Kluwer Law International 2012) 241

Litman, J, 'The public domain' (1990) 39 Emory LJ 965

Litman, J, 'Real copyright reform' (2010) 96 IoLR 1

Lucas, A, 'European copyright codification', in Synodinou, TE (ed), *Codification of European copyright law* (Kluwer Law International 2012) 373

Lucas, A and Lucas, HJ, *Traité de la propriété litéraire et artistique* (3rd edn, Litec 2006)

MacQueen, H, Waelde, C and Laurie, G, *Contemporary intellectual property. Law and policy* (1st edn, OUP 2008)

Mandel, GN, 'Left-brain versus right-brain: competing conceptions of creativity in intellectual property law' (2010) 44 UC Davis L Rev 283

McCreevy, C, 'Charlie McCreevy speaks to the European Parliament JURI Committee', Brussels, 21 November 2006, SPEECH/06/720

McGuinness, P, 'Digital downloads: the "age of free" is coming to an end'(*The Telegraph*, 8 July 2011) <http://tinyurl.com/3lw5tmy> accessed 14 June 2013

Michalos, C, *The law of photography and digital images* (Sweet & Maxwell 2004)

Miller, JS, 'Hoisting originality' (2009) Cardozo L Rev 459

Minero, G, 'Did the Database Directive actually harmonize the database copyright? Football Dataco Ltd v Brittens Pools Ltd and the ECJ's rules against subsistence of database copyright in fixture lists' (2012) 34 EIPR 728

Monseau, S, '"Fit for purpose": why the European Union should not extend the term of related rights protection in Europe' (2009) 19 Fordham Intell Prop Media & Ent LJ 629

Montagnani, ML and Borghi, M, 'Promises and pitfalls of the European copyright law harmonisation process', in Ward, D (ed), *The European Union & the culture industries: regulation and the public interest* (Ashgate 2008) 213

Montagnon, R and Shillito, M, 'Requirements for subsistence of database copyright and other national copyright in databases referred to the ECJ: Football Dataco Ltd v Yahoo!' (2011) 33 EIPR 324

Monti, M, *A new strategy for the single market at the service of Europe's Economy and Society. Report to the President of the European Commission José Manuel Barroso*, 9 May 2010

Ng, A, *Copyright law and the progress of science and the useful arts* (Edward Elgar 2011)

Ong, B, 'Originality from copying: fitting recreative works into the copyright universe' (2010) 2 IPQ 165

Pallante, M, 'The next great copyright act' (2013) 36(3) Colum JL & Arts 315

Patry, W, *How to fix copyright* (OUP 2011)

Pats, J, 'Originality standard as applied to photographs and other derivative works: a need for change' (2006) 17(2) NYSBA Entertainment, Arts and Sports Law Journal 37

Patterson, LR, *Copyright in historical perspective* (Vanderbilt University Press 1968)

Phillips, J, 'News in Slovakia: no copyright in newspaper news' (The 1709 Blog, 5 January 2012) <http://tinyurl.com/bdjs2nj> accessed 14 June 2013

Phillips, J, 'When Birss meets Bus: a study in Red and Gray' (The 1709 Blog, 22 January 2012) <http://tinyurl.com/bhdk4vj> accessed 14 June 2013

Phillips, J, 'At the apex of the Summit: "real world" invoked in copyright debate' (The IPKat, 11 September 2012) <.http://tinyurl.com/ao9u8s6> accessed 14 June 2013

Phillips, J and Firth, A, *Introduction to intellectual property law* (4th edn, Butterworths 2001)

Picard, RG, Toivonen, TE and Grönlund, M, *The contribution of copyright and related rights to the European economy based on data from the year 2000*, final report prepared for European Commission, Directorate General – Internal Market, 20 October 2003

Pila, J, 'Compilation copyright: A matter calling for "a certain ... sobriety"' (2008), *University of Oxford Legal Research Paper Series, Paper No 45/2008*, November 2008

Pila, J, 'Copyright and its categories of original works' (2010) 30 OJLS 229

Pila, J, 'The "Star Wars" copyright claim: an ambivalent view of the empire' (2012) 128 LQR 15

Pila, J, 'Copyright and internet browsing' (2012) 128 LQR 204

Posner, RA, *Law and literature* (revised and enlarged edn, Harvard University Press 1998)

Prime, T, *European intellectual property law* (Ashgate 2000)

Prinsley, MA and Byrt, S, '*Lucasfilm* fails to find the force' (2011) 105 Euro Law 14

Quintais, JP, 'Proposal for a Directive on collective rights management and (some) multi-territorial licensing' (2013) 35 EIPR 65

Rahmatian, A, 'The concepts of "musical work" and "originality" in UK copyright law – Sawkins v Hyperion as a test case' (2009) 40 IIC 560

Rahmatian, A, 'Copyright protection for restoration, reconstruction and digitization of public domain works', in Derclaye, E (ed), *Copyright and cultural heritage: preservation and access to work in a digital world* (Edward Elgar Publishing 2010) 51

Rahmatian, A, *Copyright and creativity. The making of property rights in creative works* (Edward Elgar Publishing 2011)

Rahmatian, A, 'Temple Islands Collections v New English Teas: an incorrect decision based on the right law?' (2012) 34 EIPR 796

Rahmatian, A, 'Originality in UK copyright law: the old "skill and labour" doctrine under pressure' (2013) 44 IIC 4

Reding, V, speech at IDATE Conference (Montpellier, 21 November 2005)

Reding, V, speech at Visby Agenda: Creating an Impact for an eUnion 2015 (Visby, 9 and 10 November 2009)

Reichman, JH, Dinwoodie, GB and Samuelson, P, 'A reverse notice and takedown regime to enable public interest uses of technically protected copyrighted works', in Strowel, A (ed), *Peer-to-Peer file sharing and secondary liability in copyright law* (Edward Elgar Publishing 2009) 229

Reinbothe, J, 'A review of the last ten years and a look at what lies ahead: copyright and related rights in the European Union', presentation at Fordham Intellectual Property Conference, New York, 4 April 2002

Reinbothe, J and Lewinski, S von, *The WIPO Treaties 1996 – The WIPO Copyright Treaty and the WIPO Performances Treaty. Commentary and legal analysis* (LexisNexis 2002)

Ricketson, S, 'The new Copyright Act 1997' (1997) 29 IPF 14

Ricketson, S, 'International conventions', in Gendreau, Y, Nordemann, A and Oesch, R (eds), *Copyright and photographs. An international survey* (Kluwer Law International 1999) 15

Ricketson, S, 'Threshold requirements for copyright protection under the international conventions' (2009) 1 WIPOJ 51

Ricketson, S and Ginsburg, JC, *International copyright and neighbouring rights. The Berne Convention and beyond* (2nd edn, OUP 2006)

Rodgers, M, 'Football fixture lists and the Database Directive: Football Dataco Ltd v Brittens Pools Ltd' (2010) 32 EIPR 593

Roojen, A von, *The software interface between copyright and competition law* (Wolters Kluwer International 2010)

Rosati, E, 'The Wittem Group and the Project of a European Copyright Code' (2010) 5(12) JIPLP 862–868

Rosati, E, 'Originality in US and UK Copyright Experiences as a Springboard for an EU-Wide Reform Debate' (2010) 5 IIC 524–543

Rosati, E, 'Originality in a Work, or a Work of Originality: The Effects of the *Infopaq* Decision' (2011) 58(4) J Copyr Socy 795–817, and 33(12) EIPR 746–755

Rosati, E, 'The Hargreaves Report and copyright licensing: can national initiatives work *per se*?' (2011) 33 EIPR 673

Rosati, E, 'ISPs' six strikes enforcement plan in force next July' (The 1709 Blog, 15 March 2012) <http://tinyurl.com/axkr82g> accessed 14 June 2013

Rosati, E, 'EU copyright at Fordham: a report (Part I)' (The 1709 Blog, 17 April 2012) <http://tinyurl.com/ansc3lz> accessed 14 June 2013

Rosati, E, 'EU copyright at Fordham: a report (Part II)' (The 1709 Blog, 17 April 2012) <http://the1709blog.blogspot.it/2012/04/eu-copyright-at-fordham-report-part-ii.htmlhttp://tinyurl.com/b2gkp54> accessed 14 June 2013

Rosati, E, 'ISPs' six strikes enforcement plan delayed' (The 1709 Blog, 20 May 2012) <http://tinyurl.com/axkr82g> accessed 14 June 2013

Rosati, E, 'The Orphan Works Directive, or throwing a stone and hiding the hand' (2013) 8 (4) JIPLP 303

Rosati, E and Rosati, CM, 'Copyright in diagnostic tests: not death time for fair use yet' (2012) 7 JIPLP 510

Rose, M, *Authors and owners. The invention of copyright* (Harvard University Press 1993)

Runge, D, 'Football match fixtures and European Union copyright law: answering the questions referred to the European Court of Justice in Football Dataco Ltd. v. Yahoo! UK Ltd.' <http://tinyurl.com/asyxx48> accessed 14 June 2013

Salokannel, M and Strowel, A, 'Study contract concerning moral rights in the context of the exploitation of works through digital technology' (2000), final report, <http://tinyurl.com/2fqbd8> accessed 14 June 2013

Saltarelli, A, 'Red bus suggests copyright law is not black and white: an Italian perspective' (Art and Artifice, 29 January 2012) <http://tinyurl.com/b5hdbj7> accessed 14 June 2013

Samuelson, P, 'Preliminary thoughts on copyright reform' (2007) 3 ULR 551

Samuelson, P, 'The past, present and future of software copyright: interoperability rules in the European Union and United States' (2012) 34 EIPR 229

Samuelson, P and Members of The CPP, 'The Copyright Principles Project: directions for reform' (2010) 25 Berkeley Tech LJ 1

Samuelson, P, Vinje, T and Cornish, W, 'Does copyright protection under the EU Software Directive extend to computer program behaviour, languages and interfaces?' (2012) 34 EIPR 158

Sawdy, C, 'High Court decision revisits protection of databases in the United Kingdom – Football Dataco Ltd v Brittens Pools Ltd' (2010) Ent LR 221

Scanlon, L, 'Government must change copyright law to protect website browsing' (2013) 35 EIPR 63

Schijndel, M van and Smiers, J, 'Imagining a world without copyright: the market and temporary protection, a better alternative for artists and the public domain', in Porsdam, H (ed), *Copyright and other fairy tales. Hans Christian Andersen and the commodification of creativity* (Edward Elgar Publishing 2006) 147

Schütze, R, 'Supremacy without pre-emption? The very slowly emergent doctrine of Community pre-emption' (2006) 43 CML Rev 1023

Scott Fitzgerald, F, *The Great Gatsby* (first published 1926, Penguin Books 2010)

Sechin, A, 'On plagiarism, originality, textual ownership, and textual responsibility. The case of *Jacques le fatalist*', in McGinnis, R (ed), *Originality and intellectual property in the French and English enlightenment* (Routledge 2009) 102

Senftleben, MRF, 'Bridging the differences between copyright's legal traditions – the emerging EC fair use doctrine' (2010) 57 J Copyr Socy 521

Senftleben, MRF, 'Does the Directive provide enough flexibility and sustainability?', presentation at InfoSoc @ Ten. Ten years after the EU Directive on Copyright in the Information Society: looking back and looking forward, CRIDS – IviR conference, hosted by Marielle Gallo (Member of the European Parliament), European Parliament, Brussels, 13 January 2012

Seville, C, *EU intellectual property law and policy* (Edward Elgar Publishing 2009)

Shapiro, T and Lindner, B, 'More football in pubs: European Union – Court of Justice (Grand Chamber) *Football Association Premier League Ltd and Others v QC Leisure and Others* (C-403/08) and *Karen Murphy v Media Protection Services Ltd* (C-429/08)' (2013) 3 QMJIP 43

Sherman, B and Bently, L, *The making of modern intellectual property law. The British experience, 1760-1911* (CUP 1999)

Simon, DA, 'Culture, creativity, & copyright' (2011) 29 Cardozo Arts & Ent LJ 279

Singh, A, 'The protection of photographs in French copyright law' (The 1709 Blog, 2 February 2012) <http://tinyurl.com/auz6cat> accessed 14 June 2013

Singh, A, 'Paris court rejects photographer's copyright claim' (The 1709 Blog, 10 January 2013) <http://preview.tinyurl.com/bhzf5op> accessed 14 June 2013

Smith, J and Silver, J, 'FA Premier League down at half-time in European Championship: Advocate General finds that territorial exclusivity agreements relating to the transmission of football matches are contrary to EU law' (2011) 33 EIPR 399

Smith, S and Maxwell, A, 'Premier League football cases: linguistic tactics, non-naked match feeds and the away goals rule' (2012) 18 CTLR 33

Sontag, S, *On photography* (Picador 1977)

Stanganelli, M, 'Spreading the news online: a fine balance of copyright and freedom of expression in news aggregation' (2012) 34 EIPR 745

Sterling, JAL, *World copyright law* (2nd edn, Sweet & Maxwell 2003)

Stern, S, 'Copyright, originality, and the public domain', in McGinnis, R (ed), *Originality and intellectual property in the French and English enlightenment* (Routledge 2009) 69

Stokes, S, *Art and copyright* (1st edn, Hart Publishing 2001)

Stokes, S, 'Graves' Case and copyright in photographs', in McClean, D and Schubert, K (eds), *Dear images. Art, copyright and culture* (Ridinghouse 2002) 109

Stolfi, N, *Il diritto d'autore* (Società Editrice Libraria 1932)

Synodinou, TE, 'Databases: sui generis protection and copyright protection' (Kluwer Copyright Blog, 20 December 2011) <http://tinyurl.com/aacyfgj> accessed 14 June 2013

Synodinou, TE, 'The foundations of the concept of work in European copyright law', in Synodinou, TE (ed), *Codification of European copyright law* (Kluwer Law International 2012) 93

Tjong Tjin Tai, E and Teuben, K, 'European precedent law' (2008), *Tilburg Institute of Comparative and Transnational Law Working Paper No 2008/4*

Tomasi di Lampedusa, G, *Il Gattopardo* (Feltrinelli 1958)

Torremans, P, *Holyoak and Torremans: Intellectual property law* (4th edn, Butterworths 2005)

Torremans, P, 'Copyright territoriality in a borderless online environment', in Axhamn, J (ed), *Copyright in a borderless online environment* (Kluwer Law International 2012) 23

Treacy, P and George, D, 'Football broadcasting: Advocate General opines that internal market freedoms trump copyright' (2011) 6 JIPLP 614

Tritton, G, 'Articles 30 and 36 and intellectual property: is the jurisprudence of the ECJ of an ideal standard?' (1994) 16 EIPR 422

Tritton, G (ed), *Intellectual property in Europe* (3rd edn, Sweet & Maxwell 2008)

Ullrich, H, 'Harmony and unity of European intellectual property protection', in Vaver, D and Bently, L (eds), *Intellectual property in the new millennium. Essays in honour of William R Cornish* (CUP 2004) 20

Vassiliou, A, 'Culture and copyright in the digital environment', Brussels, 4 February 2013, SPEECH/13/94

Vermazen, B, 'The aesthetic value of originality' (1991) 16 MISP 266

Vignaux Smyth, J, 'Originality in Enlightenment and beyond', in McGinnis, R (ed), *Originality and intellectual property in the French and English enlightenment* (Routledge 2009) 175

Vousden, S, 'Infopaq and the Europeanisation of copyright law' (2010) 2 WIPOJ 197

Vousden, S, 'Apis, databases and EU law' (2011) IPQ 215

Weiler, JHH, 'Community, Member States and European integration: is the law relevant?' (1982) 21 J Common Mkt Stud 39

Westkamp, G, *The Implementation of Directive 2001/19/EC in the Member States*, February 2007

Weston, S, 'Software interfaces – stuck in the middle: the relationship between the law and software interfaces in regulating and encouraging interoperability' (2012) 43 IIC 427

Wittem Group, *European Copyright Code* (2010)

Wood, A, 'The CJEU's ruling in the Premier League pub TV cases – the final whistle beckons: joined cases *Football Association Premier League Ltd v QC Leisure* (C-403/08) and *Murphy v Media Protection Services Ltd* (C-429/08)' (2012) 34 EIPR 203

Woodmansee, M, 'On the author effect: recovering collectivity', in Woodmansee, M and Jaszi, P (eds), *The construction of authorship. Textual appropriation in law and literature* (Duke University Press 1994) 15

Zemer, L, *The idea of authorship in copyright* (Ashgate 2007)

Index